YOUR HUNDRED BILLION DOLLARS

$$$

Other Books by the Author

PICTORIAL HISTORY OF ISRAEL
PICTORIAL HISTORY OF THE UNITED NATIONS
COUNTRY WITHOUT A CURTAIN
MINORITY PROBLEMS IN POSTWAR EUROPE
AT THE GATES OF HADES
POLAND REVISITED

YOUR HUNDRED

THE COMPLETE STORY OF

UNITED STATES OF AMERICA

BILLION DOLLARS

AMERICAN FOREIGN AID

By JACOB A. RUBIN

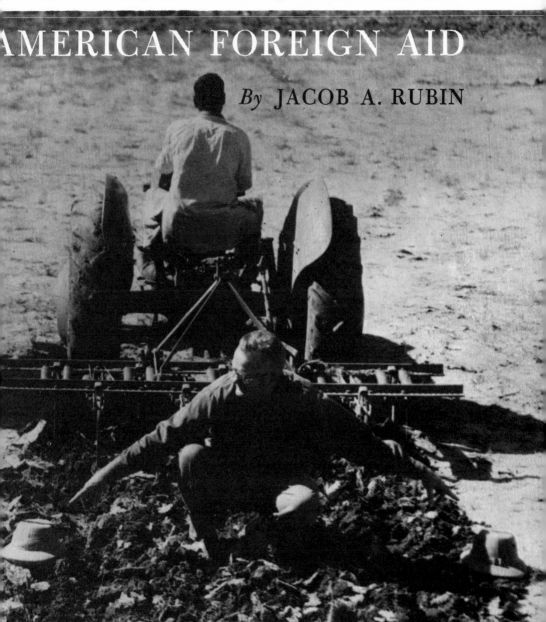

CHILTON BOOKS

A DIVISION OF CHILTON COMPANY

Publishers

Philadelphia   New York

To my daughters, NIRA *and* EDNA, *and my son-in-law,* JOEL, *who will have to carry, for years to come, the burden of mutual responsibility for the progress of man everywhere*

Why do you dislike me—I have never done anything to help you? CONFUCIUS

Our age will be well remembered not for its horrify-ing crimes or its astonishing inventions, but because it is the first generation since the dawn of History, in which mankind dared to believe it practical to make the benefits of civilization available to the whole human race. ARNOLD TOYNBEE

$$$

Preface

YOUR HUNDRED BILLION DOLLARS is not used as the title of this book to attract the attention of the public. These are really "your" hundred billion dollars—you the reader, you the taxpayer, you the average American. All these billions came from your pockets, within the last seventeen years. And all of them called for some kind of sacrifice on your part. They have reduced your spending power for your own needs, in order economically to assist foreign nations. Although a detailed accounting will show that not all these billions were outright grants, never to be repaid, and although a thorough review of the uses to which these billions were put will show that they saved many more billions which would have had to be expended to assure the measure of security America has attained through the many foreign-aid programs—these hundred billion dollars are still *your* dollars, and therefore you should be deeply concerned and involved in this aspect of American foreign policy.

Yet to write a book on this subject appears almost "un-American." Such an activity runs contrary to the spirit, if not the letter, of the provisions of the foreign-aid legislation. It was the Dworshak amendment which forbade the Administration to use the various communications media to inform the American public about what is being done and what is being accomplished with the tremendous sums appropriated annually for foreign aid. Thus the foreign-aid operations became almost a "secret" for the American public—and their presentation to the world seriously impeded in an age which has turned information and public relations into one of the most important instruments in the contest of "peaceful coexistence."

In this respect, this study entitled YOUR HUNDRED BILLION DOLLARS tries to set the record straight. The growing intensity of the controversy on all matters related to the foreign-aid program makes comprehensive and accurate information on this subject imperative. The taxpayer who has to form his judgment on basic problems of American policies before he finally makes up his mind is entitled first of all to know all the facts. If it is true that there is no better citizen than a well informed citizen, if it is true that knowledge of government affairs by the public lies at the heart of a true democracy, then a discussion of United States foreign-aid programs helps keep this country well informed about the policies of its government and the international implications of one of the major arms of its foreign policy.

In presenting as completely as possible all the major aspects of foreign aid, I have tried not to take the usual path—that of exaggerating the negative side of the aid programs and minimizing their successes and achievements. This attitude, too, seems almost un-American, when set against the background of such books as *The Ugly American* and *A Nation of Sheep*. While I have not attempted to whitewash any of the failures in the foreign-aid programs, I have made an effort not to lose the historical, political, and humanitarian perspective of this unprecedented effort to help other peoples who might differ in nationality, religion, race, social standards, and even political philosophy.

To make this study more complete and objective, an effort was made to permit those who have benefited and are benefiting from U.S. aid to speak for themselves about it. In this book, for the first time, authoritative representatives of a number of nations which have cooperated with the United States in this great mutual endeavor of human progress report directly to the American people. Unfortunately, limitations of space make it impossible to publish these reports in full, but those parts which the reader will find in this book are the most essential. It is my fervent hope that at some time in the future the opportunity will come to make these appraisals of United States foreign aid by representatives of foreign nations available in full to the American public.

Along with the deep debt of gratitude I owe to these foreign officials who have responded to my request, a word of thanks is due to the many distinguished citizens of this country who willingly contributed information, source material, photographs, and advice. These thanks go to Paul G. Hoffman, Managing Director of the United Nations Special Fund and former Administrator of the Economic Cooperation Administration, which implemented the Marshall Plan and made the miracle of European economic recovery possible, for sharing in the course of two long interviews his experience and vast knowledge; to Philip Klutznick, former member of the United States delegation to the United Nations in charge of the affairs of the Economic and Social Council, for his friendly advice and encouragement; to Clinton A. Rehling, assistant to Mr. Hoffman, whose kindness and help were most important in the progress of this book; to Joseph L. Newman, deputy director of public affairs and information for the Agency for International Development (AID), for his cooperation; to James T. McCrory, chief of the Public Affairs Division of AID, for his constant care in making the informational resources of AID available; to Dr. Taylor E. Parks, historian of the State Department, for his friendly counsel; to William McIntyre and Clyde McNair of the AID information staff for opening the vast photographic collection of the agency and for making photographs available for publication; to Jim

Klinberg of the AID Information Department for making available some most important documents on United States foreign aid; to G. W. F. Fitzgerald and Robert Asher of the Brookings Institution for their advice; to Colonel Frank E. Mason, President Hoover's assistant, and Miss Mary Dempsey, President Hoover's secretary, for supplying from the archives of President Hoover materials and photographs which very few, if any, in this generation have ever seen; to Representative Otto E. Passman of Louisiana, Chairman of the subcommittee on Foreign Operations Appropriations, for granting an interview in the midst of a most crowded session in order to make it possible to bring to my readers his point of view, one held by an important segment of the Congress and of the American public on foreign aid; and to William Stricker, in charge of the Foreign Correspondents Center in New York City, and its staff. Special thanks go to my wife Aliza for her cooperation, and for bearing the burden of the long weeks of absence from home for the intensive work involved in the writing of this book and later for her help in preparing the index.

It is my hope that this book will serve to enlighten the public on one of the central areas of United States foreign policy. I have tried my best to make the discussion on foreign-aid programs as interesting to the reader as they are fascinating in their complex actuality. Foreign aid is extremely absorbing; it is often even a sensational story, one deserving headlines no less sensational than some other matters which catch the attention of the public. These are stories which are both romantic and accountable in terms of dollars and cents, dramatic and pleasing, dangerous and challenging, thankless as well as rewarding, taxing the best in human beings and luring them with temptations which need character, understanding, and responsibility to withstand.

YOUR HUNDRED BILLION DOLLARS presents this story in words and pictures in order to bring it closer to everyone who is interested in knowing what United States foreign aid really stands for, what it has accomplished, and what are its ultimate goals.   JACOB A. RUBIN

$$

Contents

$$

Illustration Credits

The author and the publisher are grateful to the following organizations, institutions, and picture services for permission to reproduce their photographs in this book: Agency for International Development; British Information Service; the Joint Distribution Committee; CARE; American Council of Voluntary Agencies for Foreign Service; European Community Information Service; the Hoover Institution on War, Revolution, and Peace; the New York Public Library; United Nations; UNRRA Archives; U.S. Department of Defense; U.S. Navy; U.S. Information Agency; Ford Foundation; U.S. Peace Corps; Inter Nationes.

YOUR HUNDRED BILLION DOLLARS

$$$

1

$$$

The Forerunners of Foreign Aid

Foreign aid in its present form was not the beginning of American programs to assist foreign nations. For decades, the image of "Uncle Sam" bestowing his riches on people in faraway lands has been as familiar as were the images of many other nations in history, e.g., the Greeks as philosophers, the Romans as conquerors, the British as empire builders.

For over a century, people all over the world, when afflicted by famine, flood, earthquake, or other disasters, have known that there is always a country, a nation, which will try to comfort them, bring them help, and alleviate their sufferings.

This image was not created with a stroke of the legislator's pen. The people who instituted the feast of Thanksgiving in gratitude for the bounty they found in the new land derived from their religious devotion an understanding of man's responsibility for the welfare and fate of his fellow man. Charity was not the only expression of these convictions. To "help others to help themselves," the slogan of the present-day for-eign-aid programs, dates back to the days of the Founding Fathers. Benjamin Franklin expressed this thought with admirable wit and con-ciseness when, after sending ten *louis d'or* to a young friend in need, he included the following note: "I do not pretend to give you such a sum; I only lend it to you. When you return to your country, you cannot fail of getting into some business that will in time enable you to pay all your debts. In that case, when you meet with another honest man, in similar distress, you must pay me by lending this sum to him, enjoining to discharge the debt by a like operation when he shall be able and shall meet with another such opportunity. I hope it may thus go through many hands before it meets with a knave that will stop its progress."

The conviction that progress means the sharing of wealth and the promotion of its widest distribution was forcefully expressed by Abraham Lincoln in the midst of the Civil War. On his way to Washington to be inaugurated, Lincoln delivered an impromptu speech in Philadelphia, in which he said about the Declaration of Independence: "It was not a mere matter of the separation of the colonies from the motherland, but something in that Declaration giving liberty not alone to the people

1

of this country but hope for the world, for all future time. It was that which gave promise that in due time the weight should be lifted from the shoulders of all men and that all should have an equal chance." He continued: "I was about to say that I would rather be assassinated on this spot, than to surrender that concept of our Declaration of Independence."

This special meaning of the Declaration of Independence was tested very early in the independent dealings of the Congress. The representatives of the thirteen colonies had just managed to muster the means necessary to uphold the integrity of the fledgling Union when the Congress had to deal with its first problem of assistance to people in dire need, people who were outside the boundaries of its jurisdiction. The needy were refugees from Haiti, and the problem was whether the federal government had the constitutional right to use tax money for the benefit of foreigners. The Congress lived up to the spirit of the Declaration of Independence: $15,000 was voted for relief for the unhappy Haitians. And the year was only 1794.

It seems that this act opened a special chapter in the annals of the North American republic. The American continents entered an era of upheavals, and the other nations of the hemisphere, as they emerged from colonial bondage, at once started looking toward the North, where a great republic had been born.

Anti-colonial struggle and a natural disaster presented the American legislators with a new trial less than two decades after the first Congressional appropriation for "foreign aid." On Holy Thursday, March 26, 1812, an earthquake struck the cities of Caracas and La Guaira in Venezuela. Twenty thousand persons perished. The already bleeding country, in the midst of an uprising against the Spanish crown, was shocked. In this tragic hour of supreme suffering, the people, who had just declared their independence and established the Republic of Venezuela, received comfort and help from their neighbor to the North. Alexander Scott, special representative to Venezuela, was in Baltimore awaiting passage to that country when the news of the disaster reached the United States. Scott knew that people in distress should be helped immediately. In a report to the Secretary of State he wrote: "Under these circumstances, it has occurred to me that the Government might probably feel disposed to indulge their native feelings of generosity and sympathy, in administering to the wants of the unhappy sufferers, and in affording that relief, which would, no doubt, be highly acceptable. Such an act of philanthropy, besides adding to the lustre of the American character would, I imagine, be extremely grateful and popular with the Government and people of that country; to succor the distressed, and comfort the afflicted being not less noble and magnanimous among nations, than among individuals."

Within one week, on April 29, 1812, a resolution was submitted to the House, in which the Committee of Commerce and Manufactures was instructed to report a bill authorizing the President to purchase flour for shipment to the victims of the earthquake. Although the amount was not specified, the resolution was adopted unanimously. When the appropriation was set at $30,000, it was raised to $50,000 on a motion by Calhoun. There were 4,272 barrels of flour and 2,728 bushels of corn purchased at a cost of $47,840.73, and these were shipped immediately to the needy.

The magnanimous example was established. As the years passed, victims of disasters around the world found that Scott's assertion that "to succor the distressed and comfort the afflicted is not less noble and magnanimous among nations than among individuals" had become a kind of national trait of the people of the North American republic. The instances of devotion to this principle are innumerable. But the first nationwide test, which came when a whole people—millions, and later hundreds of millions—had to be saved from hunger and pestilence, faced the United States when an almost global confrontation of world powers had set the stage for the First World War.

The general indignation at the German disregard of Belgium's neutrality was hardly over when the ten million Belgians under German occupation were deprived of their usual sources of supply and were forced to become dependent on assistance from foreign countries. Although some money was available from the foreign bank accounts of the Belgian Government, the magnitude of the task of feeding the Belgians, and later the people of the northern provinces of France, made foreign assistance imperative. Consequently, the American Commission for Relief in Belgium, headed by Herbert Hoover, came into being. Soon, other nations wanted to share in the noble work. The commission was renamed the Commission for Relief in Belgium, to be abbreviated to "The Belgian Relief," and became soon, in its initials, "CRB," a password, among the interested nations, of international cooperation for humanitarian purposes.

Obtaining the money for the provision of supplies was only part of the very complex task at hand. Intricate problems arising from the war conditions had to be solved immediately. The German occupation forces had to agree to protect imported supplies and to assure immunity from attack on ships carrying the supplies; the Allies had to assure the passage of the supplies through the blockade; and means had to be devised to prevent the Germans from seizing these supplies, a development which could have turned the entire charitable effort on behalf of millions of civilians into a backdoor supply route for blockaded Germany, with profound consequences on the conduct of the war.

The problem was very serious. The German attitude was expressed by General Von Lüttwitz, the military governor of Belgium, who, when

One of the ships in fleet, in the service of the Belgian Relief, carrying assistance to German-occupied Belgium.

told by representatives of the CRB that the Germans had a duty, as the occupation government of Belgium, to keep the Belgians alive, answered coldly: "The Allies are at liberty to feed the Belgians. If they don't, they are responsible for anything that may happen. If there are bread riots, the natural thing would be for us to drive the whole civilian population into some restricted area, like the Province of Luxembourg, build a barbed-wire fence around them, and leave them to starve."

It was the job of the CRB not to leave them to starvation. The enormous dimensions of the financial and supply problem involved will be understood if one remembers that the regular, peace-time imports to this area amounted to 300,000 tons, or $30 million monthly.

A complicated system of rationing, diets, selection of food items, administration, and supervision had to be evolved. The CRB soon turned into almost a separate government, a kind of go-between in the midst of the belligerents. Special CRB passports were issued and were recognized, a CRB flag was flown on ships exempt from restrictions of blockade and submarine warfare, and huge, illuminated signs saying "CRB" identified the supply vessels miles away on the open seas.

Although the word "American" was removed from the name of the relief organization, the American contribution remained the chief factor in this enormous relief operation. The Governors of all forty-eight states organized relief committees. All religious denominations, charitable institutions, and social organizations gave their immediate support. Money and materials, the two "M's" for the relief of the Belgians and the northern French, became a main preoccupation of people of good will. Their number ran into the hundreds of thousands.

All over the country committees sprang up. Women started community sessions for the knitting of sweaters, which, after they reached Europe, were laboriously unraveled to be reknit into shawls, considered a more useful item than the sweaters which did not suit the local fashion. Donors of old clothes seemed to have a great surplus of silk hats. Dinner suits were turned into beautiful coats for children, and old evening gowns, which the men on the CRB thought useless and started to dispose of by dumping them in the waters of the Belgian ports, were rescued from destruction and turned to useful service by the practical Belgian and French women, who thought that these fine silks and fabrics were very suitable for some kind of clothes for children. In those distress-filled days, humor did not abandon these women: the Brussels women ran a unique fashion show in the local work room by displaying a long line of dressmakers' dummies, clad in the various styles they had received. Evening gowns proved to represent not less than thirty years of fashion. Another aspect of the gift clothes very soon became known: many donors would leave some cash in the pockets of the used clothes and thus a special kind of "sport" developed, that of hunting in the pockets for an additional dollar, if the officials of the CRB had not themselves collected this cash for a special relief fund.

This charitable endeavor was not without political complications on the domestic American scene. Because the CRB was mainly directed by Americans and the nature and scope of its activities had necessitated relations between the Commission and various governments, some opponents of President Wilson cited the Logan Act, which prohibits American citizens from taking part in negotiations with foreign governments. Thus the criticism of the American involvement in the CRB activities and the American government's cooperation in the program assumed proportions of a major controversy. Senator Lodge did not miss the opportunity to needle President Wilson, who reiterated on numerous occasions his full support for the relief activities and who prodded Congress into appropriations of nine million dollars per month for the needs of the Commission. (Starting in November, 1917, the appropriation was increased to nine million dollars monthly for Belgium and six million dollars for France.)

But these political encounters did not prevent the continuation of the American participation in the relief work in Europe. During the five years that the CRB existed, 5,174,431 tons of supplies were sent to Belgium and northern France, and the cost of the entire operation reached $930,518,676.93. The American share of this sum was $386,632,260.44 from the U.S. Treasury and $34,521,026 from charitable contributions.

The saving of the lives of millions, who were assured of a minimum of 1,500 calories per day, was the most urgent task of the CRB during the war years. With the approach of the end of the war, it became clear that new tasks were looming on the horizon. President Wilson soon gave clear indication that he intended to employ American wealth in the economic rehabilitation of the devastated economies of Belgium and northern France. On November 7, 1918, he wrote to Mr. Hoover, "I believe that the American people will willingly accept a large share of the burden of assisting in the now all-important work of reconstruction and rehabilitation. . . . In order that such assistance should be exerted in the most liberal, efficient and comprehensive manner, I feel that it should be organized under a single agency, which may coordinate the whole effort of the American people and Government, in the furnishing of supplies, machinery, finance, exchange, shipping, trade relations, and philanthropic aid."

President Wilson was sure that the American people were willing to carry this burden because he saw the CRB as only a small sample of the American spirit. Although the CRB was in many respects administered in a businesslike way with provisions paid for and loans to cover the expenses, it was nevertheless a manifestation of compassion for the suffering of others and readiness to alleviate their burdens by self-sacrifice, financial and personal alike. With the entrance of the United States into the war, the responsibility for the fate of the 170 million people of the Allied and neutral nations of Europe became of more direct concern to the American people and government.

Before an American soldier set foot in the trenches, an outpouring of patriotic zeal was seen in every corner of this country. Participation in the military campaigns and supplying its own forces were only a part of the American share in the war. Food became at the outset a powerful instrument in the strategy of forcing an early surrender of the enemy.

"Food will win the war"—the five-word slogan covered the billboards, shouted from the headlines of newspapers, and sounded from every speaker's platform. That this was the right approach to winning the war as quickly as possible was admitted by no other than the British Prime Minister Lloyd George, who stated, "The food [supply] decided the issue of this war. It was directly responsible for the downfall of Russia, finally was the element that led to the collapse of Austria and Germany. Indirectly it was responsible for bringing America into the war, since Germany's indiscriminate submarine warfare was her answer to our blockade."

To indicate the dimensions of this unprecedented feeding of almost 200 million people, it is enough to mention two figures: the pre-war yearly average of American exports of food was about 8.1 million tons, and, during 1918 alone, despite drought and generally poor agricultural conditions, this export reached 18.4 million tons.

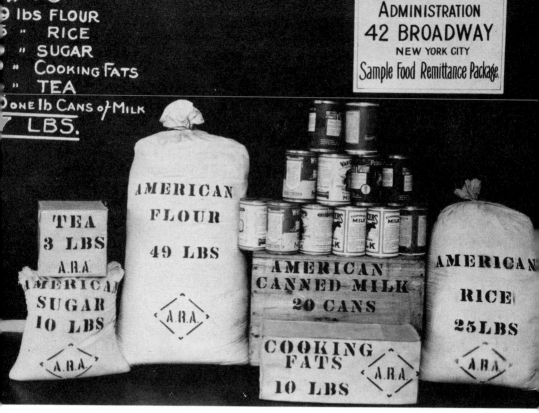

Sample food package, of which scores of thousands have been shipped to war-torn Europe.

To achieve such results, ordinary means of acquiring the foodstuffs did not suffice. The nation had to be mobilized. The producers and the consumers had to respond to the call for an increase of American food exports to Europe. The people of the United States were called to self-sacrifice. The Food Control Act of August 10, 1917, enjoyed the willing cooperation of the American citizenry. Placards were placed on the front windows or doors of those who wished to join the food mobilization effort. Cards giving methods of saving food and other commodities were distributed. Fourteen million housewives pledged to cooperate in the drive to save food—as did all public eating places. Wheatless and meatless days were instituted. (Meatless Tuesday prevails in some places until this very day, when very few can any longer explain the origin of the customary Tuesday closing of delicatessen restaurants.) The "gospel of the clean plate" became the slogan everywhere. A woman's magazine proclaimed prominently: "Never before has the American woman faced the opportunity and the responsibility that are before her today. . . . The final success of the war . . . depends upon our ability to produce more food, and upon our thrift and self-sacrifice in conserving food. . . ."

In this effort Russia soon assumed a special place. The Communist

7

revolution had removed Russia from the camp of the Allies. The peace treaty the new rulers of Russia signed with the Central Powers at Brest Litovsk, in March, 1918, freed the United States from even a moral obligation to care for the food supply of that nation. A month later, Secretary of State Robert Lansing and President Wilson's chief adviser, Colonel E. M. House, came to the conclusion that an effort should be made to arrive at better relations with the Communist government of Russia. Helping Russia solve her food problems seemed then to be the proper way. In a letter to President Wilson, Secretary of State Lansing suggested "the creation of the Commission for the Relief of Russia. This Commission, to be organized generally along the same lines as the 'Commission for the Relief of Belgium,' except that all of the funds required should be furnished, for the time being at least, out of your War Fund. This would obviate the necessity of going to Congress, for the present, for an appropriation."

Circumstances did not permit the implementation of this suggestion, which, however, became a fact some years later, when Soviet Russia received American help to rescue tens of millions of her citizens from starvation. But the overwhelming food needs of other nations left no time for special treatment of the complicated question of Russian relief. The signing of the Armistice on November 11, 1918, revealed a disastrous situation. The real results of the four years of the First World War became apparent. The worst famine in human history was on hand. It suddenly became clear that practically every country of the globe was, to some extent, involved in the struggle. A short survey of the situation showed that forty-five nations were, to a greater or lesser degree, in need of assistance. One billion four hundred million people needed either their complete subsistence or at least some additional food supplement in order to live. From the British Isles to China, people were waiting for relief from practically one source—the United States of America. In addition, the war left about 15 million displaced persons—refugees, impressed laborers, prisoners of war. They were in need of everything from their daily rations and some clothes to cover their bodies, to medical supplies, employment opportunities, housing, and transportation to their homes.

The flow of American supplies started with the loading of 600,000 tons of food for the acute famine areas in the countries of the Central Powers—Germany, Austria, Hungary, Bulgaria, and Turkey. Aid went as well to eastern Europe from Finland in the north to Rumania and Albania in the south, from Armenia to China and Communist Russia. But the American effort was hampered by a political dispute between the American government and the Allied Powers. Not all of Wilson's Fourteen Points, set forth as a basis for the forthcoming peace, were accepted enthusiastically by the Allies. Some of their leaders did not hide their suspicion that the U.S. government might turn the food "carrot" into a stick to be wielded in a way which would force acceptance of American political opinions and thereby enable it to rule the world after the signing and enactment of the peace treaty. It took many weeks of negotiations to establish the Council of Relief and Reconstruction.

The fact that America was, in the opinion of all, the major factor in the solution of post-war problems of supply and reconstruction determined in advance the selection of the man to head the new relief agency. In addition, America had already had the experience of dealing with Belgian relief and had personnel who were ready and able to assume once again the overwhelming mission of bailing the world out of its state of confusion and want. With Herbert Hoover as Director General of the Council of Relief and Reconstruction, such personalities as Vance McCormick, Bernard Baruch, Norman H. Davis, and Henry Robinson became the leading members of the American group cooperating with the Allies in the handling of the constantly worsening supply situation.

In these dire circumstances, such questions arose as whose needs should be considered first and whether the defeated enemy nations should be put on a par with the Allied ones in the supply efforts. The American thinking in this regard, expressed in a statement published in the American, British, and French press on March 21, 1919, is perhaps the best indicator of the real reasons for which America became her "brother's keeper." It sounds almost like a manifesto written by a most devoted admirer of American foreign aid, an especially practical admirer who wouldn't need to change much to make this document a contemporary appeal for the existence and extension of American foreign-aid programs. Signed by Herbert Hoover, its main points were as follows:

Why are we feeding Germany? From the point of view of my Western upbringing, I would say at once, because we do not kick a man in the stomach after we have licked him.

From the point of view of an economist, I would say that it is because there are seventy millions of people who must either produce or die, that their production is essential to the world's future and that they cannot produce unless they are fed.

From the point of view of a governor, I would say it is because famine breeds anarchy, anarchy is infectious, the infection of such a cesspool will jeopardize France and Britain, will yet spread to the United States.

From the point of view of a peace negotiator, it is because we must maintain order and stable government in Germany if we would have someone with whom to sign peace.

From the point of view of a humanitarian I would say that we have not been fighting with women and children, and we are not beginning now.

From the point of view of our Secretary of War, I would say that I wish to return American soldiers home and that it is a good bargain to give food for passenger steamers on which our boys may arrive home four months earlier than will otherwise be the case.

From the point of view of the American Treasurer, I would also say that this is a good bargain, because it saves the United States enormous expendi-

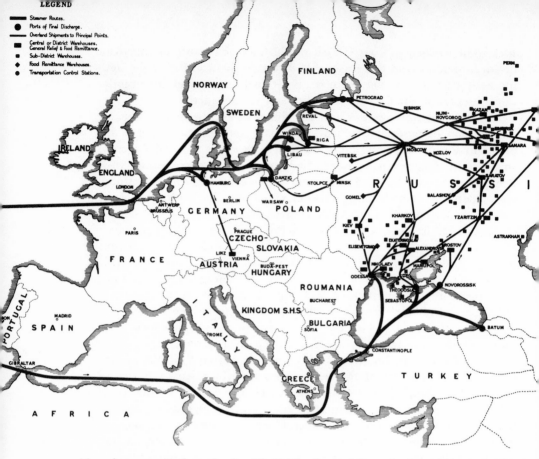

Map of movements of supply after World War I, especially to famine-stricken Soviet Russia.

tures in Europe in the support of idle men and allows these men to return to productivity.

The inclusion of Germany into the relief activities increased the number of people to be cared for by 70 million. In view of the hundreds of millions of the needy this was a rather negligible number. It only indicated the dimensions of the relief activities which had to be undertaken. Although formally a joint undertaking of the Allies, it soon developed into an American operation, with America providing most of the money, the actual supplies, the personnel, and the technical advisers, who were spread all over the world, to run railways, reactivate coal mines, restore transportation, and advise on administrative matters.

The solution of these problems involved an intricate system of loans, charitable gifts, and appropriations. By the existing standards, it amounted to an astronomical sum. From its entry into the war in April, 1917, to the signing of the Peace Treaty in June, 1919, the United States expended seven billion dollars for relief purposes. Except for cash purchases from overseas, United States government agencies had financed more than 80 per cent of the overseas supplies. The other 20 per cent came from American charitable agencies and the Allied governments. The charitable agencies themselves during the nine years of war and its aftermath spent one billion dollars for relief purposes. Four thousand Americans were active all over the world on relief work, and the official American government relief agencies maintained representatives or missions in thirty-two countries. All of this was in addition to the tens of thousands of Americans who were administering the affairs of the relief operation in the U.S. itself. The moral obligation to perform these duties found its expression in many official documents of the Wilson administration.

In the message to Congress which accompanied his request for an appropriation of $100 million for relief purposes, President Wilson wrote:

From our abundance we can surely afford to offer succor to these countries destitute of resources or credit. . . . The high mission of the American people to find remedy against starvation and absolute anarchy renders it necessary that we should undertake the most liberal assistance to these destitute regions. . . . I wish to appeal to the great sense of charity and good-will of the American people toward the suffering, and to place this upon a primarily humanitarian basis of the first magnitude. While the sum of money is in itself large, it is so small compared to the expenditure we have undertaken in the hope of bettering the world, that it becomes a mere pittance compared to the results that will be obtained from it, and the lasting effect that will remain in the United States through an act of such broad humanity and statesmanlike influence.

The great task of saving the hungry was not to be accomplished quickly. As late as 1923, it was still necessary to maintain the relief activities. And it was certainly a special test of American sincerity toward charity and humanitarian duty to fellow men, irrespective of political considerations, when tens of millions of people in Soviet Russia were threatened with annihilation by the worst famine in centuries.

The appeal for help for the millions of starving Russians did not come from the Soviet government, for this would virtually acknowledge the failure of Communism, which was supposed to alleviate all the suffering and solve all the problems of men. The first call for help was therefore issued on July 13, 1921, by Maxim Gorky, the world-renowned writer, who was close to the Russian government. "Bread and medicine" for the children and the sick were asked.

The American Relief Administration answered the call ten days later. Readiness was expressed to provide relief and medical supplies for one million children. The Commissar of Famine Relief in the Kremlin, Leo Kamenev, readily accepted the American offer. Some days later the Russian Commissar of Foreign Affairs, Georgi V. Chicherin, sent a note to foreign offices of Europe and the U.S. State Department asking for help. (Lenin also made such an appeal, but his was to the proletariat of the world.)

But the real, sizable help was to come first of all from the archcapitalist country—the United States. On August 20, 1921, an agreement was signed, in Riga, between Maxim Litvinov, the Assistant Commissar for Foreign Affairs, and Walter Lyman Brown, the director of the American Relief Administration in Europe. The twenty-seven paragraphs of the document could be considered "revolutionary" in view of the Russian willingness to afford the American Relief Agency privileges which, in fact, turned it into a state within a state.

The aid was most timely. About twenty-five million people in the Volga basin and in the Ukraine were in the midst of absolute famine. The prognosis of a medical observer was that "death for the whole population of these areas is only a few months away." Typhus, cholera, typhoid, and smallpox were common. In panic, millions were fleeing the famine without knowing where to go. Horrifying reports were reaching the central administration of the Relief Agency. From Orenburg, from Ufa, from Kazan, from Samara, from Cheliabinsk, from Petrograd (later Leningrad) alarming messages were flooding the relief workers.

To provide the money necessary to meet the growing demands for relief in Russia was beyond the existing resources of the Relief Administration. At that very time, the United States was deep in an economic depression. Five million unemployed required support, but the relief activities in Russia went on. About thirty million dollars still in the coffers of the Relief Administration were thrown into the effort. An over-all public drive for contributions met with a generous response. The Congress passed an act authorizing the use of the surplus medical supplies of the War Department for relief needs in Russia. Every possible way of collecting funds was employed.

The rescue operation was soon revealed to be insufficient. It became clear that if the famine was to be conquered the Russian people would have to produce food themselves. Seed, therefore, had to be provided for the famine areas—a job which the Relief Administration gladly undertook. In addition to the 741,573 tons of goods which were shipped to Russia, 166,973 tons of seed were distributed in the famine areas. The ingenuity shown by the leaders of the Relief Administration in the appeals which they addressed to various religious, national, and professional organizations, as well as to the organized charities, turned the assistance for Russia into a kind of a nationwide campaign which penetrated into almost every home in the United States.

But scarcely had the results of the relief action begun to be successful when obstacles from official sources started to hinder the operations in Russia. Russian employees of the American Relief Administration were arrested. Russian officials in charge of contacts with the Relief Administration were replaced one after the other. The transportation system failed. In November, 1922, the Russians demanded a revision of the agreement with the American Relief Administration. In the United States itself an organization was set up to compete with the Relief Administration. The Communists in the United States organized the Ameri-

12

Russian children waiting for their meal. Sign at entrance reads: American Relief Administration. Second line reads: Welfare Kitchen No. 1.

can Committee for Russian Famine Relief, which immediately set about appealing to American generosity. Almost two million dollars was collected by this new committee.

In the very midst of these unexpected difficulties a new blow was administered to the Relief Administration, a blow which endangered the effectiveness of its charity appeals in America. In the fall of 1922, news leaked out that the Russian authorities were contracting to export thousands of tons of grain, from harvests in areas other than those stricken by the famine. In these circumstances the relief activities lingered on for almost another year. In the summer of 1923 a decision was made to terminate the American Relief Administration activities in Russia.

These gradual changes in the Russian attitude toward the practical activities of the Relief Administration were reflected in the official appraisals of them over the years, by the highest Soviet authorities. At the beginning all was praise. Chicherin, the Commissar for Foreign Affairs, acknowledged in June, 1923, that "the work of the American Relief Administration is the work of broad masses of the American people, who at a most difficult moment have come to the assistance of the Russian people and have thus laid a firm foundation for the future unalterable

13

U.S. Navy turning over seventeen American vessels to Russian Fleet at Dutch Harbor, Alaska. Capt. William S. Maxwell at microphone. Rear Adm. Boris Popov, center.

relations of friendship and mutual understanding between them. . . ." And the official organ *Izvestia* on July 20, 1923, reported a speech by another member of the Russian government, Kamenev, who stated:

The Sovnarkom [Council of Commissars or Ministers] passed a resolution, thanking the American people . . . for responding, in the trying year of a great elemental calamity . . . coming self-sacrificingly to its aid, organizing on a tremendous scale the importation and distribution of products and other articles of prime necessity. Thanks to the tremendous, utterly unselfish effort of ARA millions of people of all ages were saved from death and whole villages and even cities were saved from the horrible catastrophe that was threatening them. At the present time, when with the termination of the famine, the grandiose work of the ARA has come to an end, the Soviet of Peoples Commissars, in the name of the saved millions, and of the whole toiling people of Soviet Russia and its united Republics, considers it its duty to express before the whole world, to this organization, its head Herbert Hoover, Col. Haskell, its representative in Russia, and his co-workers, its profoundest gratitude, and to declare that the people populating the Union of Soviet Socialist Republics will never forget the help given by the American people through the ARA.

How these professions of eternal gratitude were preserved in the written history in Soviet Russia, is best exemplified in the 1926 edition of the official *Great Soviet Encyclopedia:*

The work of the American Relief Administration was limited to supplying children foodstuffs. In 1922 five million children were receiving ARA rations. In that year ARA undertook also to supply adults and a total of ten million people were receiving the rations. . . . In all, 1,814,900,000 daily rations, 602,292 pairs of shoes, 1,929,805 meters of clothing etc. were distributed. . . . The total cost of this relief was estimated at $1,455,861.

The 1950 edition of the *Encyclopedia* had this to say about the ARA:

The capitalist world tried to use the difficulties of U.S.S.R. Saboteurs and spies were setting fire to Soviet plants or attempting to blow them up. The ARA helped this enemy activity.

These were not the only expressions of Russian "gratitude." Soviet First Deputy Prime Minister, Frol Kozlov, while on a visit to the United States in 1959, told President Eisenhower that the U.S. contributions to stem the famine were "a loan that the United States forced Russia to repay in gold." The American retort came immediately from the most authoritative person in this field, former President Hoover: "It was not a loan and not a dime was ever asked for or paid. At the direct request of the Soviet Government we raised about $62,000,000, and provided the Russians with more than 700,000 tons of food, clothing and medical supplies as an absolute gift."

The vast amount of debts incurred by other European countries during the First World War and in the period of the war's aftermath, and the billions which were supposed to be loans to enable these countries to purchase American supplies, have never been repaid. These loans were $4,715,000,000 to Great Britain, $4,230,000,000 to France, $1,000,000,000

The Belgian Relief took care not only to supply food, but efforts were also made to fight unemployment and its consequences.

to Belgium, and many more billions to a host of other countries. These low-interest loans, to be repaid in installments over a period of sixty years, represented only a part of the actual debts, which were considerably reduced. After paying for a few years, the debtors ceased payments in 1933. With the exception of Finland, these initial payments did not exceed 5 per cent of the total. In fact, as it turned out, these loans, and the millions of tons of supplies which (unlike the free donations) were supposed to be paid for, became in fact an outright gift by the American people to peoples from almost the entire world.

Hardly had the accountants of the Treasury and the banks acquiesced to the discontinuation of payments by the European debtors of the First World War when new rumbles of a coming world conflict reached the shores of the United States. Hitler's armies were rolling their tanks on the lowlands of Poland and, the Luftwaffe was getting ready for an assault on the British Islands. Europe was at war. Great Britain's imperial might was challenged. The Royal Navy was threatened by an all-out attack by the German submarines. But the United States, whose shores were protected by the first line of defense of the Western Hemisphere, the British Royal Navy, was divided in its appraisal of the German menace. The Neutrality Act, the legal basis for the American foreign policy of aloofness toward foreign international conflicts, was still very much alive.

Despite the general popular mood of detachment from the outcome of the European war, when even the victorious German armies seemed to have put a *de facto* end to the war by stopping their march at the gates of the Maginot Line on the frontiers of France, the leaders of the American administration were well aware of the coming crisis. As early as December 17, 1940, at his weekly press conference, President Roosevelt spoke openly of his grave concern with the European war. Using one of his famous parables, President Roosevelt told the assembled newsmen: "Suppose my neighbor's house catches fire, and I have a length of garden hose—400–500 feet away. If he can take my garden hose and connect it up with his hydrant, I may help him to put out the fire. Now what do I do? I don't say to him before that operation: 'Neighbor, my garden hose cost me $15—you have to pay me $15 for it.' What is the transaction that goes on? I don't want $15—I want my garden hose back after the fire is over."

The journalists, and with them the entire country, understood the moral to be drawn from the story. They knew that the "cash-and-carry" policy of previous deliveries of war materials to Great Britain, France,

Lunch for children being served with food provided by American relief in a school in Austria.

and, to a limited extent, their allies, was coming to an end, as those nations were nearing the end of their gold reserves. A disregard for American neutrality was inherent in the cash-and-carry policy, which had become law on November, 1939, and had made possible American assistance to the powers fighting Nazi Germany and her allies. This was an evident prelude to changes which had to occur in the American policy toward the European conflict. America had clearly expressed her political sentiments in the transfer on September 30, 1940, of fifty American decommissioned destroyers to Great Britain in exchange for naval bases which Great Britain ceded to the United States in her territories stretching from Newfoundland to British Guiana.

The true meaning of the President's words at his December press conference came to full light only some three weeks later. In his State of the Union message, read on January 6, 1941, Roosevelt notified the legislators that he "found it unhappily necessary to report, that the future and safety of our country are overwhelmingly involved in events far beyond our borders." Speaking about the role America should play, he continued:

Our most useful immediate role is to act as an arsenal for them as well as for ourselves. . . . The time is near when they will not be able to pay for them in ready cash. We cannot and will not tell them they must surrender, merely because of present inability to pay for the weapons which we know they must have. . . . For what we send abroad, we shall be repaid, within a reasonable time following the close of hostilities, in similar materials, or, at our option, in other goods of many kinds which they can produce and which we need.

The wheels of Congressional legislation started moving quickly. Senator Alben Barkley introduced in the Senate, on January 10, the bill dealing with Lend-Lease, and Representative John McCormack did the same in the House. After it was passed, the Clerk of the House stamped it with the number H. R. 1776. Thus H. R. 1776 entered the history of the Second World War to become one of the most decisive factors in the winning of the war and later the example and basis for many acts of American foreign policy related to various forms of assistance to foreign nations.

The general phrases of the President's message were translated into the language of the law, which defined the countries eligible for Lend-Lease as "any country whose defense the President deems vital to the defense of the United States."

The bill authorized the President to "sell, transfer title to, exchange, lease, lend or otherwise dispose of . . . any defense article" to any nation he found vital for the defense of the United States. There were, of course, stipulations concerning the remuneration the United States would receive for materials thus given to foreign nations. According to the bill, this could be "payment or repayment in kind or property, or any other direct or indirect benefit which the President deems satisfactory."

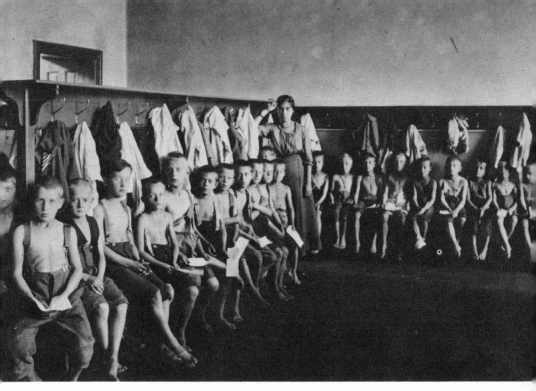

American Relief providing for medical care of children in Vienna.

This was a sweeping piece of legislation as far as accepted standards of dealing with foreign nations were concerned. It was revolutionary even in view of the already established tradition of assistance to foreign nations. Bitter opposition could therefore be expected. Harsh words filled the political air of the country. One of those opposing the bill termed the Lend-Lease "the New-Deal Triple—A Foreign policy to plow under every fourth American boy." From such an attack even Roosevelt, hardened in bitter political campaigns, could not remain aloof. This is "the rottenest thing that has been said in public life in my generation," retorted the President. But the real answer in this heated dispute was already given by the legislators: on March 9, 1941, the House of Representatives approved the bill, and the Senate followed suit.

The House acted speedily. Soon after passing the bill, Congress authorized an initial appropriation of seven billion dollars. Within three hours after the President signed the Lend-Lease Act, on the afternoon of March 11, 1941, he issued directives putting the Lend-Lease program in motion. Directive One declared Great Britain vital to the defense of the United States; Directive Two applied the same criterion to Greece.

The mobilization of industry for the production of implements of war was facilitated by the very fact that under the "cash-and-carry" act a considerable effort, in this direction, had already been made. Secretary of War Henry L. Stimson stressed this point in a letter to Senator D. A.

George, on February, 1941, during the debate on the Lend-Lease bill. "Without the head start given industry by these foreign orders we would, at the present time, be in a very grave situation, as to the plants and facilities which we now need for the pending emergency," Stimson wrote.

But the powers struggling against the Axis were soon in as dire need of food as they were of war material. As early as April 3, 1941, the Department of Agriculture announced that its granary program was to be greatly expanded. The government announced the policy of supports of prices of pork, dairy products, eggs, poultry, and other foods "at levels remunerative to producers."

This was to be a total mobilization. In a nationwide broadcast, Secretary of Agriculture Claude R. Wickard stated that "for the first time in the history of agriculture in this country, production goals for all essential farm commodities have been established." The "Food for Freedom" program was launched, with goals calling for the biggest total farm production in history: nine billion more pounds of milk, 500 million dozens more eggs, ten million more hogs, two million more head of cattle, one and a half million more acres of soy beans, three million more acres of peanuts.

Shipments of food were being sent swiftly and in large quantities. The first Lend-Lease transfer of food was authorized on April 16, 1941. At the President's direction 100,000 cases of evaporated milk, 11,000 tons of cheese, and 11,000 tons of eggs were transferred to Great Britain. By the end of 1941 the food shipments passed the million-ton mark.

The growing operations under the Lend-Lease Act required appropriate administrative arrangements. In October, 1941, the Office of Lend-Lease Administration was established as an independent agency of the federal government. When it was established it was already known that it would have a much more extended field of activity than anticipated. Soviet Russia was in the fourth month of its life and death struggle with the invading German forces, and she needed assistance badly. The initial Soviet orders were paid for in cash, but pressure mounted to acknowledge Soviet Russia as eligible for Lend-Lease aid under the provision of the Act, according to which the defense of Russia should have been seen as "vital to the defense of the United States." On October 1, 1941, an agreement was signed with Russia, providing for supplies valued at about one billion dollars.

The real character of this assistance to Russia was expressed in President Roosevelt's letter to Stalin, on October 30, 1941: "In an effort to obviate any financial difficulties immediate arrangements are to be made so that supplies up to one billion dollars in value may be effected under the Lend-Lease Act. If approved by the government of U.S.S.R. I propose that the indebtedness thus incurred be subject to no interest and that the payments of the U.S.S.R. do not commence until five years after the war's conclusion and be completed over a ten-year period thereafter." Stalin's

Russian child waiting for his relief ration.

answer came without delay. In a letter dated November 4, 1941, he wrote: "Your decision, Mr. President, to grant the Soviet Union a loan in the amount of one billion dollars subject to no interest charges and for the purpose of paying for armament and new materials for the Soviet Union, is accepted with sincere gratitude by the Soviet government as an unusually substantial aid."

And this was only a beginning. Once the lines of delivery had been opened, assistance flowed in a steady, ever-growing stream. Thousands of planes, hundreds of thousands of trucks and jeeps, one million tons of steel, and almost two million tons of food reached Russia by the mid-

American nurses take care of Austrian children.

dle of 1943. Fifty ships sailed every month from American ports loaded with supplies for Russia. Many other ships moved across the sea lanes on all the oceans. Ports, highways, and railroads, especially built all over the world, carried the goods of the United States, which had become the arsenal of the forces fighting against Germany and her allies. A most vivid description of these enormous Lend-Lease deliveries and their presence all over the world was given by the head of the Lend-Lease Administration, Edward Stettinius, in his testimony before the Committee on Foreign Relations of the Senate and the Committee on Foreign Affairs of the House:

As I put together the story of Lend-Lease, I found that I had to speak of almost all the theatres of war: Egypt, China, Russia, and finally the great combined offensive in North Africa. The story included air-routes to China, over the South Atlantic to Africa, and across the deserts of Africa itself. It told of ports built on the Red Sea and Persian Gulf, of a railroad in Iran, assembly depots in Egypt, a naval base in Northern Ireland, a road and railroad through Burma to China. It told of guns, tanks, planes, ships, food, copper, machine tools, of training pilots. . . .

All this was done to the tune of billions of dollars, with America doing its best even to suit the culinary tastes of the recipients. For Russia, a special Russian recipe was used to prepare *tushonka,* a canned pork preparation. Similarly, for other countries, other national dishes were made so that the soldiers at the front felt that somebody cared for them. And

22

the "somebody" was well identified in the eyes of the fighting men everywhere—in the snow-covered plains of Russia, the sands of North Africa, and the jungles of Asia. Those who received this aid did not care about the correct name of the program under which it was given. Whether it was Lend-Lease, or Lease-Lend as some wanted to call it, or Defense Aid or Mutual Aid, War Aid or Reciprocal Aid—the many names used until Lend-Lease became standard terminology—it was always the most welcome signal that *America* was with them, and, to so many, this meant their only hope for victory.

Having allies in a world war, the United States was soon in need of the services of others. The basis for these services was defined in the Reciprocal Aid Agreement of September, 1942, with Great Britain, the Free French, Australia, and New Zealand. Called popularly "reverse Lend-Lease," it gave American troops stationed on the territories of these countries, and of others to which this agreement was later extended, everything they needed to make their service possible, and their duties meaningful. We can get an idea of the extent of this reciprocal aid from the fact that up to June 30, 1943, "reverse Lend-Lease" by the countries of the British Commonwealth added up to $1,175,000,000 worth of assistance given to American troops. All forms of reciprocal aid, by all the countries involved, reached, at the end of the war, over seven billion dollars, as against over fifty billion dollars of American aid under the Lend-Lease Act. The bulk of this aid went to Great Britain ($31,385,000,000), Russia ($10,982,000,000), and France ($3,224,000,000), with the balance distributed among the many nations allied with the United States. This great flow of American aid was not discontinued even after the formal termination of the Lend-Lease operation by President Truman, in August, 1945. Shipments which had been arranged before that date were sent to the countries which ordered them, chiefly to Great Britain and China. By March, 1948, the value of these goods reached almost two billion dollars.

But the most impressive act of American generosity was still to come. In December, 1946, President Truman announced that 70 per cent (about thirty-five billion dollars) of the total amount expended by the United States was considered repaid. For the repayment of the rest, negotiations were conducted and successfully concluded with Great Britain in July, 1948, and with other nations as well, while with Soviet Russia these negotiations dragged on for years, and no final agreement was ever reached.

Coming only about two decades after renunciation of the First World War debts to the United States in the amount of about ten billion dollars, this similar experience was liable to prompt future American administrations to be somewhat more careful in their generosity to foreign nations. The multi-billion-dollar loans which became outright gifts, nevertheless, turned into something completely contrary to what might have been expected: they became rather elements in the evolution of the American attitude toward the problems of providing assistance to other nations. Instead of drawing businesslike conclusions from history, America chose rather to give the wisdom embodied in the Latin saying *historia magistra vitae* ("history is the teacher of life") a new meaning, namely that of the mutual responsibility of all men and the success which such responsibility, in the last count, assured. This basic approach proved also the most appropriate, even from the point of view of the selfish interests of the United States. One of the basic stipulations of the Lend-Lease agreements (Article VII) became the guiding beacon of American policies on all matters of international economic cooperation. This article stated:

> There we agree that the final Lend-Lease settlement shall include provision for agreed action, open to participation by all countries of like mind, directed to the expansion, by appropriate international and domestic measures, of production, employment, and the exchange and consumption of goods, which are the material foundations of liberty and welfare of peoples, and, in general, to the attainment of all economic objectives set forth in the Joint Declaration, made on August 14, 1941, by the President of the United States and the Prime Minister of the United Kingdom [the Atlantic Charter].*

Lend-Lease, while it helped the armies win the war, did not present an answer to the problems of the civilian populations in war-torn areas. The country which decided to become the "arsenal of democracy" made itself ready to become as well the "granary" of the liberated areas. Military victory would be meaningless if its aftermath would be only pestilence and starvation.

Plans for solving this problem were initiated about a year after the Lend-Lease program was born. On November 18, 1942, President Roosevelt delegated to the Secretary of State the responsibility for developing United States policies towards the peoples of the territories occupied by the armed forces of the United Nations, the great alliance of forty-four nations fighting Germany, Italy, and Japan. As in the case of the Lend-Lease, speed was of essential importance. Three days later, Herbert H. Lehman, then Governor of New York, was appointed director of the Office of Foreign Relief and Rehabilitation Operations (OFFRO) to "undertake the work of organizing American participation in the activities of the United Nations in furnishing relief and other assistance to victims of war in areas reoccupied by the forces of the U.N."

Similar measures were taken by other agencies of government. The War Department established a Civil Affairs Division in March, 1943, and the Combined Chiefs of Staff organized a Combined Civil Affairs Committee in July, 1943. With the invasion of Italy, the armed forces took on responsibility for government and relief in the occupied areas. Three hundred and fifty million dollars were appropriated for GARIOA

* Point Five of the Atlantic Charter dealt with problems of securing improved labor standards, economic adjustments, and social security for all men.

Inoculation supplied by the American Relief in what was then Petrograd, later Leningrad. Typhus was raging in Russia, and these shots were indispensable in saving the masses.

(Government and Relief in Occupied Areas) independent of the American contribution to what was to be called UNRRA.

The American initiative was not intended to become an American monopoly. Simultaneous with the American preparations for the relief activities in the territories liberated by the armies of the United Nations, the groundwork was being prepared to turn this relief operation and relief responsibility into a common task for all the nations with whom the United States was allied. November 3, 1943, was the historic day at which these negotiations were concluded. On that day, President Roosevelt was able to announce:

To my friends, on this historic occasion, on November 3, 1943, here, in the White House, seated about a table in the historic East Room are representatives of forty-four nations, United Nations and those associated with them. Representatives of these forty-four nations—you gentlemen here have just signed an agreement creating the United Nations Relief and Rehabilitation Administration—commonly known by a simpler word as UNRRA. All of the United Nations agree to cooperate and share in the work of UNRRA—each nation according to its own resources—and to provide relief and help in rehabilitation for the victims of German and Japanese barbarism. . . .

When victory comes there can certainly be no secure peace until there is a return of law and order in the oppressed countries, until the peoples of these countries have been restored to normal, healthy, and self-sustaining existence. This means that the more quickly and effectively we apply measures of relief

Major General Lewis H. Brereton, left, Commanding General of the U.S. Army Ninth Air Force, conferring with Russian officer at the assembly center where American planes were being turned over to Russia.

and rehabilitation, the more quickly will our own boys overseas be able to come home.

These aims, as defined by President Roosevelt, became part of the UNRRA agreement. In the preamble, the contracting parties expressed their determination that immediately upon the liberation of any war-torn area, the population thereof should receive "aid and relief from their sufferings, food, clothing and shelter; and in the prevention of pestilence and in the recovery of the health of the people; and that preparations and arrangements should be made for the return of prisoners and exiles to their homes" and "assistance in the resumption of urgently needed agricultural and industrial production and the restoration of essential services."

To assure the implementation of these lofty goals, money was needed. One of the officials of the United States Treasury, Harry Dexter White, suggested a formula for the raising of money for the UNRRA operations: one per cent of one year's national income would be contributed to the UNRRA budget by each member government whose territory was not overrun by the enemy. The suggestion was accepted and under this scheme the United States had to contribute $1,350,000,000, the United Kingdom $320,000,000, and Canada about $90,000,000. The concept of taxing governments on the basis of national income was new. The London *Economist* wrote about it: "The concept of national income, hitherto regarded as an obscure academic plaything, became an instrument of statesmanship."

The acceptance of this principle turned UNRRA into a basically American operation. The Congress responded eagerly. The first 1 per cent contribution was authorized by the Seventy-Eighth Congress on March 28, 1944, in the amount of $1,350,000,000. The first appropriation in the amount of $800,000,000 was voted in June of the same year. In sum, the American contribution amounted to 73 per cent of the total operating funds of UNRRA which came from government contributions.

Many in the nation considered this an overgenerous contribution. These feelings were reflected in the hearings before the House Committee on Foreign Affairs. Representative Sol Bloom, chairman of that committee, tried to overcome misconceptions about UNRRA. In one of the Committee hearings he said:

One of these errors was the idea that the United States was committing itself to a vast and undefined expenditure abroad, while other nations were shirking their corresponding responsibilities for the relief of people in liberated territories; and that countries liberated would not help to relieve their own peoples. It was soon made clear that the object of UNRRA is *to help people to help themselves;* that ninety per cent of the expense of relief and rehabilitation would be borne by the nations overrun by the enemy, that UNRRA would operate through governments, and not by distributing alms to individuals.

This was a rebuff to the critics of American outlays for foreign nations who argued that the United States was assuming the role of provider for the whole world. Though the American contribution was great, supporters of the program pointed out that it did not exceed 10 per cent of the general financial burden of relief borne by the suffering nations themselves.

But the criticism did not harm the public and private efforts to build American grassroots assistance for the UNRRA activities. The government was most anxious to have the country mobilized behind this relief effort. A campaign for the "Victory Food Program" was initiated all over the country. It began in the summer of 1945 and set as its target the collection of ten million cans of fruit and vegetables. The UNRRA Committee also called for the preparation of the cans in community canning centers. Millions of people, young and old, were engaged in this work. People collected vegetables and fruit and spent evenings together working for UNRRA. An unprecedented community spirit evolved. Even when the program was extended to include the collection of commercially canned products, the community canning effort continued, giving people a feeling of direct participation.

But the success of this campaign bore in itself the seeds of its failure, for the success was not economical. When Fiorello LaGuardia succeeded Herbert Lehman in the post of director general of UNRRA, he had to call off this part of the program. "People," said LaGuardia, "out of the goodness of their hearts, purchase all kinds of canned food not suitable, such as soups, vegetables containing considerable water, and we would be shipping water instead of food, and there is plenty of water in all these countries. . . . The cost of boxing alone is eighty to ninety cents for every twenty-four cans. In addition, contributors pay retail prices, and we are shipping in wholesale quantities. This makes a difference of some thirty per cent. Therefore a cash contribution is desirable, because meats, fish, milk, dehydrated food is acquired all ready for shipments."

The Government was embarrassed. The masses of people were disappointed. But they did not permit their personal disappointment to interfere with the aid effort. Cash gifts for the Victory Food Program brought in $2,836,150, while the value of canned food collected reached the amount of $2,156,852. And this was only a small fraction of the total contributions from non-governmental sources, which amounted to $209,895,377. This was one-third larger than the contribution of the Canadian government, the third largest governmental contributor to the UNRRA budget.

Not only food was needed. A United Nations Clothing Collection was planned on the scale of a War Loan Drive. President Roosevelt appointed Henry J. Kaiser chairman of the drive, in which fifty thousand tons of clothing were collected and shipped to twenty liberated countries in Europe and Asia. The third clothing drive, known as the Victory Clothing Drive, organized early in 1946, realized a total of twenty thousand tons of clothing.

Popularly UNRRA was identified with food relief, with clothing, and later overwhelmingly with the problems of the D.P.'s—Displaced Persons. As one of the UNRRA officials wrote: "The UNRRA Displaced Persons operations in Germany received an amount of publicity disproportionate to its importance in relation to the whole UNRRA program—because human beings were more appealing copy than tractors, or sacks of wheat."

That this was a most compassionate effort for the relief of the sufferings of fellow men and that people were the most urgent concern of Americans was demonstrated in the appeals of the people responsible for the operations of UNRRA. Fiorello LaGuardia expressed these American feelings in his opening address to the UNRRA Council:

28

Russian resolution of appreciation for American assistance by Council of Commissars submitted to Herbert Hoover, head of the American Relief Administration.

United States sent oil and tank cars to Russia during the war, enabling her soldiers to keep their mechanized forces in the field.

I cannot help repeating again: this is all so new, it is all so hopeful. Have ever in the history of the entire world forty-eight nations come together to save lives? We are united to preserve life, to build, not to kill, not to destroy. There is no precedent in international law. But there is precedent for the spirit of UNRRA in the Old Scripture, and in the New Scripture: to love our neighbor, to aid the needy—that is not original. It has just not been carried out. . . . In every land, in every dialect which is spoken by men, the prayer is spoken: Give us this day our daily bread. Our task is to respond to this prayer. That is our call. That is all there is to it—to respond to that prayer. We then become a great army of mercy, a great army carrying out God Almighty's response to the call for daily bread. . . . That is the mission of UNRRA and that is the army I am willing to lead.

The "daily bread" was only part of the UNRRA relief mission. Its activities spread all over. Because the terms of UNRRA's charter restricted its activities only to territories liberated after they have been overrun by the enemy, a special clause was necessary to make other needy countries also eligible for UNRRA assistance. The so-called "India clause" stated that "areas important for military operations, stricken by famine or disease may be included in benefits of UNRRA." In addition to food and clothing UNRRA provided for shelter, equipment, restoration of transportation facilities, and means of production. A Polish minister of the present Communist regime admitted at the unveiling of a plaque commemorating Poland's gratitude to UNRRA that "every child and old person knew that UNRRA meant bread, milk, sugar, and clothing; to the sick it meant medical assistance; to the peasant it meant tractors; to the factory workers it meant machines."

To keep this enterprise operating, a constant stream of shipments flowed from the Western Hemisphere. During 1946 more than one million long tons were shipped overseas monthly. Among the recipient nations, China received $945,000,000 worth of goods, Poland $479,000,000, the Ukraine $189,000,000, Belorussia $61,000,000, Czechoslovakia $256,-000,000, and Yugoslavia $405,000,000. These amounts assured two thousand calories daily for many millions and clothing which was often allocated by means of a coupon system. For example: a man's overcoat—eighteen coupons; a pair of trousers and jacket—twenty-one coupons; two shirts—ten coupons; two vests—eight coupons; two pairs of pants—eight coupons; two pairs of socks—four coupons. This represented what was considered the minimum wardrobe a needy man was entitled to receive from UNRRA—a minimum which even today in some countries is certainly still in the realm of dreams.

The benefactors were not anonymous. A resolution of the UNRRA Council recommended that member governments "permit the use of special labels or other designations on supplies and equipment belonging to or furnished by the UNRRA administration." The resolution did not deal with the controversial issue of whether the national flag of the contributing country should be used as a label. But even with the later decision that no flag be used, it was not hard to find out that the United States was the main supplier and contributor to the UNRRA operations. In regard to this matter the official history of UNRRA states:

> It is less certain that there was a wide-spread, clear understanding of the international character of UNRRA, or of the principles under which it operated. Indications were, in fact, encountered in all receiving countries of a frequent tendency to regard UNRRA a "help from the American people." It arose primarily from the fact that such commodities as canned goods, drugs and equipment, assembled in the receiving country, being shorn of their UNRRA labeled outer wrappings, revealed only the brand or manufacturers markings which included the country of origin—and the largest portion of UNRRA supplies came from the United States of America. The major contributing country had, therefore, little cause for concern that its generosity was not well known.

As future developments showed, this generosity soon had to prove itself in new conditions, on a new basis, and with a much more convincing and far-reaching philosophy than that which prevailed in times of emergency, of war, or of postwar circumstances.

2

$$

The Plan That Worked

The test came very soon. The last shipments of UNRRA's more than three billion dollars worth of materials had reached their destinations. The program arrived at the last stage of its phasing-out operation. Peace seemed to have been won; but now new clouds began to gather on the European horizon. It seemed that the victors had been overcome along with the vanquished. America's allies were lying prostrate. The situation threatened the very foundations of the Western civilization which the Second World War had been supposed to save.

There seemed to be almost no hope. Food was rationed more strictly than in the days of war. France had to return to a two-hundred-gram daily ration of bread. Sugar was not available. In restaurants liquid saccharin was served as a substitute. It was kept in bottles which had special devices to ensure that not too much liquid would flow into the cup of what was supposed to be coffee, but which was in fact some burned vegetable with a dreadful taste. Englishmen had to live on a diet of substitutes or strict rationing, which, the doctors warned, would produce a generation of undernourished and weak people. And so the story went in country after country of postwar Europe. At the same time, the entire machinery of production seemed to be moving toward a complete standstill. The people froze throughout the extraordinarily cold winter because the small supply of fuel had to be saved to keep the economy running. The undernourished and underpaid workers were quick to respond to any call for a protest or a strike. Hardly a week went by in which some kind of a public utility would not stop functioning. This was generally caused by either lack of materials with which to maintain operations, or by a strike, which was the workers' only recourse in their desperate situation.

Europe was approaching a state of complete economic chaos, a situation which would be only one step away from a total breakdown of the normal functioning of the state. To provide the minimum subsistence requirements for their populations, western European countries had to import goods in an amount beyond their ability to pay. During 1946 and 1947, western Europe financed dollar-cost imports valued at approximately fourteen billion dollars. These imports were made possible through loans and grants as well as the use of dwindling dollar reserves. The dollar deficit in 1947 alone reached $8,000,000,000.

32

The United States could not and did not let the victorious alliance succumb. As years went by without visible improvement in the economic situation of these countries, America continued to supply them with the means of survival. From the end of the war till the middle of 1949, the United States gave to the rest of the world nearly $16,000,000,-000 in aid. Of this amount about $11,500,000,000 went to western and southern Europe. This sum may be further broken down into about $4,500,000,000 as grants (which included the allotments to UNRRA, post-UNRRA and "interim" aid programs) and $6,800,000,000 in the form of credits.

While these programs of aid were being implemented, a new situation developed in Greece and Turkey: Great Britain announced that it could no longer carry the responsibility for the security of the eastern Mediterranean region. Greece had been devastated by the war and was now torn by guerrilla warfare being waged by Communist forces; the Communists hoped to win this strategically located country and to draw it into the Russian orbit. Turkey was under growing pressure from Russia. There was not a moment to lose. On March 12, 1947, President Truman asked Congress to appropriate $400,000,000 for economic and military aid to Greece and Turkey. The President's message proclaimed "a policy of active support to free peoples resisting subjugation by armed minorities or by outside aggression." Thus the "Truman Doctrine," which was to become a permanent feature of American foreign policy, was born.

In 1946, Great Britain was accorded a loan of $3,750,000,000 to enable her to reduce trade and exchange controls. And because of the obstacles that the Soviet Union created in the UNRRA operations in eastern Europe, President Truman recommended that an additional $350,000,-000 for relief assistance be administered directly by the U.S.

But the demand for aid to Greece and Turkey, to which the Congress promptly responded, was only a stop-gap operation in a limited area, and on a limited scale. By no means did it solve any of the major problems western Europe was facing. The depth of these problems was not generally understood. Dean Acheson, one of the most influential personalities in the Truman Administration, stated that everybody had a "misconception regarding the nature and depth of the problems after World War II. No one had a picture of the completeness of the disruption that had occurred. This was true of both European and Asiatic countries. We had operated on a theory dealing with hunger, disease, and unrest until one or two good crops could come in. But the problems were more far-reaching and it grew upon us toward the end of 1946 that we were heading for very bad trouble."

This "bad trouble" was recognized by American policy makers. The Policy Planning Staff of the State Department was advised to prepare a memorandum on how to deal with this critical situation. In its report, which was ready on May 23, 1947, it discussed conditions prevailing in

Europe and suggested means of dealing with them immediately. This report, which provided the policy guide lines that later produced the Marshall Plan, repudiated the idea that Communism is the sole source of all troubles and that the fear of Communist expansion dictated America's policies of aid to suffering countries. "The Policy Staff," read the memorandum, "does not see Communist activities as the root of the present difficulties in Western Europe. The Policy Planning Staff recognizes that the Communists are exploiting the European crisis and that further Communist successes would create a serious danger to American security. It considers, however, that American efforts in aid to Europe should be directed not to the combating of Communism as such, but to the restoration of the economic health and vigor of the European society."

To make this point even clearer, the memorandum further asserted that two principal misconceptions about the Truman Doctrine had to be dispelled: "that the United States approach to world problems is a defensive reaction to Communist pressure and that the effort to restore sound economic conditions in other countries is only a by-product of this reaction and not something we would be interested in doing if there were no Communist menace," and "that the Truman Doctrine is a blank check to give economic and military aid to any area in the world where the Communists show signs of being successful."

But discounting, to a degree, the Communist drive did not mean closing our eyes to the needs of Europe. When the needs of all of war-devastated Europe were discussed at the Big Four Foreign Ministers Conference in Moscow in March, 1947, the Western diplomats had no difficulty in sensing that Russia was not in any great hurry to relieve the difficulties of Europe. Secretary of State George C. Marshall soon became aware of the main obstacles in the way of a cooperative effort to put Europe on its feet. The Foreign Ministers' conference had dragged on for almost a month before Marshall seized upon an opportunity to have a frank talk with Stalin himself. As Marshall later revealed, this was a most instructive private conversation since Stalin did not even try to conceal that Russia's interest was in keeping the European kettle boiling and in intensifying European distress.

Marshall knew then that Europe would have to be helped without Russian cooperation. He outlined the problem with his advisers and sought for an appropriate solution. George F. Kennan, head of the Policy Planning Staff, saw eye-to-eye with Marshall. Marshall gave him only one instruction: "Avoid trivia."

"Avoiding trivia" was only part of the problem. There was another, more serious one: how to assure the support of the country and of Congress for any new program of assistance to needy nations. Some years later Marshall wrote: "The feeling seemed to be that any new proposal for more funds to be appropriated would be ruthlessly repulsed. Therefore the manner of statement, the first approach, and similar factors had to be most seriously considered. It is easy to propose a great plan, but exceedingly difficult to manage the form and procedure so that it has a fair chance of political survival."

To ensure this "political survival" Marshall undertook a series of consultations with leaders of both parties. The problem of securing bipartisan support was discussed with the leading Republican in the Senate, Arthur H. Vandenberg. He was rather upset by the magnitude of the figures yet showed understanding for the magnitude of the task.

When the stage was set and the groundwork laid, Secretary of State Marshall chose the commencement exercises at Harvard, on June 5, 1947, to announce the decisions the U.S. Government had reached regarding problems of European recovery. It is somewhat striking that Marshall's address, which marked the beginning of what was later to be known as the "Marshall Plan," did not elaborate on any plan at all. Speaking in rather vague terms—such as "assistance"—he called mainly for a new "approach" to the problems of European recovery:

> The truth of the matter is that Europe's requirements for the next three or four years are so much greater than her present ability to pay that she must have substantial additional help or face economic, social, and political deterioration of a very grave character. Aside from the demoralizing effect on the world at large and the possibilities of disturbances arising as a result of desperation of the people concerned, the consequences to the United States economy should be apparent to all. It is logical that the United States should do whatever it is able to do to assist in the return of normal economic health in the world, without which there can be no political stability and no assured peace. Our policy is directed not against any country or doctrine, but against hunger, poverty, desperation, and chaos.

Having stated these intentions, Marshall felt obliged to explain the role that the American involvement was supposed to assume in the process of European recovery. "Such assistance," said Marshall, "must not be on a piecemeal basis as various crises develop. The initiative has to come from Europe. The program should be a joint one, agreed to by a number, if not all European nations. An essential part of any successful action on the part of the United States is an understanding on the part of the American people of the character of the problem and the remedies to be applied."

As future developments proved, Marshall's "approach" had been one with understanding on both fronts: in Europe, in the Cabinets of the nations which were involved and among the people of the United States who had, in the end, to bear the entire burden of turning Marshall's approach into a plan for European recovery.

Europe's leaders responded promptly. Barely a week after Marshall's address, French Foreign Minister Bidault spoke with British Foreign Secretary Bevin. To demonstrate that the American proposal was not merely an anti-Russian stratagem, the two Foreign Ministers agreed not to move further without the participation of the Soviet Union. On June 23, Foreign Minister Molotov accepted the invitation, and four days later a Big Three conference opened in Paris.

Acting in accordance with Secretary Marshall's suggestions, the British and French proposed to elect a steering committee to survey the resources of the European countries and develop the outlines for a European recovery program. Here the first snag developed. Molotov objected to any survey of resources. This would mean, he said, meddling into the internal affairs of sovereign nations. Instead, he proposed that the United States be asked to supply details about the amount of help it was ready to grant and that each country prepare its own survey and estimates.

The British and French Ministers disputed this approach. It then seemed to be a normal diplomatic dispute, which everybody hoped to resolve. But in the midst of the diplomatic bargaining something unexpected happened. Molotov's position hardened, and it became clear that he was looking for a way to break up the conference. Writing about this development, Dean Acheson noticed an interesting detail: "It seems that Molotov has a bump on his forehead, which swells when he is under emotional strain. The matter was being debated, and Molotov had raised relatively minor questions and objections at various points, when a telegram was handed to him. He turned pale and the bump on his forehead swelled. After that his attitude suddenly changed and he became much more harsh. I suspect that Molotov must have thought that the instruction sent to him from Moscow was stupid; in any case, the withdrawal of the Russians made operations much more simple."

The cable, certainly from Stalin, and the subsequent withdrawal of Russia from the deliberations, did not disrupt the practical work of preparing plans for the start of the European recovery program. But it did start a series of Russian efforts to make the plan unworkable, to label it an "American imperialist device," to mobilize European workers to sabotage it, and to neutralize its influence on the European economy. On June 25, *Pravda* made the first attack, calling the Marshall Plan "a plan to prolong the postwar boom in the United States." On June 29, the official Russian news agency Tass called the Marshall Plan "another instance of American imperialism."

The Russian attacks did not stop the Western powers from acting. On July 3, Bidault and Bevin invited twenty-four European nations to a conference to be convened in Paris on July 12. Austria, Belgium, Denmark, France, Greece, Iceland, Ireland, Italy, Luxembourg, the Netherlands, Norway, Portugal, Sweden, Switzerland, Turkey, and the United Kingdom sent representatives. Czechoslovakia, which had agreed to attend, was forced to withdraw as a result of Russian pressure.

Preventing the eastern European countries from participating was not Russia's only response to the Marshall Plan. In July, *Pravda* announced the establishment of a new organization of the Communist countries, the Cominform, with headquarters in Belgrade, Yugoslavia. In addition to the countries under Communist rule—Russia, Yugoslavia, Poland, Bulgaria, Czechoslovakia, Hungary, and Rumania—the Communist parties of France and Italy became founding members of the new organization. The task of these latter was clear: the sabotage of the Marshall Plan in their countries, both crucial to Europe's survival. Moreover, this political move was strengthened by an economic plan for cooperation between Russia and the eastern European countries: instead of the Marshall Plan they were given the Molotov Plan, based on trade agreements involving grain deliveries and various barter arrangements.

The Communist attacks notwithstanding, western Europe moved quickly towards cooperation, a basic condition for American help. The Committee for European Economic Cooperation (CEEC) began an analysis of the economic resources and capabilities of the sixteen nations which subscribed to the program. The CEEC engaged in developing the principles for the European recovery program, defined the specific functions of each participating country, and determined the aid which each was to receive through the general assistance plan. Subcommittees for food and agriculture, iron and steel, fuel power, and transport worked on details. By September 22, the CEEC presented to the American government a report which suggested four main tasks: (1) a concentrated effort to increase production; (2) the creation and maintenance of internal financial stability; (3) the establishment of a permanent organization and of greater economic cooperation among the participating countries in the fields of production, development of resources, trade, transportation, and movement of persons; and (4) the solution of the problem of the dollar deficit—primarily through expansion of exports.

Simultaneously, the pace of American action was quickened. On June 22, President Truman appointed committees to make studies for the preparation of a program which could be submitted to Congress—and have a chance of meeting its approval.

The President's Committee on Foreign Aid, composed of eminent private citizens, under the chairmanship of W. Averell Harriman, then Secretary of Commerce, started work. The task set for this committee was to formulate principles to guide the aid programs and to investigate the needs and capabilities of the European countries, the volume of assistance required, and its relation to the American economy, and problems of finance and administration.

Two other committees, one under the chairmanship of the Secretary of Interior, Julius A. Krug, and the other headed by Edwin G. Nourse, were engaged in studying America's ability to launch a large new aid program and the probable effect of aid exports upon domestic production, consumption, and prices.

Thus the preparation was made most thoroughly. The Administration had to be ready to meet every possible inquiry, to answer every question, to eradicate every doubt. All over the country voices had been raised against continuing high taxes which had one purpose: to "bail out Europe." The reports of the three committees arrived at similar conclusions, that aid to Europe was a necessity and that if aid were not extended, free institutions everywhere, including those in the United States, would be in jeopardy. The Nourse report went even further, predicting that without an aid program American exports would decrease sharply. "In the longer run," said the report, "the economic restoration of Europe will benefit our own economy by enabling us to obtain more goods by advantageous trade." The report of the President's Committee on Foreign Aid devoted even more attention to the interdependence of the United States and Europe. "Our position in the world has been based for at least a century on the existence, in Europe, of a number of strong states, committed by tradition and inclination to the democratic concept. . . . Our goal should be to bring about a condition where exports from this country are more nearly balanced by a return flow from abroad of services and materials essential to our economy."

To "put Europe on its feet," as the saying was in those days, required an immense amount of money. The Committee did not hesitate to point out that to finance the European recovery program $12.5–17.5 billion would be necessary over a four-year period. Most of this would have to come through grants and loans from the United States Treasury, along with $58,000,000,000 from the World Bank and other sources. But the Committee understood quite well that even such sums would be only a fraction of the over-all effort which Europe would have to make. The Committee, therefore, added that this aid should be viewed not as a support for Europe, but only as a "spark which can fire the engine."

A troublesome problem which arose at this time was the question of official American assistance to economic enterprises which were not run on a "free-enterprise" basis. This matter, which has since accompanied almost every discussion of foreign aid, seemed to be crucial at that time also. There was considerable dissent within the committee, and it required the mediation of Paul G. Hoffman, the man designated to head the aid agency and a leader of the highest standing in the business community, to resolve it. What has come up again and again in reports of various Presidential Committees on Foreign Aid, and most recently in the Clay Report, in 1963, was settled, at that time through a compromise as follows:

Aid from this country should not be conditioned on the methods used to reach these (agreed-upon) goals so long as they are consistent with basic democratic principles. Continued adherence to such principles is an essential condition to continued aid, but the condition should not require adherence to any form of economic organization or the abandonment of plans adopted and carried out in a free and democratic way. While this Committee firmly believes

38

that the American system of free enterprise is the best method of obtaining high productivity, it does not believe that any foreign aid program should be used as a means of requiring other countries to adopt it. The imposition of any such conditions would constitute an unwarranted interference with the internal affairs of friendly nations.

The preparations accomplished, the final plan could be drafted. On December 19, 1947, President Truman sent to Congress, then in special session, a message on "A Program for the U.S. Support to European Recovery." The general sentiment expressed in the message was summed up in the following sentence: "Our deepest concern with European Recovery is that it is essential to the maintenance of the civilization in which the American way of life is rooted."

The message did not reach an unprepared Congress. On July 29, 1948, the House of Representatives established a Select Committee of nineteen members to study the proposals of Secretary of State Marshall. Representative Charles A. Eaton, chairman of the Foreign Affairs Committee, presided over this Select Committee, and Representative Christian Herter was vice chairman. The Committee members did not satisfy themselves with holding hearings. They traveled to many countries. They learned on the spot. Their impressions were best defined by a question which one Congressman formulated: "What would it cost us not to aid Europe?"

Representatives of both parties on the Committee agreed that aid to Europe was imperative. A leading Republican, Congressman Everett M. Dirksen, went further than giving only formal support for the program. He said,

I see three choices before the American people. One is to withdraw from Europe and be prepared to let the Kremlin take over. Another is to give niggardly aid. There is a third choice, and that is this choice that we must make. I want to make it. I have been back home. People have talked to me about giving away my country, and I have talked to them. . . . And I have said "Look, let us examine this whole picture." And it is amazing to me to see how the people back home have changed minds on the basis of such facts as you disclose to them. I am not afraid of the reaction in this country. I am confident that in proportion as we do our jobs as representatives to bring them the story—that they will go along with the third choice, and the third choice in my book is immediate, adequate, aggressive aid. My formula, Mr. Chairman, is very, very brief. Do it, do it now and do it right.

Of course there was opposition, and some of it from important and respected leaders. Former President Hoover called for more safeguards. He asked that the aid in the first fifteen months be limited to around three billion dollars. Another prominent Republican, Senator Robert A. Taft, agreed to the idea of the proposed aid but opposed its dimensions. "Aid to Europe," said Taft, "at the rate proposed by the European nations, means eight billion dollars in taxes in 1948, on the American people, over and above what they would otherwise pay. The adoption

39

of the Marshall Plan has a direct tendency to inflate prices further in the United States. I am prepared to support, to some reasonable amount, the general principle of aid to European countries to enable them to help themselves."

On the other hand, at the grassroots level, there were many who had not even heard about the program. A Gallup poll, released on December 7, 1947, stated that in four and a half months the proportion of the population which had not read or heard about the Marshall Plan had dropped from 51 to 36 per cent. During the last five weeks of that period, the percentage of those with "no opinion" on the plan dropped from 38 to 27 per cent, and the percentage of those favoring the program had risen from 47 to 56 per cent, with 17 per cent opposed.

The dissemination of information about the Marshall Plan and the forthcoming discussion in Congress was greatly intensified especially through the activities of a Citizens Committee for the Marshall Plan. Former Secretary of War Henry L. Stimson called for support. As head of the Citizens Committee, Stimson secured the cooperation of another former Secretary of War, Robert P. Patterson, who became chairman of its executive committee. Among the members were Mrs. Wendell Willkie, chairman of the women's division, Dean Acheson, Winthrop W. Aldrich, James B. Carey, David Dubinsky, Herbert H. Lehman, Philip Reed, and Herbert Bayard Swope.

The Committee, in a huge information and education effort, published leaflets, pamphlets and weekly "fact sheets" concerning the Marshall Plan. Speeches, lectures, and radio programs were devoted to the same theme. Thus, when the President suggested in his message that $17 billion be made available for the four-year program of European aid ($6.8 billion for the first fifteen months), the immense figures did not shock the members of Congress. The Senate and House committees concerned with foreign affairs opened hearings without delay. Week after week witnesses appeared before them. Their testimonies before the Senate Committee filled 1,466 pages and those before the House Committee 2,269 pages. Not a single aspect of the problem was overlooked. Each side had a chance to air its grievances, reservation about, or support for the Marshall Plan.

The American determination to turn the European recovery program into a working plan provoked intensified Russian propaganda attacks. The "plan of American imperialism" was renamed the "instrument of preparation for war," and the "means for the economic and political enslavement of Europe." The Communist parties of western Europe followed the same propaganda line devised by the Cominform. When the price of wine declined in France, Coca-Cola was the cause; when a motion picture industry went bankrupt, the invasion of Hollywood films was blamed. Because of the strength of the Communist parties in France and Italy, the leading countries of the European recovery effort, this propaganda was at least partially effective. The French Institute of Public Opinion reported in September, 1947, that the results of a poll it took indicated that only 18 per cent believed that Secretary Marshall's proposal was a result of a sincere concern with the welfare of Europe; 17 per cent were of the opinion that the Marshall Plan was an American means of meddling in European affairs; 47 per cent saw in the Marshall Plan a way to assure foreign markets for American production; and 18 per cent had no opinion.

The vehemence of the opposition had an effect diametrically opposite to the one the Soviets expected; it hastened Congressional deliberations and aroused the country to support the program. The New York *Times* summed up the influence of the Russian attack in a sentence: "The Kremlin, as usual, comes to the rescue of the European Recovery Program."

The House and the Senate quickly advanced towards the final vote. The stop-gap measure to assure an Interim Aid Program took the form of a $522 million grant for France, Italy, and Austria and was approved by a special session of the Congress. On March 1, 1948, Senate Republican leader Vandenberg was able to state that "with the unanimous approval of the Senate Foreign Relations Committee, I report the Economic Cooperation Act of 1948 in its perfected text." Continuing, Senator Vandenberg tried to explain the real considerations which moved the Senators in their deliberations and decisions.

There are no blueprints to guarantee results. We are entirely surrounded by calculated risks. I profoundly believe that the pending program is the best of the risks. It strives to help stop World War III, before it starts. It fights economic chaos which would precipitate far-flung disintegration. It sustains Western civilization. It means to take Western Europe completely off the American dole at the end of the adventure. It recognizes the grim truth—whether we like it or not—that American self-interest, national economy, and national security are inseparably linked with these objectives. . . . It is the final product of eight months of more intensive study by more devoted minds than I have ever known to concentrate upon any objective in all my twenty years in Congress. It has its foes—some of whom compliment it by their transparent hatreds. But it has its friends, countless, prayerful friends not only at the hearthstones of America, but under many other flags. It is a plan for peace, stability, and freedom. As such it involves a clear self-interest of the United States.

The foes were mighty and they were persistent. Senator George W. Malone, a vehement opponent of the plan, held the floor of the Senate for two days. Others, in both Houses of Congress, also tried to defeat it. But they could not turn the tide. The Senate voted 69 to 17 in favor of adoption of the Act; in the House of Representatives the vote was 329 to 74. Thus on April 3, 1948, the Economic Cooperation Administration came into being. The activities of the ECA encompassed not only the administration of aid to western Europe, but also of U.S. aid to countries in other parts of the world. The most important of these were East and Southeast Asia.

41

Flanked by Marshall Plan officials and Congressional leaders, President Truman signs into law a bill authorizing new appropriations to carry the European Recovery Program until July 1, 1950. President Truman is seated. Standing from left to right: Howard Bruce, ECA Deputy Administrator; Representative John Kee, Chairman, House Foreign Affairs Committee; William C. Foster, Deputy Special Representative to Europe; W. Averell Harriman, Special Representative to Europe; Paul G. Hoffman, ECA Administrator; U.S. Senator Tom Connally of Texas, Chairman of the Foreign Relations Committee; and Dean Acheson, U.S. Secretary of State.

The wording of the new act embodied some decisions about ways to implement both the program and its long-range goals. One of these goals was to encourage European countries to achieve, through joint organization, economic cooperation among themselves. This attempt to create a domestic market as large as that of the United States has proved itself the most decisive factor in the movement of western Europe towards unity. The act also provided for bilateral agreements which obliged each country to increase its production, take adequate measures for achieving financial stability, and cooperate in striving towards the reducing of their trade barriers. An important passage dealt with "counterpart funds" of local currency, which were equal to the amounts received in the form of grants. Each government had to deposit the funds in a special account. Of the money in these accounts, 95 per cent had

General Marshall flanked by leading officers of foreign aid. From left to right: William C. Foster, Paul G. Hoffman, General George C. Marshall, and Harold Stassen.

to be used, with the concurrence of the United States government, for domestic recovery; the remaining 5 per cent was reserved to help meet American administrative and procurement costs. Each country was also supposed to assist in the accumulation of strategic materials required by the United States. To assure employment for the American Merchant Marine a clause stipulated that 50 per cent of all assistance goods had to be transported in American ships and that 25 per cent of the U.S. wheat shipments had to be shipped in the form of flour.

The organizational problems were resolved speedily in the creation of the ECA, which set up headquarters in Washington and established an office in Paris, with special missions in each participating country. A Public Advisory Board of twelve members was set up to assure public support and supervision, and a Joint Congressional Committee was appointed to review all foreign-aid programs. The latter soon became known as the "watchdog committee." The importance of the new administrative machinery to implement the Marshall Plan was stressed by the decision of Congress to make the head of the new agency (the Administrator of the Economic Cooperation Administration) appointed by and responsible directly to the President. It further decided that he should have equal status with the heads of executive departments and that he and the Secretary of State should keep each other "fully and currently informed on matters including prospective action pertinent to the duties of the other."

Paul G. Hoffman, a leading Republican and industrialist, was appointed to head the new agency, which would supervise the biggest plan for economic assistance in the history of the United States. The choice of a Republican was advised by Senator Vandenberg, who considered it a good device for assuring bipartisan support in the many problems the new program was expected to encounter. (Hoffman himself remarked at his appointment: "it seems that I was the least obnoxious of the Republicans.")

To deal with the Economic Cooperation Administration the European Marshall Plan countries established among themselves the Organization for European Economic Cooperation (OEEC). The American government decided to encourage this development towards European unity. It urged the OEEC to take the responsibility for recommending the division of aid in the fiscal year 1948–1949. The importance of such a development was not underestimated. It would not only ease the American burden of having separately to allocate aid for each country but would also be a most potent means of promoting European unity for it would provide the western European nations with a major exercise in close cooperation.

Russell H. Dorr, chief of Marshall Plan Mission in Turkey, and Emdjet Yektay, Turkish official, join Turkish farmer in inspecting varieties of wheat. Nearly five thousand tractors were imported and sold in Turkey under the Marshall Plan.

Fine herds of livestock in Italy resulting from Marshall Plan aid being inspected by group of American farmers who toured Marshall Plan countries.

45

Marshall Plan Administrator, Paul G. Hoffman, celebrating the first anniversary of the Marshall Plan.

These sentiments of the American government were also voiced in many other forms. An official statement of the U.S. government said, "it is further declared to be the policy of the United States to encourage the unification of Europe." A report on the European Recovery Program made clear that "persons most familiar with attitudes in Congress are afraid that a continuation of the European Recovery Program at the minimum necessary level of aid cannot be expected unless Western European countries have clearly embarked on the course of economic unity." In this spirit, Hoffman called for "building of an expanding economy in Western Europe through economic integration."

European leaders did their best to comply with America's wishes. The European Payment Union was soon formed by the OEEC in consultation with the European Office of the ECA, and on May 9, 1950, the French Foreign Minister, Robert Schuman, proposed the pooling of the European coal and steel industries. This marked the beginning of the creation of a group of economic and political institutions for western European integration, of which the Common Market is the latest, but probably not the last development.

The practical launching of the European Recovery Program was effected without delay. Two weeks after Hoffman assumed office, on April 9, 1948, the freighter *John H. Quick* sailed from Galveston, Texas, for Bordeaux, carrying 9,000 long tons of wheat. By June 30, goods and services worth $738 million had been authorized on a grant basis. Together with other programs which were being negotiated or had been completed, a total of $1.3 billion was promised within ninety days after the Economic Cooperation Administration had come into being. In the first fifteen months, $6.8 billion was piped into the economies of the Marshall Plan countries. Although Congress was unwilling to make commitments for more than one year, no hitches developed and appropriations for the sixteen countries participating in the European Recovery Program (ERP) were forthcoming each year. In the field of foreign aid, Congress continuously demonstrated a degree of cooperativeness with the Administration which has never been matched.

The sixteen countries of the ERP, together with the three occupied zones of West Germany (later the Federal Republic of Germany) speedily supplied proofs of their efficiency in using American assistance. Production indicators of the April–June quarter of 1949 showed a steady increase in agricultural and industrial output, not only when compared with postwar levels, but even with the levels of 1938. The rate of growth continued to climb steadily. In the second quarter of 1950, industrial production in ERP countries was 18 per cent higher than in 1938 and 28 per cent above the first quarter of 1948. The largest production increases over prewar levels occurred in Norway (47 per cent), Sweden and Denmark (69 per cent each), and in the United Kingdom (49 per cent).

This economic miracle was made possible in spite of the fact that American aid in 1948–1949, for instance, amounted to no more than about 4 per cent of western Europe's gross national product. In his testimony before Congress, Hoffman said that "for every dollar of our aid to Europe, Europe puts six dollars into capital formation." For example, an allocation of $300 million which made possible the purchase of thermo-equipment (power production machinery), also made possible an investment of some $6 billion, or twenty times as much in thermo-generating power, over a period of five or six years.

Everything was developing according to the plans made during 1947

47

Dedication ceremony of Berlin City Hall built with Marshall Plan funds.

and 1948. The smoothness of the operations surpassed all expectations. At the time President Truman submitted his message to Congress, an expenditure of $17 billion was anticipated; even higher estimates were made by some of the many committees which worked on the plans for the program. However, when the ERP was formally dissolved on December 31, 1951, the funds which Congress had made available totaled only $13,015,000,000. Even the expected duration of the program had been overestimated: The program was completed six months before its four-year cycle was to have ended. The program's official inauguration was in April, 1948, and by the end of 1951 its administrators were able to announce proudly that the task had been successfully completed. Thus was vindicated an earlier report of the American ECA: "The two and a half years since the start of ERP has witnessed a profound change in Western Europe and . . . it can be truthfully asserted that much of the heritage of destruction left by World War II has been overcome and the most difficult part of the reconstruction task has been accomplished." Likewise confirmed was the report of the Committee of European Economic Cooperation, which stated at the end of 1950 that the "Marshall Plan was the blood transfusion which sustained the weakening European economies and gave them the strength to work on their own recovery."

Almost a decade and a half later, on April 2, 1963, in his message to Congress introducing the proposed Mutual Defense and Assistance Programs, President Kennedy praised in the highest terms this major effort in American aid: "History records that the Marshall Plan made it possible for the nations of Western Europe, including the United Kingdom, to recover from the devastation of the world's most destructive war, to rebuild military strength, to withstand the expansionist thrust of Stalinist Russia, and to embark on an economic renaissance which has made Western Europe the second greatest and richest industrial complex in the world today—a vital center of free world strength, itself now contributing to the growth and strength of less developed countries."

The vast amounts of American aid to Europe have also contributed to the economic well-being of America itself. Of the over-all amount allocated for aid to Europe, over two-thirds were designated for procurement in the United States. Special organizational arrangements—procurement agents, commodity specialists who advised the private commercial channels making the purchases in the United States—were all aimed at effecting a balanced distribution of procurement in the United States, geographically and within each industry. Industry and agriculture profited almost equally, as almost equal amounts were spent to purchase the products of each, and the shipping industry had its share in the more than one billion dollars of ocean freight costs.

The Economic Cooperation Administration, therefore, had good reason to be satisfied with its accomplishments, as had Administrator Paul G. Hoffman and W. Averell Harriman, the head of its European Office.

Bakery in Oslo, Norway, after bread and flour rationing was lifted in March, 1949, in part the result of plentiful imports of grain from the U.S. under the Marshall Plan.

From the perspective of more than a decade, Hoffman drew many far-reaching conclusions when I interviewed him recently on his experience in the foreign-aid field. "The whole expression 'foreign aid,'" said Hoffman, "is most unfortunate. If these were really only foreign-aid programs, I doubt whether there would be a legal basis to tax for such purposes. The fact is that the Marshall Plan was vital to the interests of the United States, to its security, and commercial situation. Any investment in European recovery will come full back to us, if it has not come already." As far as United States security is concerned, Mr. Hoffman stated emphatically that "any military person will admit that it would have cost many billions more to build the defense system of the United States if Europe were not saved and if there would have been no possibility to build the NATO defense alliance." About the economic problems, which many seem to view, at present, only in the light of the difficulties with the French and the Common Market and the latter's relationship with American trade, Hoffman stated: "In 1948 there was almost no flow of normal trade between western Europe and the United States through normal trade channels—and now the United States export to western European countries has reached the seven-billion-dollar mark."

In this regard it is of interest to quote some little publicized remarks which Hoffman made in Washington on April 6, 1963, to mark the fifteenth anniversary of the start of operations of the Economic Cooperation Administration. Speaking before his associates in the Marshall Plan venture at the same hotel in which the ECA had its first office (the Statler-Hilton), Hoffman said that perhaps he,

Averell Harriman, Bill Foster, and Dick Bissel can take some credit for recognizing that the role of the ECA in speeding the recovery of Europe was that of a junior partner. We knew that only the Europeans can save Europe. It was because we recognized this that we placed upon every country the responsibility for developing its own recovery program and upon the OEEC the responsibility for coordinating these programs and recommending to us contributions which should be made to each country. In other words, we did not over-administer—if anything we underadministered.

May I conclude by calling attention to a rather exciting fact which has been but little publicized. It was originally estimated by the European Economic

The primitive methods of making and selling bread in Italian villages are still the order. But the Marshall Plan has meant more wheat, and therefore more bread for the village bakerwoman to deliver from house to house.

51

Committee, headed by Sir Oliver Franks, that approximately twenty-nine billion dollars of assistance would be required to restore industrial and agricultural production in western Europe to prewar levels and that it would take four years to reach that goal. Later the Harriman Committee, of which I was a member, estimated that the job could be done for seventeen billion. The actual result was that, after only two and a half years of the Marshall Plan, the work of reconstruction had gone forward with such a will that industrial production in western Europe had jumped to 40 per cent above the highest prewar figure, and even in agriculture the West Europeans had registered a 20 per cent gain. In the end, the job of European recovery was accomplished with U.S. aid of only about thirteen billions, of which almost two billions have since been repaid.

Why did this happen? Because of the tremendous upsurge in the spirit of the European people and the enthusiasm with which they went about their job. Thus once more it was proved that you cannot measure or forecast, by statistical analysis or otherwise, the potentialities of the human spirit.

These potentialities had since to match for many years the American aid programs to cover tens of countries over all continents. With the Marshall Plan a success, new vigor might have been expected for aiding foreign nations in their development and in increasing production and raising their standard of living. However, these expectations were not fully realized. International political complications forced a change in the priorities of foreign aid. Economic aid was to a large extent replaced by military aid, and instead of concentrating on one area American aid had to be spread out over all continents. The level of economic, social, and political development of the additional recipient nations was far below that of the western European countries, and thus new tasks, new measures, and new forms became the order of the day for foreign-aid programs. The era of foreign aid as a permanent element of American policies, not linked any more with postwar reconstruction or emergencies, had arrived.

3

$$$

Who's Who in Foreign Aid—
The Parade of Initials

A lover of alphabet soup would delight in the concoction of initials that marks the changing nomenclature of the agencies which have been called upon to administer foreign-aid programs. The decade and a half of American economic assistance to foreign nations has not been especially marked by consistency in either the programs or the names of the agencies administering them. The search for the most suitable name has been unceasing. It is hard to avoid the impression that those in responsible positions have thought of a change of name as a panacea which was supposed to alleviate all the troubles which too often beset aid programs. The old saying that "a change of name is followed by a change of fortunes" seems to have been the guiding maxim for those who so often have made these changes.

It has been confusing indeed. A *Who's Who* in foreign aid agencies would be a record of continual change. Stories are told in Washington about Congressmen who, while debating foreign-aid programs, have mentioned—through a slip of the tongue—the name of some aid agency which has long been extinct. No wonder that foreigners are sometimes at a loss for the correct name and that Russian propaganda so often hinges criticism of these programs on their titles which—in the Russians' opinion—signify anything but conviction of success or belief in the propriety of American methods for dealing with foreign nations. An article called "The Golden Big Stick," published in the Moscow *New Times* of July 31, 1963, says: "That all is not well with the aid program is evidenced by the frequent reorganization of its operative machinery." While the Russian writer went on to speak in exaggerated terms about the "eleventh Administrator," David Bell, who was appointed in December, 1962, as Director of the Agency for International Development, the plain truth would be sufficient to point to the permanent uneasiness of the Administration itself in matters pertaining to foreign aid. It is the same uneasiness which has dictated not only the frequent changes in the agency names but also the appointment of special committees to investigate the entire program, including its various

Entrance gate and main factory building of Chunggu Paper Manufacture Company, Taegu, Korea.

phases of application and its usefulness for the United States. Congressional committees and committees of private citizens have alternated in this effort to overcome criticism by opponents of foreign aid. As Paul Hoffman has remarked, "againsters are being heard much more than are heard the for's." The Fulbright Committee of 1956, which conducted an extensive study of foreign aid, the Citizens Advisers Committee, headed by Benjamin F. Fairless, the Gray Committee, and the Draper Committee are only a few of the groups which have studied and made recommendations on foreign aid before the Kennedy Administration started a new series of committees on the same subject and for the same purpose.

One of the first acts of President Kennedy, only two months after his inauguration, was the appointment of a task force on Foreign Economic Assistance, "to work out the program, legislation and organization." This task force, which worked in three groups (on Legislation and Congressional Presentation, Organization and Administration, and Program Development), was supplemented by panels of private consultants and private citizens. It prepared a new program for foreign assistance after "drawing heavily on the accumulated experience of this country in administering foreign economic aid over the past two decades." But even after such a thorough research effort and revamping of the program, President Kennedy saw the necessity of the appointment of still another new committee. This panel's work reflected one of the necessities for presenting foreign aid programs to Congress: after a concentrated effort had been made to effect a clear division between economic aid and the various forms of military aid, the new Committee again consolidated all forms of assistance under one heading and chose "security" as that aspect of the aid program under which the entire program was to be promoted. The name of the committee manifested these parliamentary necessities. There was no mention of aid—it was a Committee to Strengthen the Security of the Free World, commonly known, after the name of its chairman, General Lucius D. Clay, as the Clay Committee.

The changing moods and changing political winds on Capitol Hill have never augured well for foreign-aid programs. A joke circulating around Washington likens the permanent scrutinizing of foreign-aid programs to repeatedly removing from the soil a plant which is just beginning to send out roots—to see whether the roots are growing fast enough and in the right direction. Unfortunately, this is not merely a joke. That seven major aid agencies have come into being in the seventeen years of centrally organized assistance, an average of one new agency (or new name) every two years, is sufficient proof of how much truth there is in this joke and of how many handicaps have been encountered by those responsible for the administration of foreign aid.

The great venture in aiding foreign nations began in an atmosphere of idealism. Though there were many—and among them several most influential people—who were unhappy about the direction embodied in the establishment of the Economic Cooperation Administration (ECA), the first independent foreign-aid agency, the overwhelming majority of both houses of Congress committed itself and the nation to a mission which at the outset entailed outlays that appeared huge even when the costs of the war, only recently terminated, were fresh in men's minds. The Economic Cooperation Act of 1948, which established the ECA to administer the European Recovery Program (Marshall Plan), seemed to many a one-time effort which would come to an end with the attainment of its goal—the economic recovery of western Europe. The aim was clearly defined, the method was worked out in all its details, and the real problems in the countries to be coped with and helped in their solution were known. In addition, and most importantly, there was a fixed time limit. Congress was called upon to support a plan which had to be terminated after four years.

The time limit was preserved, even advanced. The European Recovery

(*Above*) Before U.S. aid this is how earth was moved; (*below*) now work methods are revolutionized with the supply of earth-moving equipment to Thailand.

Program had made its intended, considerable impact even before four years had elapsed. And yet with the approaching end of this period, the end of the aid programs seemed even more remote than at the start. Aid to foreign countries had lost its simplicity. It had lost its initial unity and clarity of purpose, its strictly defined objectives, its geographical limits. It had become complicated, much in the same way that a war effort becomes complicated. The Cold War was on. The Berlin blockade and later the Communist aggression in Korea had their full impact on all aspects of United States foreign policy, including, naturally enough, the foreign-aid programs.

The name of the aid agency, the Economic Cooperation Administration, seemed rather inappropriate and even irrelevant in view of the new developments. The four-to-one ratio of economic to military assistance that had prevailed in the 1949 appropriations was now reversed. Of the $8.5 billion in new funds for 1950, $5.7 billion was allocated as assistance to allies who had to arm to face the Sino-Soviet threat. The change had to be sanctioned by a new legislative act. The Economic Cooperation Act was replaced by the Mutual Security Act of 1951, and the Economic Cooperation Administration had its functions transferred to the Mutual Security Agency (MSA) on December 30, 1951.

It was not only the new name that symbolized the growing concern with making foreign aid an efficient tool in achieving security for the non-communist world. On the initiative of various members of Congress, stipulations were added to make this purpose even clearer than the name itself would indicate. The Mutual Defense Assistance Control Act sponsored by Congressman Laurie C. Battle (the so-called Battle Act) provided for mandatory termination of United States aid to any country shipping arms and munitions to Soviet-dominated areas. The same Act provided for termination of aid to countries shipping strategic goods, other than arms, to Soviet-dominated areas unless the President found such termination detrimental to national security. The concern with Soviet pressure found its expression in still another development in the policies of the foreign-aid programs. After Yugoslavia broke with Moscow, Congress found it advisable to approve the extension of aid to a country governed by a declared Communist regime. This was a formal and unequivocal departure from the basic provisions of the Mutual Security Act, which provided aid to strengthen countries opposing the spread of Communism. Even the increase in the lending authority of the Export-Import Bank, from the ceiling set in 1945 of $3.5 billion to $4.5 billion, was also accompanied by a provision justifying this increase by the need to finance the production of strategic materials abroad.

In spite of all these provisions so clearly linked to the national security, hopes for a quick end to aid programs did not fade. Although a thorough analysis of the world political situation could hardly have given reason to believe that an end was in sight to international tensions, the first

(1951) Mutual Security Act provided for a termination of the entire program within three years. As every political observer could have predicted, and as a majority of Congress certainly anticipated, the conclusion of this three-year period found no significant change in the world situation. The 1954 Act did not renew the general provisions for ending foreign aid: in rewriting the earlier law, Congress stipulated that *economic* aid would end in 1955, making no mention of termination of military aid. But after an additional year of experience, even the provision for terminating economic aid was dropped.

All this, reflecting a growing recognition of the imperatives of a changing world, could not have left uninfluenced the organizational structure of the agency administering the United States assistance programs. When it became clear that economic aid programs would have to be definitely continued with no predictable and definite end in sight and when the

DDT and spray equipment are unloaded in the high plateau of Darlac province in Vietnam.

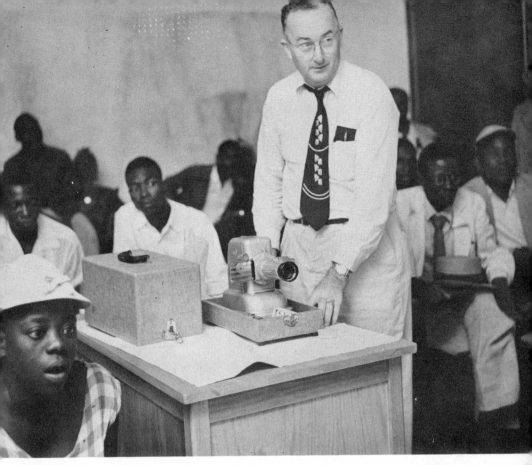

Dr. D. J. Hays, International Cooperation Administration elementary education specialist, shows slides to group of teachers attending a district-wide rural teachers workshop in Liberia.

armistice in Korea had been signed, a new name for the aid agency appeared overdue. It did not make too much sense to emphasize security considerations exclusively in a program which also provided emergency relief to flood-stricken areas in neutral countries like India or the construction of elementary schools in African villages. Although the annual presentations to Congress of proposals for foreign-aid expenditures continued to be enveloped in phrases stressing national security, the undeniable fact was that the desire to give aid to foreign nations did not stem exclusively from considerations of national security, but frequently was stimulated by humanitarian motives as well. It thus appeared to a growing body of opinion that the rhetoric of foreign aid distorted the truth unnecessarily, and to the detriment of the U.S. position in the world of nations.

In view of this general feeling prevailing in the Administration and in Congress, the latter did not interfere with Reorganization Plan Number 7, submitted by the Administration June 1 and effective August 1,

Well in Bastar Madhya Pradesh, India, first built under community development program, provides the only clean water source in the aboriginal area. The villagers posed for the picture themselves in response to a question from Technical Cooperation Administration to illustrate what the well meant to them.

1953, by which the Mutual Security Agency ceased to exist and its functions were transferred to the new Foreign Operations Administration—FOA.

The name "Foreign Operations Administration" did not seem to express clearly enough the real tasks and activities of the government agency entrusted with the administration of all forms of foreign aid. That the new agency also incorporated the functions of the Technical Cooperation Administration and the Institute of Inter-American Affairs did not do much toward defining the special character of the agency. "Foreign operations" was too general. Such a title could just as well be used for a host of other activities of the Department of State.

This feeling was greatly strengthened by a growing understanding of the new character of the manifold challenges which United States policies were facing all over the world. Hopes for an early termination of aid had faded almost completely. Almost all the new nations on the international scene were in urgent need of assistance, and the Soviet Union appeared as a competitor in the area of direct assistance to underdeveloped nations. There is no doubt that the short thaw in the Cold War, heralded by the 1955 Big Four agreement to restore Austria's sovereignty, was not without influence on the thinking of the Administration. These developments, together with the hopes raised by the approach of the summit conference in Geneva, scheduled for July 18, 1955, made a change in the conception of the aid agency imperative.

The new name chosen—International Cooperation Administration (ICA)—came to symbolize the new approach to the intricate problems of foreign aid. The element of cooperation with other nations seemed to be uppermost in men's minds. The new name would stress the values of partnership and give the recipient nations a feeling that they were not clients of wealthy Uncle Sam, but partners in a great venture of development and progress. Established by Executive Order 10610 of July 1, 1955, the ICA was organized as a semi-autonomous agency within the Department of State.

The trend towards cooperation seemed to be strengthened by the "revisionist" policy initiated at the Twentieth Congress of the Soviet Communist Party on February 14–25, 1956. But succeeding developments—the suppression of Hungary, the Russian arms deal with President Nasser of Egypt—dealt a shocking blow to these new approaches by the U.S. Administration. The withdrawal of the American offer to help finance the Aswan Dam in Egypt was a major event in the history of U.S. aid policies. Foes of the United States seized on this decision to inspire propaganda which asserted that American aid is never free of political strings. And the Soviet Union appeared as a major contender in the field of foreign aid when it announced its decision to fill the gap created by America's withdrawal of aid from the Aswan Dam project.

These developments brought about a far-reaching reappraisal of for-

(*Above*) Village mothers in Cameroon carry water for mixing mud to plaster new self-help temporary school. (*Below*) Village mother in Cameroon rubs new temporary school she is helping to build through self-help.

eign-aid programs. Political developments were seemingly imposing a change in the basic ideas underlying United States policies. The concept of giving aid only to those nations allied or in some way cooperating with the free world gave way to the new concept that U.S. aid can and should be given to any nation as long as it had not become involved in expansionist Communist bloc policies. The prevailing principle had been expounded by Secretary of State John Foster Dulles: that neutrality is immoral because there can be no neutrality between right and wrong. This principle started to recede from control of U.S. foreign policy in general and accordingly from foreign assistance policies, in particular. In his foreign aid proposals of 1956, President Eisenhower took notice of the new developments. Referring to the Soviet "challenge to competitive co-existence," President Eisenhower stated that "aggression through force appears to have been put aside, at least temporarily, and the communists are now making trade approaches to many nations of the free world."

The awareness of these new realities prompted a new series of studies of foreign aid programs as effective instruments of foreign policy. The Senate Foreign Relations Committee commissioned and published a score of such studies by independent experts before making its own final report, and the President also appointed a committee, which prepared another report. Though these various reports differed on some aspects of aid policies, one basic conclusion was shared by all: that aid be substantially increased to the newly independent, underdeveloped countries of Asia and Africa in the form of long-term loans. To implement these recommendations, the President asked Congress to establish a Development Loan Fund, with an initial appropriation of $500 million and authority to borrow another $750 million in the fiscal year 1959 and again in 1960. Explaining this request, President Eisenhower related it to the fact that the "moderate leaders" of the non-industrial nations of Asia and Africa "must be able to obtain sufficient aid from the free world to offer convincing hope for progress. Otherwise their peoples will surely turn elsewhere."

Thus, even in the non-military field, the idea of a contest with the communist world had to be employed to prod Congress into action and assure the annual appropriations for the aid programs.

In the situation then prevailing, the International Cooperation Administration seemed best fitted and adjusted to the new trends in international affairs. The search for new names for the aid agencies that would best reflect the tasks at hand seemed to have reached an end. The International Cooperation Administration had gained a long lease on life. It lasted longer than any previous aid agency, from 1955 to 1961. But, under Executive Order 10973, on November 3, 1961, the new Democratic Administration replaced it with the Agency for International Development (AID), again a semi-autonomous agency within the Department of State. The new agency incorporated the Development Loan

63

African boy learns English through improved teaching methods in self-help school.

Fund (DLF) established by the Mutual Security Act of 1957, as the lending arm of ICA, and later, in 1958, reorganized as a government corporation.

A decade of "mutual security" in foreign-aid legislation came to an end. This was not done only by implication, through a change in nomenclature. On March 22, 1961, two months after his inauguration, President Kennedy made clear his intention to replace the ten-year-old Mutual Security Act with a new mandate separating the military from the nonmilitary programs. The President logically contended that military-aid programs should be included where they belong—in the Department of Defense—so that the over-all basis of economic aid might not be blurred by military considerations, deforming its real character and aims. This was not the only change the President had in mind. Speaking about the new methods of aid programming, he called for a new approach to the entire concept of aid to foreign nations. The coming decade, he said, should become a "Decade of Development on which will depend, substantially, the kind of world in which we and our children shall live."

"There exists in the 1960's," said the President, "an historic opportunity for a major economic assistance effort by the free industrialized nations to move more than half the people of the less developed nations into self-sustained economic growth." The new trend found its expression in the name of the new Congressional act which authorized appropriations for the 1962 fiscal year: the Foreign Assistance Act.

The Congress went along with these changes without major opposition because the President's message merely called by name what had already been generally felt for some time. Senator Mike Mansfield clearly expressed these views some time before the Kennedy Administration took over. In a speech on foreign aid he said: "We have watched the emphasis in these programs shift from economic aid during the days of the Marshall Plan, to military aid in subsequent years. If my perceptions are accurate, we are now at the beginning of a shift back to an era of economic emphasis. We have also observed a change in the principal focus of these programs, from western Europe to the Far East and then the Middle East. Again, if my perceptions are accurate, the focus may now be shifting toward Africa and Latin America."

On the whole, Senator Mansfield's perceptions were accurate in tracing the changes in emphasis in the various forms of aid, and they were correct as regards the areas of concentration of the major aid effort.

In this most recent shift towards the underdeveloped countries of Asia, Africa, and Latin America, one problem assumed new importance—that of the development of human resources. American aid planners long ago understood that economic assistance could be properly utilized only by a nation which has the appropriately skilled people necessary for progress. No amount of assistance could help develop a country that

Stones carried by hand to build low walls to protect fertile valley from run-off water. Part of Moroccan National Development Program financed partly by P.L. 480, Title II.

lacked engineers, technicians, and planners, or schools and health facilities.

Awareness of this problem was translated into practical action in the early stages of the large-scale foreign-assistance programs. The Economic Assistance Act of 1950 provided for the establishment of the Technical Cooperation Administration (TCA) within the Department of State, and it later became an integral part of the major aid agencies as they evolved through the succeeding years.

The importance of this factor in the planning of aid was indicated by its inclusion in President Truman's inaugural address as part of his program for the coming four years. It was the fourth point in the program,

Children helping in distribution of pamphlets, leaflets, and posters in the Philippines.

and as such it has become known everywhere as Point Four. In many countries Point Four is a synonym for all forms of American aid, and it may indeed be said to have opened a new era of international cooperation in economic and social development.

"A bold new program for making the benefits of our scientific advances and industrial progress available for the improvement and growth of underdeveloped areas" were the words of President Truman in introducing the fourth point of his program. Other passages in this part of his address show that this was no casual remark.

Viewed against the background of the 1960's—with the advent of the newly independent countries in Africa and the problems of development encountered by many of the Latin-American countries—the concept of Point Four and the way it was presented now appear as a piece of far-sighted statesmanship. President Truman spoke about "their poverty being a handicap and a threat both to them and to more prosperous areas," about "aid for the efforts of the peoples of economically underdeveloped areas to develop their resources and improve their living and working conditions by exchange of technical knowledge and skills and by the flow of investment capital to countries which provide conditions under which such technical assistance and capital can effectively contribute to raising standards of living, creating new sources of wealth, increasing productivity and increasing purchasing power."

67

As these words indicate, Point Four had quite a task to perform. But at no time was there any attempt made by the Administration to direct considerable amounts of money into this part of the foreign-assistance program. The first budgetary provision for Point Four was for $45 million, which was later cut by Congress to $25 million. The first head of the Technical Cooperation Administration, Dr. Henry Garland Bennet, president of Oklahoma University, never missed a chance to voice his opposition to any attempt at combining technical assistance with any provisions for investment funds, at least in direct connection with his program. It is only in later years that this strict delineation has become somewhat blurred by the practical necessities of the work to be done in various countries. In the request for appropriations for fiscal year 1964 for the foreign-assistance program, technical cooperation appeared lumped together with development grants, and the amount requested was $257 million.

The outspoken promotion of the program of economic assistance by the President did not find full support even in the Department of State itself. The economic section of the State Department did not understand its meaning and, as some observers have remarked, never liked it. This should be considered something of a surprise. Technical assistance, though not called by this name, was not new among American responses to the needs of others. Former President Hoover's relief mission after the First World War was largely directed to giving technical assistance to the war-torn and devastated areas. Coal mines in Silesia, rail transportation in Austria, and health services in the Baltic states were all returned to operation with the help of American engineers, technicians, physicians, and nurses. But this tradition seems to have been forgotten. The head of TCA had to concentrate not only on his new agency, but also had to search for people who would be able and ready to take over assignments in faraway lands, often in primitive areas that would not only test their technical abilities but also their idealism and their belief in the moral obligation of developed nations to help others in their quest for progress.

The Department of the Interior became a natural source of personnel for the TCA. The organizers of the TCA felt that the problems likely to be faced by the members of technical assistance teams would resemble those the Department of the Interior has encountered in the Indian Service, the Office of Islands and Territories, and in places such as Puerto Rico and Alaska. And indeed many of the heads of the United States Operations Missions, as the offices administering technical assistance have been called, have come from the Department of the Interior—though their experience has not always proved adequate to the new tasks they had to perform.

The program also found ardent and devoted supporters. As on so many occasions in the nation's history, the Bible became a source of in-

A typical team of U.S. aid mission at U.S. Operations Mission in Vietnam.

spiration. The one most often quoted passage was from the Prophet Amos: "Who calleth forth the waters of the sea, and poureth them out upon the face of the earth—the Lord is his name." Supporters of technical assistance pointed to these words as divine advice to carry progress wherever possible, recalling the age-old vision of turning the sea-water into usable, fresh water. Besides quoting the Bible, supporters of the technical assistance concept also pointed to a Chinese saying—"if you plant for years, plant grass; if you plant for decades, plant trees; if you plant for centuries, plant men." Such a philosophy accorded the technical-assistance effort a dimension divorced from immediate and practical considerations, and placed it in the realm of a mission working for a transcendently important goal.

The technical-assistance program, conceived out of the desire to help bring progress to other nations, could not have been implemented without the reservoir of technical skill which the United States had at its disposal. There are perhaps many other countries which would have gladly helped others, but they simply lacked the means to do so, and many were barely managing to help themselves. The United States had the capability to institute this program, and President Truman considered it advisable to stress this fact explicitly. He said: "Our imponderable resources in technical knowledge are constantly growing and are inexhaustible."

This little fellow is making sure that he cleans up his plate of food made possible mainly through the U.S. Food for Peace Program. The shipments are provided by the U.S. Agency for International Development (AID) and are administered under the Peruvian National School Nutrition Program.

Technical knowledge was not all that the United States had in abundance. The abundance in food products had always suggested some use more practical and beneficial than piling them up idly in government or rented warehouses, at the expense of hundreds of millions of dollars each year. (In fiscal year 1962 alone the United States spent nearly $400 million for storing accumulated farm surpluses.)

It was, therefore, only natural that the Administration and Congress concluded quite early that in the over-all United States aid effort, food could and would play a most important role. The Agricultural Trade Development and Assistance Act of 1954, Public Law 480, initiated this new policy. It authorized the sale of $700 million worth of surplus farm commodities to friendly nations, to be paid for in the currency of the recipient, and the gift of $300 million worth of such commodities over a three-year period for famine and relief. Like all other forms of American aid, in order to be accepted by Congress and the general public this program has had to be rationalized as being very much within the best and most practical interests of the United States. Thus, for example, President Eisenhower, in signing the act on July 10, 1954, stated that it would "lay the basis for a permanent expansion of our exports of agricultural products, with lasting benefits to ourselves and peoples in other lands." This was a fitting commentary to the words of Public Law 480, whose purpose was defined as providing for the use of surplus farm products "to expand international trade, to promote the economic stability of American agriculture and the national welfare . . . to encourage economic development . . . to promote collective strength and to foster . . . the foreign policy of the United States."

Thus, the American public received the explanation for the introduction of this new avenue of United States aid. But those nations that became the recipients of this new form of aid did not care about the wording of the law, nor about the comments of the President. What did concern them were the U.S. agricultural commodities which prevented famine, and were instrumental in assuring useful employment, promoting development, and helping to build schools, roads, and bridges.

The name given by President Kennedy to the programs carried out primarily under Public Law 480, Food for Peace, was appropriate. Some 2,500,000 Algerians, about a fourth of the entire population of that country, were fed with these commodities; the "food for wages" program in that same country has put 60,000 Algerians to work on soil conservation and irrigation. This Food for Peace program helped effect the following pilot projects: the school building on the shores of Lake Titicaca, more than 12,000 feet high in the mountains of Bolivia; the afforestation of large stretches of Tunisia; the saving from famine of hundreds of millions (over 450 million people in India) who were thus able to develop their country by the $3.7 billion worth of farm commodities shipped from the United States under Public Law 480; the sustenance of

71

families of South Vietnamese troops with shipments of grains, condensed milk, and fibers. The people in 112 countries and territories who have benefited directly from the fruits of the unprecedented productivity of the American farmer—these are day-to-day demonstrations of American abundance and generosity.

It is clear that an operation which has expended more than eight billion dollars since legislation was formally adopted in 1954 had to be based on its own distinctive laws and regulations. The three sections, or titles, of the original Agricultural Trade Development and Assistance Act of 1954 divide the shipments of farm commodities into various categories according to their use, the form of payment, and the use of these payments, as well as the system of delivery.

Title I, which embraces the lion's share of this program, authorizes the sale of farm goods to friendly countries in their own currencies, with the United States financing the dollar cost of the commodities; U.S. shipping is required. The American farmer receives full payment for his product, in what is really a special form of government subsidy. The hope has already been realized that this subsidy will, in time, produce new markets. In the year ending June 30, 1962, United States farm exports reached an all-time high of $5.1 billion, of which $3.5 billion were commercial cash transactions. Grain export alone rose in 1962 by 23.7 per cent and poultry by 66 per cent.

But these sales under Title I do not result in any immediate monetary return. The payments made by recipient countries are deposited in those countries, in the name of the United States, and not more than 10 per cent of these funds may be spent on local United States operations, e.g., the administrative expenses of the embassy. With the permission of the United States government the local currencies may be used as loans and grants for economic development, and up to 25 per cent of these funds may be lent to private American undertakings in those countries, or even be lent to foreign business firms if they are considered helpful in expanding markets for United States farm products. These foreign currencies also finance official Congressional committees while on tour in such countries and are used to pay for translations of American books into local languages, agricultural marketing programs, and international educational exchanges.

But the ordinary foreign citizen hardly realizes that these commodities were practically given away by the United States. He must pay the full price, in local currency, of course, for the purchases he makes of American goods. As far as he is concerned, he is spending his own money in normal business transactions. It demands special intelligence and even a certain degree of good will on his part to acknowledge that he owes a debt of gratitude to the American government for making it possible for him to feed his family. As far as he is concerned, he is buying an imported article in hard currency, just like any other which his govern-

Clarke A. Anderson, USOM (bending right), assisting Lebanese Prime Minister planting cane on the sand dunes of Khalde (sand stabilization project).

Feeding children in Yugoslavia with products of United States abundance.

ment has to pay for. In view of these circumstances, the argument against foreign aid because "it demoralizes the people" falls rather flat. It is the foreign *government* which benefits from this agricultural aid, the sales of which generate the funds necessary for development plans. Only after the completion of development projects does the average citizen benefit.

Of course, this "handicap" in making United States aid in the form of farm products is remedied proportionately to the degree of local intelligence and literacy. A total of 246 commodity sales agreements under Title I, representing a total cost of $5.4 billion, have been signed with thirty-nine countries as of June 30, 1962. These have generated so much local currency and, through this, so many development projects that it is hard to imagine that awareness of this aid will not soon become felt throughout the population in these countries. But there are other uses for surplus agricultural products which are free of this "handicap," if it should be called a handicap.

Title II of Public Law 480 authorizes the use of agricultural products as emergency relief and as grants for development purposes. The $1.4 billion worth of these commodities that had been granted as of June 30, 1961, had helped to save millions of people stricken by disaster, famine, or political developments which turned them into refugees. A tribe in Kenya whose crops were wiped out through drought . . . masses of people in the northeast states of Brazil in need of relief after a drought . . . refugees in the Middle or Far East . . . earthquake-ravaged areas in Chile or Yugoslavia . . . flooded provinces in Pakistan—all have greatly benefited from this program. The legend printed on the gift bags and containers, *Donated by the People of the United States,* tells the story all over the world—and should reassure anyone who is not satisfied with a humanitarian act as such.

The same legend identifies the donor of the food shipments under Title III, which authorizes allocations of farm commodities to voluntary American agencies recognized by the United States government. This Title has made possible the distribution of $2.1 billion worth of goods in the three years ending June 30, 1962. In fiscal year 1962 alone, the volume of these donations amounted to more than 2.7 billion pounds, valued at $224,500,000. Sixty-eight million people in 112 countries and territories, including 32 million children, have been assisted with the produce of American fields and farms. The American Red Cross, CARE,

Died in line of duty: Flower-banked tablet of Dr. Henry Garland Bennett Memorial in Teheran, Iran, where first director of International Cooperation Administration was killed in air crash, December, 1951.

Lebanese government members and U.S. aid representatives at arrival of wheat shipment.

Church World Service, Catholic Relief Services, Lutheran World Relief, United Nations agencies such as the United Nations Children's Fund (UNICF) and the United Nations Relief and Work Agency (UNRWA) administering aid to Arab refugees, and other organizations are distributing this aid, which very often means the difference between life or death by starvation.

Somewhat awkwardly, Title III, which deals with relief through voluntary organizations, covers barter agreements with foreign countries as well. The $1.3 billion worth of commodities that have been exported in the seven years ending June 30, 1961, as payment for what this Title calls "strategic and other materials for stockpile and other purposes," such as tin from Bolivia or chromite from Turkey, can hardly be considered unusual transactions which depart from accepted trade practices. In the same category is Title IV. An addition to Public Law 480, this Title deals with sales of United States farm commodities at regular market prices, for dollars, with the only special accommodation being that payment may be deferred for as long as twenty years. Venezuela, the Dominican Republic, Ethiopia, the Republic of China, Chile, and Yugoslavia are among the countries which have purchased American goods on these conditions.

These many ways of supplying foreign countries with American farm products must be, and are, employed with the utmost care to avoid inter-

Israel's Finance Ministry presents Bruce McDaniel, first at left of map, head of USOM in Israel, with a relief map of Israel marked with the irrigation network and mineral resources, two of the fields in which USOM provided technical and financial assistance.

fering with the operation of normal commercial markets. Only commodities declared surplus by the Department of Agriculture are handled in these programs. The fact that United States exports of farm products have grown constantly and considerably in recent years is the best proof that the fears that Public Law 480 would put an end to exports of United States farm products have not materialized.

Such a vast and multifaceted assistance effort has long deserved some more precise definition, at least by Americans themselves, than that couched in terms of disposal of agricultural surplus. When President Kennedy established the White House Office of Food for Peace, he no longer spoke in terms of security and enlightened self-interest, as did Public Law 480, but rather stressed the fact that "American agricultural abundance offers a great opportunity for the United States to promote the interests of peace." This new-old meaning of the multi-billion-dollar program of aid through farm products casts a new light on this entire program.

Its dimensions are expressed in numbers which are astronomical: under the program wheat alone, for example, accounted over the eight-year period for 2.5 billion bushels, an average of three shiploads a day. The program at present is under the Director of Food for Peace, who is appointed by the President and is a member of the White House staff. From his office, Food for Peace is made available to those countries whose requests have been approved as justified and useful by our embassies and by the missions of the Agency for International Development. The use of American farm products has thus evolved from Food for War in the First World War, through Food for Freedom in the Second World War, to Food for Peace.

4

$$$

A Change in Outlook

Since about 1950 new economic forms of international cooperation have come into being. In the past, various forms of aid were available, but most of the time one characteristic prevailed: the goods, the services, the commodities which were to assist a foreign country were drawn increasingly from the United States. Whether the assistance was intended to help restore economies or to strengthen the military posture of countries by showing them how better to utilize their human and natural resources, the process of furnishing aid was still a complicated one. While the terminology employed was standard economic nomenclature, the real meaning of certain terms became difficult to determine. Grants had a way of becoming loans; loans were in fact a rather euphemistic name for grants; payment in local currency became something less than true payment because this local currency was really at the disposal of the recipient government; and finally some loans were *really* loans, some even short-term, at the commercial rate of 5¼ per cent annually.

The various forms of aid have had differing receptions. Outright grants, which constituted a large part of foreign aid at the beginning of the programs, very soon became the target of many attacks. The billions of dollars granted under the Marshall Plan were sharply criticized, and the success of the European recovery operation, which obviated the need for further grants, did not placate the opponents of "giveaways." Some of these critics felt that the success of the aid to Europe proved that they were right in contending that help should be extended in the normal terms of international finance and credit.

But even in their original form, the United States grants were far from being true grants, with the funds at the absolute disposal of the recipient. Only in special cases were the grantees permitted to spend the aid dollars on purchases of materials from the lowest bidders on the international trade market. Nearly always, they were obligated to buy the merchandise and commodities in the United States, and only on the United States market were they permitted to buy from the lowest bidder. The grantees' purchases in the United States were in fact regular commercial transactions. They paid full price, but in effect they were paying in their own local currency. What the United States had done was to open a line

A special platform was prepared for the dockside ceremony marking the arrival of the first shipment of grain for Tripolitania to counter a serious drought there.

of credit, in hard currency, to finance these vital imports. Thus, national reconstruction and progress was made possible abroad, and the American producer benefited as well.

But the end of the Marshall Plan period, which might be called "grant period" in the history of United States aid, did not mean the end of all grants. They have remained an important part of the assistance programs, both economic and (especially) military. But with the passing of the "emergency" period of postwar reconstruction, a growing awareness of the needs of the developing countries began to influence the thinking of the framers of United States aid policies. The fact that development is long-term has dictated the "phasing out" of grants and a gradual movement toward loans, and this change has been supported by internal pressures against "giveaways."

The establishment of the Development Loan Fund in 1957 was a manifestation of the new trend. But the change from grants to loans was a very careful operation, designed to prevent abrupt shocks to the economies of the countries in need of foreign assistance. The loans were given

The dome of St. Paul's Cathedral towering above the flames and smoke of London blazing after one of World War II air raids which brought devastation and havoc not only to the capital but to much of Britain.

on the most acceptable terms even to countries with extremely modest means and barely developed economic establishments. Repayment of such loans (which came to be known as "soft loans") was to be made in local currency, and even these payments were to begin after a period of grace, sometimes several years, with the repayment to run over decades, up to forty years, at an interest rate of less than 1 per cent. (Though very recent legislation implies a higher interest rate, the conditions on which such loans are given still remain most favorable to the receiving country.)

Grants and soft loans are supplemented by what are termed "hard loans." These lines of credit differ from international loans secured in the regular way only in that they provide for long-term repayment. Such loans, to be repaid in hard currency at an annual interest rate of up to $5\frac{1}{4}$ per cent, are usually given through the Export-Import Bank. As its name indicates, the bank's activities are aimed at promoting the efforts of the United States to increase its exports and, thus, to further the progress of the national economy.

In fiscal year 1964, nearly 60 per cent of all economic assistance will be given in the form of loans. When we compare this figure with those

St. Paul's Cathedral, London, and the new buildings which have risen about it on wartime bombed sites.

of previous years, the change from grants to loans is seen to be rather rapid: In fiscal year 1963, loans amounted to 54 per cent, and in 1961, to only 30 per cent. Since 1958 the Development Loan Fund (which was transferred to the Agency for International Development in 1961) and AID together have made more than three hundred loans, totaling $3.5 billion.

The trend toward loans involves important implications in the way assistance is furnished. Loans are free of the connotations of "giveaways" and certainly act to encourage the recipient countries to economize and to put the aid to the best possible use. To receive such a loan a detailed plan for its utilization must be submitted, and it must pass the strict scrutiny of American experts, who on this occasion can and do lend a great deal of their experience to the newly developing countries. Furthermore, the United States can expect repayment, even though the repayment will extend over decades.

The distinction between grants and loans is not always rigid. It has happened and doubtless will continue to happen that countries convert grants into loans by their own consent and start repayment in hard currency. This was the case with some of the Marshall Plan countries in

AID provided training machines and equipment worth approximately $910,000 for this institute; it also financed a contract with an American institute to provide advisory services for this Bombay training center.

Western Europe after they had achieved economic stability. For example, their gratitude for United States aid was demonstrated in 1959, when France, West Germany, and Great Britain prepaid more than $400 million due on outstanding loans from the United States, thus alleviating to some extent the United States balance-of-payments difficulties. That a great many of the loans were really normal financial transactions may be seen by the steadily rising payments of principal on outstanding loans. These sums rose from $300 million in 1950 to an average of about $700 million per year in the period from 1957–1960 and have continued to rise since.

Of course, dollar repayment is only one way that such loans are repaid. As in the case of assistance in the form of commodities or services, there are certain loans which can be repaid in the currency of the receiving, country. These funds are either deposited to the account of the United States, with the borrower agreeing to a maintenance-of-value clause preserving the dollar value of the original loan against eventual devaluation of the local currency, or to the account of the country making use of the aid, with the provision that these funds can be used only with the concurrence of the United States.

To anyone unaware of the intricacies of such operations, such accumulation of foreign currencies would appear to be a boon to the country in which these currencies are accruing. But, in fact, in the political realities of our world this is no simple problem. For instance, United States holdings of Indian rupees have reached the equivalent of $2.5 billion. What this amount in foreign ownership means can be understood if we realize that this amount, compared with the Indian gross national product would be like a foreign government owing $35 billion in the United States.

These "counterpart funds," the equivalent in local currency of United States materials delivered under aid programs, play a most important role in the attainment of American goals. They can be released only upon the agreement of the United States, which has always been careful that the funds be used only for constructive purposes. During the flow of billions of dollars to the Marshall Plan countries these counterpart funds were a most important factor in the European economic recovery. Franz Bluecher, vice chancellor of West Germany at the time of the Marshall Plan, asserted that "one reason for this recovery which we experienced is that there were such strict controls over counterpart [funds] that the economy had been like a regiment drilling under a colonel. Due to this control, counterpart [funds] was spent almost entirely for investment and increase of productivity."

Within this multifaceted program, principles had to be arrived at in order to establish priorities in the allocation of aid. This was not an easy task. The number of requests and the amounts requested have at all times far exceeded the funds that the aid agencies could dispose of.

United States Operation Mission exhibit at the Ghana Agricultural Show in Accra.

After some experimentation, aid officials introduced a scheme which classified countries on the basis of the speed with which they would be able to achieve considerable progress and economic development. Using this system, nations were divided in what became known in the language of aid programs as "country groupings." Group One, which comprises about thirty countries, is considered to be the most promising in terms of economic development and social progress.

About 90 per cent of all development lending is concentrated in this grouping. And although United States assistance to these nations amounts to no more than 3 per cent of their national incomes, it comes to about 20 per cent of their expenditures for development. Some of the countries in this group, such as Greece, Israel, Taiwan, Venezuela, and Mexico, are already approaching the stage of self-sustaining growth, and others, such as India, Pakistan, Nigeria, and Colombia, while still far from self-sufficiency, are following successful methods of economic development. Unfortunately, this group also contains countries which are much less promising but are included because of the appraisal of their genuine efforts, through maximum use of their resources and the greatest possible

Ambassador Galbraith inspects construction work on the Chandrapura thermal power station in India.

measure of self-help. The borderline between this sub-category of the first group and the second grouping is rather blurred.

The second group is composed of countries in which development is a long-term problem. Many of these countries are subject to permanent political and military pressures, and are threatened by external and internal subversion; military aid constitutes a major part of the United States aid to them.

The last group—the third—comprises more than half of the nations that benefit from United States aid. In the forty-seven members of this group, United States aid is rather limited. Only 11 per cent of economic aid funds and 8 per cent of military assistance are earmarked for these countries in the aid request for fiscal year 1964. In these countries, many of which are in Africa, United States assistance plays a minor role. In these areas, western European countries are carrying the main burden of assistance, and American aid programs serve as an appropriate medium for assuring a United States presence, for the use of certain strategic facilities, or as the alternative to the lures of Russian aid.

The bulk of all aid, in whatever form, has had to be directed, by its very nature, through governmental channels. The natural need to plan to ensure the best use of American aid and the equally natural employment of government agencies in the recipient countries have contributed to a permanent strengthening of the public sector in the economies of the many countries which receive aid. Many Americans with a traditional philosophy of economic development based on private initiative find this trend towards a planned economy distasteful. This development was inherently linked to the requirement that United States aid do the most good. But this is not always convincing for many Americans. Two consecutive Republican Administrations have recognized these conditions and based their foreign-aid operations on them. This fact, however, has not changed the minds of those who criticize the foreign-aid program as a catalyst in the spreading of "socialism" throughout the world.

It was this kind of criticism, alone, with a genuine concern for the role of private enterprise in those areas aided by the United States, that caused the drafters of the foreign-assistance acts as early as the beginning of the 1950's to provide for special measures to encourage private initiative as an integral part of the aid programs. President Truman's Point Four proposal included a special section on incentives to private investment abroad. It was followed by Congressional authorization for the Export-Import Bank to guarantee $250 million in investment against expropriation.

Since 1950, promotion of American investments abroad and the furthering of private initiative in countries receiving assistance have become permanent features of the foreign-aid programs. Many measures have been inspired by the awareness that private enterprise must have its

U.S. aid helping to extend higher education facilities in Burma.

place in the national economy to assure the development of a free society. The Agency for International Development gives, for instance, dollar loans to private borrowers where financing is not available from other sources on reasonable terms. The AID allows local currency to be used as loans for sound private enterprises and shares of costs with potential investors in investment surveys. All this is in addition to the long-standing policy of investment guarantees, which frees the American investor from risks in his investment ventures abroad. In fiscal year 1962, for instance, ninety-two guarantee contracts were signed, with a total value of $306,658,200. During the first seven months of fiscal year 1963, loans benefiting private enterprise totaled $451.2 millions.

Although these steps have made foreign aid more acceptable in the United States, even among people who are not over-enthusiastic about the idea at all, its effects on the various foreign countries have raised many problems. One of these is the frequent absence of any element in the population which could take advantage of American readiness to assist private initiative. In many of the newly developing countries, the economy is still so primitive that it is hard to find people ready or able to initiate, much less to conduct, a successful private economic venture of the dimensions necessary to influence the pace of development of the national economy. President Eisenhower, who certainly cannot be suspected of prejudices against private initiative, acknowledged this state of affairs in one of his messages on foreign aid: "Private investment is useful: . . . but for many areas it will clearly fall short of requirements."

No amount of American prodding or generosity can create such entrepreneurs overnight, and thus the stimulation and furtherance of conditions which will make the appearance of such people possible is one of the goals of foreign aid in many areas of the world.

This, however, is not the only problem. In countries in which the volume of United States private investment reaches the dimensions of billions of dollars, these investments have become targets of violent opposition by local political factions, both on the extreme Left and Right. United States enterprises in Latin-American countries are attacked as exemplars of "Yankee imperialism," which exploits "the economic riches of the countries." An agitator can cause the worker in an American-owned factory to see his employer as either a capitalistic exploiter or a foreign invader who endangers national independence. One result of this trend is that even in such developed economies as those of France or West Germany concern is being voiced over the pace and volume of United States investments. President De Gaulle has officially initiated a campaign against the "American take-over of the European industry," and a recent congress of German industrialists dealt most seriously with the problems of "United States raiding actions on German industry."

Reporting on this development, the New York *Times* of September 14, 1963, said that "West German businessmen are growing increasingly uneasy about rising foreign investments, particularly by Americans. . . . This uneasiness takes practical forms: industrial groups appear to be building up pressure for fiscal reforms to correct the advantages available to 'big foreign capital.' The critical fire is centered now on tax laws blamed for having given foreign investors, particularly Swiss and Americans, a financial edge over West Germans."

The basic forms of assistance that we have discussed are complemented by a series of other measures which are essentially part of the aid program. American-sponsored schools, libraries, hospitals, and medical centers abroad have been provided with assistance from aid funds. In 1963 the Administration recommended an amendment to the Foreign Assistance Act which would authorize an appropriation of $20 million for such institutions.

Another special form of aid was added by the Kennedy Administration. A special provision of the Foreign Assistance Act authorizes the Agency for International Development to acquire equipment declared excess for government requirements. This provision makes possible considerable

MSA Mission Chief in Vietnam, Wilbur R. McReynolds, acknowledges a big grin from one of the little Hoa Khanh refugees from Northern Vietnam.

savings and increases the demand for new equipment in the United States itself—and, eventually, overseas as well, as the time arises when spare parts and renewals are needed.

In the attempt to make use of non-governmental resources in the aid program, American business firms, industries, colleges, and service organizations have been entrusted with special functions. Contracts with such organizations have made them instrumental in spurring the growth of cooperatives for housing, savings, agricultural credit, rural electrification, and the marketing of consumer goods. The Credit Union National

Association, the National Rural Electric Cooperative Association, the Cooperative League of the U.S.A., the Foundation for Cooperative Housing, the Farmers' Union, and many other organizations perform special functions in their respective fields. In addition, many colleges and universities are working with local authorities to bring American education and skills to several new nations.

In this effort to spread education and technical skills, a special form of cooperation was developed in the form of the Participant Training Program for Foreign Nationals. As its name indicates, this program is aimed at the development of the most important resource of every nation—its people and their capabilities.

The costs of the program, including the participants' transportation to and in this country, living expenses, study materials, and training fees and charges, are shared by the United States government and the participating country. Since the Participant Training Program began in the 1940's, more than 60,000 foreign nationals have been trained by over 7,000 business firms, farm groups, labor organizations, colleges, and universities. The scope of the training offered is so wide that there seems to be no area of human activity in which people from foreign lands have

Entrance of Keelung dockworkers housing project in Taiwan.

not had the opportunity to learn with the help of some American institution or organization.

This program, going far beyond the usual confines of technical education, is an experiment in human cooperation of unprecedented dimensions. Tens of thousands of foreigners are subjected to direct contact with tens of thousands of Americans, live with them, and learn about life in America. Upon returning home they become missionaries of progress, very often devoted to the United States and everything it stands for. Channels of communication are opened, existing channels are widened, viewpoints meet and adjust to each other, creating the basis for better understanding and international cooperation.

Of similar importance and characteristics are the student exchange programs. The history of this form of United States assistance precedes by decades the aid programs of the forties, fifties, and sixties. As early as 1872 some Chinese teen-age students were sent by their government for specialized training in the United States. Of course this was a limited operation with no conspicuous developments until the post World War II period, when the student exchange programs brought tens of thousands of foreign students to the shores of this country. In the years 1952–53 alone, 34,000 foreign students attended United States colleges and universities. In the academic year ending in 1963, this number reached a record high of 64,000, an 11 per cent increase over the 1961–62 period, and a ten-year gain of 92 per cent. In the same year 6,000 professionals, teachers, researchers, and scholars as well as 7,000 medical internes and residents arrived in the United States to improve their professional skills, to widen and deepen their knowledge.

The statistical distribution of these students among countries of their origin is, in many respects, similar to that prevailing in the distribution of foreign aid programs: the number of European students has declined in the last year and the ratio of Far Eastern students rose from 23 per cent of the total in 1952–53 to 37 per cent in the current year. The percentage of students from African countries rose within the last decade from 3 to 11 per cent.

In this sphere of activity another program deserves mention: The Fulbright Scholarship Program, initiated by Senator J. William Fulbright and conducted by the Bureau of Educational and Cultural Affairs of the Department of State. In the fiscal year 1960–61, 7,048 persons were exchanged between the United States and foreign countries. Of this number, 2,040 were Americans and 5,008 were foreign visitors to America. Many of the grantees who have visited the United States under this program occupied or are bound to occupy positions of high responsibility in their respective countries.

Though conducted separately from the aid programs, this form of educational and cultural diplomacy complements foreign aid in its basic philosophy and general aims.

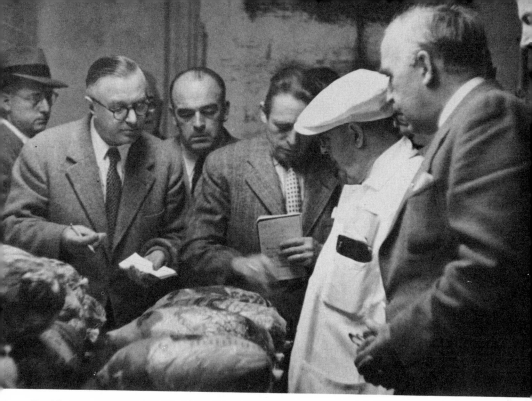

Danish meat experts studying American meat-packing methods on tour under the sponsorship of ECA's technical assistance program.

Administering the huge programs of assistance very early became one of the most important problems for each succeeding Administration. The experience of Lend-Lease proved that such operations involving billions of dollars, scores of countries, and many thousands of people could not be handled through the Department of State, where they otherwise naturally belonged. The relationship of separate foreign-aid agencies to the Department of State posed specific problems. As the identities of the aid agencies continuously fluctuated so did these relationships: sometimes the aid agencies had a status separate from and independent of the State Department, and at times they were completely incorporated into the framework of the Department.

It was not only a striving for improvement that drove Administrations to seek ways of improving the administration of foreign aid programs. Congress was always there to spur the Administration to improve standards and to prevent waste and duplication.

The reorganization program of the Kennedy Administration, which established the Agency for International Development (AID) included in one agency all assistance programs: capital financing, development, and food and commodity supply. This Administration's conviction that this change would open a new chapter was not accepted enthusiastically

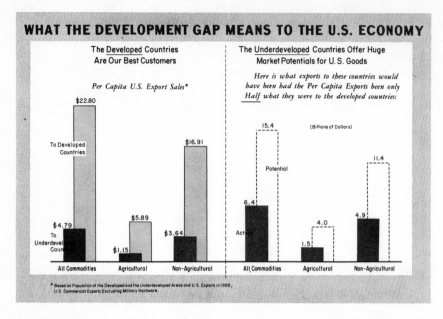

WHAT THE DEVELOPMENT GAP MEANS TO THE U.S. ECONOMY

The Developed Countries
Are Our Best Customers

Per Capita U.S. Export Sales*

$22.80

To Developed
Countries

$16.91

$5.89

$4.79
To
Underdevel
Coun

$1.15

$3.64

All Commodities   Agricultural   Non-Agricultural

The Underdeveloped Countries Offer Huge
Market Potentials for U.S. Goods

*Here is what exports to these countries would
have been had the Per Capita Exports been only
Half what they were to the developed countries:*

15.4   (Billions of Dollars)

Potential

11.4

6.4

4.9

Act

4.0

1.5

All Commodities   Agricultural   Non-Agricultural

* Based on Population of the Developed and the Underdeveloped Areas and U.S. Exports in 1959,
U.S. Commercial Exports Excluding Military Hardware.

by Congress. Representative Otto E. Passman of Louisiana, chairman of the Subcommittee on Foreign Operations Appropriations, exemplified the Congressional attitude at a hearing in 1962 at which Secretary of State Dean Rusk testified. Rusk asserted that "much has been done during this time [the seven-month existence of the new agency (AID)] to provide the strong direction and leadership this program should have, both in Washington and in our missions abroad." But Passman hastened to remark that AID "is the successor to the International Cooperation Agency—ICA was the successor to other agencies, but the objectives, the aims and the programs are in effect about the same."

This attitude of the Congress dictated and continues to dictate many of the organizational provisions of the aid agencies. Wherever possible, the Administration tries to assure public cooperation in the administration of aid programs and tries to establish instruments of control which would serve as "watchdogs" of the entire operation. A Development Loan Committee shares the burden of responsibility for loan allocations and the Management Inspection Staff helps to keep an eye on this operation, which administers aid programs in some eighty-one countries—twenty-four in Latin America, thirty in Africa, sixteen in the Near East and South Asia, nine in the Far East, and two in Europe.

To run that kind of far-flung operation, the head of the agency—the administrator—had to be given special status. He is an Undersecretary of State, reporting directly to the Secretary of State and to the President. His immediate office includes two Deputy Administrators, the Program Review and Coordination Staff, the International Development Organizations Staff, and the Information and Congressional Liaison Staff.

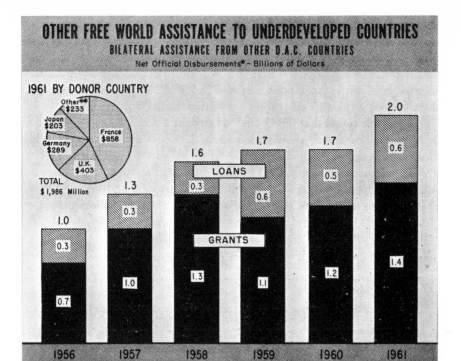

Of course it is necessary to maintain offices to administer the aid programs in the various regions and countries where AID operates. Four regional bureaus, headed by assistant administrators for the Far East, Near East with South Asia, Latin America, and Africa together with Europe, adjust the programs to the needs and conditions of their respective regions. These regional administrators also supervise the activities of mission directors or, in the instances of smaller countries, especially those in which United States assistance is rather limited, of United States embassies managing the aid programs there. United States Operations Missions (USOM) which had been administering technical assistance programs (and in some cases all other aspects of American aid), have been generally incorporated into the new organizational scheme, thus strengthening the authority and the influence of ambassadors in all matters of aid. Recently a Consolidated Administrative Management Organization (CAMO) has been set up to advise ambassadors and provide administrative support to all elements of the United States team.

Thousands of people are employed to staff all the aid operations. But the number of people working for AID at a given time is not definite and indisputable. Quite to the contrary. The official figure, reported to Congress as of April 30, 1962, was approximately 6,500 "direct-line" employees on the rolls of AID. A Department of State publication of

1963 states that AID employs directly 15,000 persons, of whom about 13,000 serve overseas. An additional 2,000 are employed abroad under contract, and they include experts from more than 150 occupations. But even this higher figure is questioned by Congress. Questioning Secretary of State Rusk, Representative Passman asserted that the number is "approximately 60,000 for all personnel concerned with the foreign aid program." The discrepancy between these two figures was explained by Passman himself, who said that he included in his figure military, AID, and State Department personnel concerned with foreign aid.

Compared with the appropriations for aid, the administrative budget of these operations is rather modest: $57,250,000 in the AID request for fiscal year 1964, which amounts to 1.7 per cent of the appropriation requested for economic assistance. For fiscal year 1963, $52,240,000 was available for administrative expenses, which amounted to about 2 per cent of the economic assistance funds. Over half of these expenses cover administration of the operations overseas.

To administer these vast aid programs and to supervise the operations of this complex machinery, persons with special aptitudes had to be called upon to lend their talents. At various times some of the most

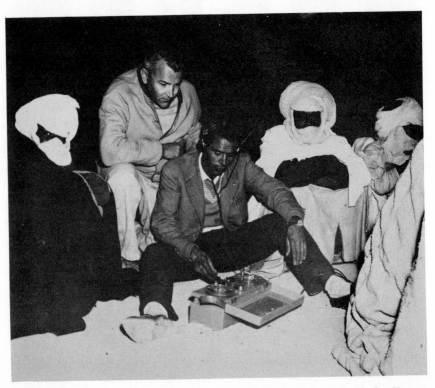

United States representatives prepare to tape the rhythmical music of the Tuareg people, deep in the desert of Libya.

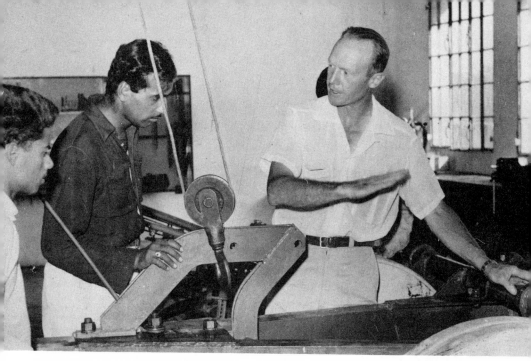

Curtis Johnson, International Cooperation Administration farm machinery advisor, explains point in the assembly of a heavy duty "ripper" machine to mechanics at the Agricultural Engineering Development Center at Quetta, Pakistan.

intelligent and experienced people in the United States have led the aid operations. The great responsibility, the pressure of the work, and the complications of the assignments have contributed greatly to the rather excessive rate of turnover among heads of aid agencies. But these were not the only reasons for the fact that within over a decade and a half of the great aid programs the Administrators have changed more than once every two years, and with them many of their principal assistants and heads of departments. People in Washington say that Congress has really got the aid agencies, and their administrators, permanently "on the run."

But the personalities "on the run" have always been of an outstanding caliber. The administrator of the first independent foreign-aid agency, the Economic Cooperation Administration, Paul G. Hoffman, brought to his new post all the qualities such an outstanding position required: administrative abilities, vast experience in big financial operations, excellent contacts with leading personalities of the country, the highest possible standing in American political life, and what was not less important, a warm heart, a deep human understanding for people who suffer, and a feeling of a moral obligation to help them in their distress. President of the Studebaker Corporation, chairman of the Automotive Safety Foundation, president of the Ford Foundation, member of the U.S. delegation to the United Nations, Hoffman did not limit his activi-

a)

b)

c)

d)

e)

f)

g)

h)

i)

j)

Heads of foreign aid agencies 1949–1964:
a) Paul G. Hoffman, b) William C. Foster,
c) Averell Harriman, d) Harold E. Stassen,
e) John B. Hollister, f) James H. Smith, g)
James W. Riddleberger, h) Henry R. Labouisse, i) Fowler Hamilton, j) David E. Bell.

ties to the practical implementation of his ideas. His books, such as *Peace Can Be Won* and *World Without Want,* are a serious attempt to put his ideas on foreign aid in historical perspective. As the Managing Director of the U.S. Special Fund, Hoffman is considered an authority on aid problems to developing countries and has rightly achieved the position of a generally acknowledged ideologist of foreign aid.

The man who succeeded him as administrator of the Economic Co-operation Administration, William C. Foster, was no newcomer to his task. As Deputy U.S. Special Representative in Europe for the Economic Cooperation Administration and later as Deputy Administrator under Hoffman, Foster acquired inside knowledge of the aid operations before assuming the leading position in this field, on October 1, 1950. A former Under Secretary of Commerce with a business past, Foster served as the second and last Administrator of the ECA, before it was renamed, with functions redefined, the Mutual Security Agency.

The man who was called to lead the foreign-aid program, when the emphasis shifted from economics to security, was W. Averell Harriman. His past posts included administrator of Lend-Lease for two years (1941–1943), overseas administrator of the European Recovery Program, U.S. Secretary of Commerce, ambassador to Soviet Russia and Great Britain.

The change of the Administration in January, 1953, relieved Harriman of his position. The new Republican Administration of President Eisenhower, reorganizing the main branches of the Executive, chose Harold Edward Stassen to replace Harriman. The one-time youngest governor of Minnesota, at thirty years of age, Stassen had been a member of the U.S. delegation to the founding conference of the United Nations in San Francisco, a contender for the Republican presidential nomination, and president of the University of Pennsylvania. He had to steer the foreign aid programs through Congress as a member of an Administration constantly repeating its credo of economies, of trimming of government spending, of defending the integrity of the dollar.

Stassen also had to supervise the change in the administrative setup of the foreign aid agency. Under Stassen's leadership, the Mutual Security Agency was replaced by the Foreign Operations Administration, FOA—which at the end of Stassen's term of office in June, 1955, was replaced by the International Cooperation Administration, ICA.

The administration of the new aid agency was entrusted to John Baker Hollister, a Cincinnati lawyer and former Republican Congressman. The new agency was supposed to be new, not only in name but also in character, scope, and outlook. Announcing the establishment of the ICA and the appointment of Hollister as its Director, President Eisenhower stated on April 19, 1955: "The placing of general responsibility for economic operations as well as for policy in this field within the Department of State offers assurance that, under a permanent government establishment, we are providing a long range basis for this kind

Cement provided by the U.S. aid program is used by Korean refugees.

of international cooperation. It is an emphatic recognition of the principle that the security and welfare of the United States are directly related to the economic and social advancement of all peoples who share our concern for the freedom, dignity, and well-being of the individual."

Hollister, a law partner of Senator Robert A. Taft and John L. Stettinius, had been a member of President Hoover's American Relief Administration, head of the U.N. Relief and Rehabilitation Administration to the Netherlands, director of a number of financial and industrial corporations, and a consultant to Secretary of State Dulles. When he

99

resigned, after two years of service, in September, 1957, the International Cooperation Administration seemed to have found the appropriate way of handling foreign aid programs and had gained a longer lease on life than the foreign aid agencies, which preceded the ICA.

Hollister's successor, James Hopkins Smith, was also to serve what had become almost a customary two-year period as head of ICA. A World War II veteran who won the Bronze Star Medal with Combat V, three Air Medals, and a Presidential Citation, Smith had been a consultant to the State Department, Assistant Secretary of the Navy for Air, and a consultant to private business enterprises on international agreements.

With his two years of service over, Smith vacated his post in January, 1959, and the leadership of the aid agency was assumed for the first time by a career diplomat, James W. Riddleberger. In addition to long and distinguished service as a U.S. diplomat abroad, including posts as ambassador to Yugoslavia and Greece, Riddleberger had vast experience in the field of aid to foreign countries. A specialist in problems of economic warfare in the Department of State at the beginning of World War II, he came into direct contact with problems of postwar rehabilitation as chief of the Office of Central European Affairs, political adviser to the U.S. High Commissioner for Germany, and later political adviser for the Marshall Plan.

Riddleberger's successor, Henry R. Labouisse, whose term of office was the shortest (from March 1, 1961, until November 3, 1961), had special experience in international relief work. A former director of the United Nations Relief and Works Agency for Palestine refugees, Labouisse had served for ten years with the Department of State. As deputy director of the Office of Foreign Economic Coordination in 1943, minister for economic affairs at the U.S. Embassy in Paris in 1944, special assistant to the Assistant Secretary of State for Economic Affairs, and economic adviser to the director of the Office of European Affairs at the end of the fifties, Labouisse was most directly involved in the great foreign aid programs of the post World War II era. Complications on the internal, political scene were the cause of Labouisse's resignation, which brought into this office Fowler Hamilton. He had served as director of the U.S. embassy's Economic Warfare Division in London. Later he was head of the enemy section of the Foreign Economic Administration during World War II. When the war was over, he returned to professional activity. As a specialist in international law, Hamilton visited countries in Europe, Latin America, and Africa, where he negotiated business transactions between American and foreign firms.

Peter Edson, a Scripps-Howard columnist, had once given a vivid description of what it means to head the aid agency of the United States. Though his column was dealing particularly with Hamilton's work, it

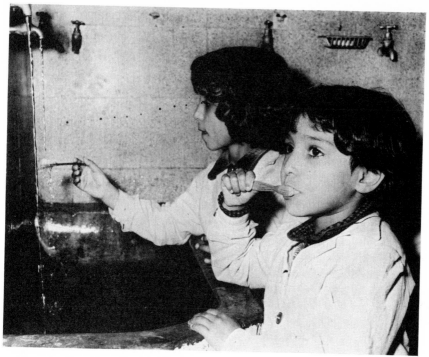

Tunisian children who participate in Child Feeding Program, financed by Tunisian Government and U.S. surplus food.

could easily have applied to any of the administrators (or directors) of the foreign aid agencies. Wrote Edson:

His [Fowler Hamilton's] secretary made a tabulation of what he did in his first month on the job, accounting for every ten minutes, the way lawyers do in charging their clients. He attended ninety-six conferences, thirty-five official luncheons and dinners. He took 312 telephone calls and wrote 285 official letters and 485 answers to messages congratulating him on his new job. This gives a pretty good idea of the way a new bureaucrat here puts in his time. He spent 259 hours on the job, a better than 9-hour-day average in twenty-eight working days, including Saturdays. For this he was paid $1,345 or $5.20 an hour which is low pay for a guy running a $2 billion business with 12,000 employees —2,500 here in Washington.

When Hamilton resigned after about one year of service, the new administrator was drawn from the ranks of the Administration. As director of the Bureau of the Budget, David E. Bell appeared to be a natural choice for administrator of the Agency for International Development at a time when the clamor for greater economy, savings, and trimming of government expenditures gained momentum in Congress. A man with academic experience in the Graduate School of Public Administration at Harvard University, early in his career Bell came into direct contact with economic problems on the government level. Bell

101

joined the staff of the Budget Bureau in 1942, and resumed his government service after release from the Marine Corps. As administrative assistant to President Truman until the President left office, and later as field supervisor to the Planning Board of the Government of Pakistan, Bell got to know directly the problems and needs of undeveloped countries. This field experience proved to be of special importance in view of the new trends in foreign assistance. A man of Bell's standing and authority was needed during the transition from the system of outright grants to development credits and during the time other industrialized nations were being pressured to assume a greater share in aiding undeveloped nations. Changing moods in Congress in relation to foreign aid have added special strain to the many already strenuous functions of the AID Administrator. In this new atmosphere Bell's budgetary schooling, business-like thinking, and administrative experience were of special importance to the Administration's struggles against sizeable cuts by Congress in proposals for foreign aid spending. No one could call Bell an internationalist dreamer, an unaccountable dispenser of American wealth who was "easy-going in spending money which is not his." And this appears a major asset among the many characteristics of the AID administrator in the seventeenth year of U.S. foreign aid programs.

Each of the administrators has left his mark on the history of American aid programs all over the world in scores of countries which have benefited from U.S. aid. These are marks which no revolution can erase; these are monuments which no violent change of regime can destroy, monuments which changed countrysides, physical conditions of life, standards of living, introduced new methods of production, new crops, made people read and write, and gave birth to realities which people have learned to cherish.

5

The Annual Battle of Appropriations

In pursuit of the high ideals of foreign aid, the aid administrators have faced innumerable obstacles. A world-wide operation involving about one hundred countries of the most diversified cultures and economic standards and many thousands of officials and many billions of dollars is by itself an almost superhuman operation. Even if the problems that are natural to such an operation were the only ones the aid administrations had to encounter, they would be sufficient to define a high order of "occupational hazard." But other difficulties have beset the programs, which always have to pass a major trial period at home before they get a chance to confront the overseas problems. They have to earn the approval of Congress, and first they must make the grade with Congressional committees.

Every year the Administration must struggle, first for the authorization for its program and then for the appropriations, which are usually less than the amount first authorized. Observers on the Hill call this the "battle of appropriations."

The phrase does not exaggerate what happens annually on Capitol Hill. The contending parties are clearly identified: the Administration vs. foresworn opponents of foreign aid—with some onlookers who prefer to adopt a "neutral" position (which is often a neutrality for and sometimes a neutrality against foreign aid). And, though the weapons are words, the going is sometimes quite rough. Representatives of the Administration are often kept for three and more hours on the witness stand before Congressional committees, where the witnesses' every word is weighed by the committees and no slip of the tongue is overlooked.

One illustration of this situation was provided at a hearing of Secretary of Defense Robert L. McNamara before the Subcommittee on Foreign Operations Appropriations. Secretary McNamara asserted that the Communists were reacting violently to the economic development of South Vietnam and to the development, as it were, of a showplace there of the Western World because North Vietnam has not developed nearly as well economically. Representative John J. Rhodes of Arizona caught on this statement and retorted: "Would it be a fair assumption to state that if the Communists react violently to the prosperity of these

The Fairless Committee on its fact-finding study about foreign aid at Bangkok, Thailand, airport, January 27, 1954.

small nations around the world after we have helped them, we are putting them in mortal danger of their independence by giving them economic aid?" The logic of this question is obvious and it requires no answer, just as no answer is needed to the assertion that the best remedy against thefts is to have people who possess nothing; but the very fact that such a "conclusion" is drawn from successful aid operations is indicative enough of the general atmosphere in which testimony on foreign aid is sometimes taken.

In another occurrence Representative H. R. Gross of Iowa demanded that the Secretaries of State and Defense be prosecuted for the "crime" they had perpetrated in writing a letter to members of Congress, explaining the importance of foreign aid for U.S. foreign policy objectives. Gross called it "lobbying" and based his demand on Section 1913, Title 18 of the United States Code, which forbids use of appropriated funds "to influence any member of Congress" by letter or otherwise to favor or oppose pending legislation.

In this continuous skirmishing against the foreign aid programs, the Congressional forces opposing them have their acknowledged leader—Otto E. Passman, Representative from Louisiana's Fifth District. As chairman of the powerful Subcommittee on Foreign Operations Appropriations, Passman takes pride in the fact that since he became chairman of this subcommittee in 1955, he "almost singlehandedly" cut $4.8 billion from requested foreign aid appropriations totaling $26.4 billion.

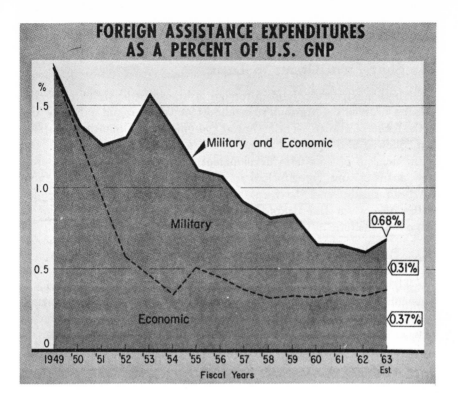

Passman's passion in fighting the foreign aid programs is not a casual whim of a sometimes disgruntled legislator. He considers his fight against what he calls "the greatest give-away in history" as a kind of a crusading mission to save "the dollar and the American economy." In his office on the Hill, he and his assistants were kind enough to supply me with materials on foreign aid—official materials of the Subcommittee, and publications which Passman issues in his own name to illustrate his views on foreign aid.

This written material was amply reinforced by Passman orally. When speaking with this Congressman on foreign aid, one feels that here is a man who misses no opportunity to proselytize. "Perhaps with the exception of the Roman empire, there has never been a state which gave away its wealth as we do," he says. Foreign aid is a new concept in foreign policy—it is the first time in history (says Passman) that a nation has tried to assure its security by giving away its wealth. "And this has been a dismal failure. Foreign aid has upset normal channels of commerce. When nations get used to receiving free what they previously had to pay for, it does not help international commerce; it kills it."

Within this general criticism of foreign aid programs, Passman has some specific criticisms of its extent; he believes that it is "spread out too much, self-defeating and over-extending the U.S. resources." It also

105

defeats many aspects of foreign policy, he says, because "any time we enter into a treaty with a nation, we immediately give something, and how could you know whether those people are sincere?"

This kind of thinking exemplifies his treatment of all arguments in support of foreign aid. The argument that foreign aid helps to increase exports he ridicules by saying that it is "as phony as a three-dollar bill." The assertion that 90 per cent of aid expenditures are in fact spent within the United States for the purchase of United States products he ridicules with the remark that "when ships leave, we get nothing in return and the invoices go to the United States Treasury and not to the recipient nations." This, he says, has very harmful effects on the American dollar since the gift of our products releases their own wealth for speculative purposes, and this in turn creates growing pressure on United States currency.

To Passman, Russian competition in the field of aid does not matter too much. He has his own appraisal of the extent of foreign aid from Russia and other Communist countries. He does not accept the official computation that Communist aid expenditures total over $7 billion. On Passman's books, this aid amounts to the equivalent of no more than some $5 billion dollars. And even this reduced amount is given in the form of high-interest loans or barter agreements, and furthermore represents only paper agreements; actual disbursements, he says, have reached only "something around one billion dollars."

In his sweeping condemnation of foreign aid, Passman ignores all changes which have been recently introduced into foreign aid programs. The gradual replacement of grants by long-term loans he calls "disguised grants," and in his estimates of the total amount of foreign aid since the inception of these programs he discounts the repayment of loans (some of them initially considered grants), which has already passed the amount of $7 billion.

Of course, this criticism does not extend to aid to people in emergency. Passman feels that the United States has always been, and should remain in the future, a country to which people hit by disaster could look for help. He is, therefore, in favor of the many relief operations in which the U.S. aid agency is now engaged and will be engaged in in the future. But regular foreign aid programs should be terminated. Of course not abruptly, he says, but within, let's say, a five-year phasing-out period in order not to upset projects based on U.S. aid and to keep promises that the United States has made to other nations.

Listening to these remarks, I found it hard to refrain from a question pertaining to the endurance of the program and its support by a majority of the Congress for seventeen years, including the eight years he has been chairman of a committee that almost controls the extent of the annual foreign aid appropriations.

Passman is no less outspoken on this than on other problems of foreign

106

aid. He is highly critical of those members of Congress who vote for the aid bills. "Congress abdicated 60 per cent of its prerogatives to the Executive," he says. "Many of them don't care to be no more than rubber stamps, and they care more for being supported by the party leadership for their re-election than for the interest of the people. . . . I was elected to represent the people—I don't want to be a follower, I want to be a leader in my own small way."

But he acknowledges that there are some members of Congress who are honestly supporting the foreign aid programs. These are the so-called liberals. And for them Passman has an original definition: "A liberal is too often a person with high-pressure feelings, low-pressure thinking, and a constant urge to give away that which belongs to somebody else."

It is to combat this kind of feeling in Congress that Presidents have appointed citizens' committees in the hope that their voices would help convince the opponents of foreign aid that they do not have the monopoly on representing "the real interest of the people." But the intentions and hopes of the Presidents in appointing these committees have not always been fully realized. The best illustration of this is provided by the most recent committee under the chairmanship of General Lucius D. Clay. The report of this "Committee to Strengthen the Security of the Free World" corroborates fully the Administration's assertions that foreign aid is a necessity and must be an important component of United States foreign policy as an excellent means for the strengthening of the security and general interests of the United States and the non-communist world in general. The report is full of such appraisals as these:

There should be no doubt . . . of the great value of properly conceived foreign aid programs to the national interest of the United States and of the contribution of the foreign assistance dollar in such programs to the service of our nation's security. We live in a world in which poverty, sickness, unstability, and turmoil are rife and where relentless communist imperialism manipulates this misery to subvert men and nations from freedom's cause. A foreign aid program is one instrument among many which we and other developed countries adequately can afford and vigorously must use in the defense and advancement of free world interest.

Declarations of this nature are distributed throughout the twenty-five-page report, designed to prove decisively the importance of this aid to United States security:

To examine the utility of our assistance programs objectively, one must bear in mind their basic purposes. In this year's programs, over $1 billion was allotted for direct military assistance to countries on the bloc's periphery which are allied with us or each other in defense against communist attack. These countries also received about $700 million in economic aid to support their military effort and otherwise add to their stability and growth. These funds represent 44 per cent of the total foreign assistance appropriation. If we add to this the military and economic support of Vietnam and Laos and of other border countries which wish to retain their independence, though not allied with us, or

General Lucius D. Clay, head of Committee whose report became a most important factor in the debate on foreign aid.

Congressman Passman, Chairman of the Subcommittee on Foreign Operations Appropriations.

with other countries in common defense, total expenditures for military support and accompanying economic aid in the border areas aggregate $2.8 billion or 72 per cent of total appropriations. If one adds to this sum our assistance under the Alliance for Progress, about 15 per cent of the total program, and our contributions to international organizations of which we are members, amounting to $150 million, the total reaches 91 per cent of current foreign assistance appropriations. This does not mean, of course, that these programs are exempt from constant re-examination in the light of their necessity and effectiveness, but it indicates the major purposes which foreign assistance presently serves.

Clearly this is not only an endorsement of the foreign aid programs, but a brief which presents it in a light that should make it immune to any criticism. But the public consequences of the Clay Report were totally opposed to those which could have been expected on the basis of such findings, that put 91 per cent of foreign aid appropriations in the category of an indisputable expense for the benefit of the United States's most vital interests. In fact the Clay Report became a rallying point for all opponents of foreign aid programs. People opposing foreign aid found a lofty banner under which to gather, and Representative Passman was so delighted with the report that he suggested "a sixth general's star for General Clay."

How and why this happened is certainly no mystery. The favorable appraisals of foreign aid came in the later parts of the report while the critical remarks preceded them at a considerable remove. The negative facts appear on the very first page of the report. They catch the reader's eye before he begins to tire—an important consideration in a factual report (though this report is very readable)—and lend themselves easily to slogan-making: "We are trying to do too much for too many too soon. . . . We are over-extended in resources and under-compensated in results . . . that no end of foreign aid is either in sight or in mind." These phrases, repeated over and over since their publication, have been presented as the standard arguments against foreign aid.

The Clay Report, or rather its misrepresentation before the public, was only one of many assaults against foreign aid programs. In any public matter, the opponents of a cause, or as Paul Hoffman calls them, "the againsters," are always much louder than those who are for it. If a government official of a country which has received even the smallest amount of United States aid, makes a remark slightly critical of some aspects of United States policies, the "againsters" immediately gain an argument against any foreign aid at all. If some hundreds of hired mobsters were to storm the United States Embassy in an aid-receiving country, or if such a country were to make a trade agreement with a Communist-bloc state, or if a representative of the country were not to support a position taken by the United States delegation at the United Nations, such a clamor would issue forth not only against aid to this particular country but against foreign aid in general! Frank Coffin, the deputy administrator of the Agency for International Development in 1962, gave a crushing answer to all those who expect foreign aid to turn the hundred-odd nations receiving this aid into docile supporters of each and every U.S. move on the international scene. In a speech at the University of Nebraska on June 21, 1962, he said:

We exaggerate the power of the United States in a world of over a hundred sovereign nations. Only rarely in history has a single nation had the power we have and yet it is not without limit. When our power to control events proves inadequate, we become frustrated, blame our administration, its officials and policies. And we weaken in our purpose at the very time when we should be steadfast.

We expect too much of aid as an instrument of national policy. We expect it to "buy friends." We expect it to produce favorable votes by all countries we help on all issues in the United Nations. We expect it to cause all nations we help to sever all relations with the Sino-Soviet bloc. We expect it to cause all nations we help to adopt the same combination of parliamentary democracy and private enterprise which we have developed over 175 years. We expect it to silence all hostile spokesmen in the other countries. We expect it to prevent all other countries from defaulting on debts to U.S. business firms and from expropriating their properties.

This I submit is too large an order to expect from $7/10$ of 1 per cent of our gross national product. More than that, no matter what the amount, it raises the basic question if our basic purpose is to help channel the energies of the developing peoples into doing those things which will lead toward orderly development within an open society, how many other purposes can we serve at the same time? On how many shoulders can we hope to carry water?

We expect too much too soon of the developing nations. We forget our own labored progress toward decent, competent government. We forget how difficult it is, even for us today, to put through any major reform or change in our own country.

We overestimate the waste in foreign aid. How often we read in the United States of a road scandal, an embezzlement, a bribe, a Billie Sol, a grotesque public building costing far more than it should, a questionable defense subcontract. Yet we do not condemn in wholesale manner local, state, or national government, nor our highway, agriculture, or defense efforts. But in foreign aid, where we have mounted thousands of projects, over fifteen years, in over eighty countries, all we need is a handful of operations which have been mishandled to give us the basis for wholesale condemnation. Here again, we must guard against erosion of our national purpose by the loss of perspective. Of course, we are going to have some waste—hopefully a minimum. To expect otherwise is to be unrealistic. But the fear of some waste should not erode our national purpose in foreign aid.

Coffin knew exactly what he was aiming at when he spoke about the charges of waste and corruption in foreign-aid operations. Some of them have become a standard argument against foreign aid. They have been repeatedly brought up in Congressional hearings. They have been reiterated to the voters. They provide catchy themes for editorials, like the one in the Beaumont, Texas, *Enterprise* of June 7, 1963 (carrying the headline "Pap from Uncle Sap"), which concluded: "Of 112 nations in the world 101 are now receiving, or have received pap from Uncle Sap." This produced a series of letters to the newspaper and to Congressmen expressing "disgust with the people in Washington."

What is the substance of these charges? Here are some samples of those which gained the greatest currency:

The story of "jungle television sets": The coupling of these two words, "jungle" and "television," seems to suffice to ridicule an entire project of the Agency for International Development. The charge was investigated, AID officials went to work, and what they found was something different from the charge about distributing T.V. sets in the jungle. As became customary, in matters of Congressional charges, AID supplied Congress with the following explanation:

Early in 1962, AID contracted for the manufacture of 1,000 battery-powered television sets, designed to receive educational television broadcasts in villages without electric power and sturdy enough to withstand tropical climates and field conditions. The project was not carried out because defects were found in the way the contract for manufacture was let. However, there is still interest in the project. Education is a priority in many developing countries, yet trained teachers are scarce. Several African countries have established educational television stations as a way of bringing education to villages without trained teachers. . . . Battery-powered receivers would bring education to more villages which lack both teachers and electric power at present.

Then comes the story of "suits for Greek undertakers." AID's explanation:

This statement goes back many years. The answer to the House Foreign Affairs Committee on March 12, 1958, was: "Procurement records in Greece show no aid procurement of clothing of any kind with the exception of footwear for the Greek Army. Civilian clothing, as a matter of United States and Greek policy, has been ineligible for United States aid financing in Greece since the inception of the aid program in Greece."

And the story of "Wife buying in Kenya," which AID presented to Congress as follows:

In the early 1950's, the government of Kenya, entirely with its own funds, launched a pilot program for loans to traders and small manufacturers. During this pilot period, one trader borrowed $600, got himself a wife, and went on a prolonged holiday on which he used up the money, ruined his health, and lost his new wife. The incident was widely publicized, but it had no connection with United States aid or, for that matter, the success of the small loan program. After the pilot period, the loan program was organized as a regular operation, rigid controls were set up to prevent any misuse, and the United States then permitted the use of some United States-controlled counterpart funds (pound sterling) in the program. Although the small loan program was designed to provide credit in cases where commercial credit might not be available, the actual record of repayment to date has been better than that of some of the commercial credit establishments in Kenya.

But the explanations setting the record straight seldom reach the public. What has remained are the stories about "American dollars spent on wife-buying, dressing undertakers, and jungle television sets." The charges were sensational; the explanations deprived these stories of sensationalism and the explanations seem, therefore, to have been not worth printing. A similar course was run by other charges, like the one concerning highway building in Vietnam where allegedly an estimated cost of $18.3 million grew to a figure of $129 million. The critics took no notice that the bid of $18.3 million submitted in 1956 provided for a limited amount of road and bridge construction and the $129 million was cited in 1961 as the then applicable estimate for *all* expected costs of the Vietnam highway and bridge program.

Or the charge about a "yacht for the Emperor of Ethiopia" which was in fact part of the arrangements with the Ethiopian government for maintaining important U.S. communications-relay facilities. The entire deal was made by the Department of Defense and stemmed from U.S. interest in efficient patrolling of Ethiopia's coast. It was under this program, AID points out, that "a decommissioned World War II ship, the S.S. *Orca,* was refitted for use as training ship and flagship for the Ethiopian patrol fleet. Because of climatic conditions in the Red Sea, the vessel was air-conditioned, as are U.S. Navy ships operating in this area. The total cost of taking the S.S. *Orca* out of the U.S. 'mothball' fleet and refitting it for duty again is estimated at about $3.1 million."

These are the most widely advertised charges. As the refutations of them by AID indicate, they do not stand on very solid ground. But even if there were some instances of misuse or of waste of aid funds, as there certainly are, could these really serve as an argument against aid? Would anybody assume for a moment that, because the findings of the space agency have made some contractors responsible for the waste of about $100 million, the entire space program should be thrown overboard? Said former Vice President Nixon, when speaking on waste in foreign aid, "I think military leaders will be the first to admit that there is waste in defense."

And military aid represents an important part of the foreign aid programs. The Clay Report, which did not spare remarks critical of the aid programs, states:

In examining our national interest in foreign military and economic assistance, the direct relationship to free world security is most evident in the defensive strengths of those nations which, in their contiguity to the communist bloc, occupy the frontier of freedom. Many of these countries are our allies, and some belong to alliances with which we are associated. Several of these nations are carrying defense burdens far beyond their national economic capacities. These countries are now receiving the major portion of U.S. foreign assistance, but are also providing more than two million armed men ready, for the most part, for any emergency. While their armies are to some extent static unless general war develops, they add materially to free world strength so long as conventional military forces are required.

In concluding this paragraph, this report arrives at what could well be defined a most daring assertion. "Indeed it might be better to reduce the resources of our own defense budget rather than to discontinue the support which makes their contribution possible."

And this opinion of a committee of civilians headed by a retired general is not the only voice of its kind. Consecutive chairmen of the Joint Chiefs of Staff have expressed similar opinions at Congressional hearings. General Nathan F. Twining made a most emphatic statement on this matter in 1959 when he said:

> The cold facts of the matter are that the security of the United States depends upon our collective security system, which, in turn, depends upon our military assistance program.
> There may be some alternative to collective security and military assistance. Maybe those who make the broad charge that all money spent in these areas goes down the hole—know what that alternative is—but so far no responsible military man has been able to think of it.
> We simply don't have the manpower, the material or the money to take on the entire defense of the free world ourselves and the defense of the free world is a condition precedent to our own defense. If a substantial part of the free world falls or slips behind the Iron Curtain, our chances of being able to defend ourselves dim in proportion.

The present chairman of the Joint Chiefs of Staff, General Maxwell D. Taylor, has repeated these assertions. He stressed a fact which is not hard even for a non-military man to understand, that the system of U.S. defenses overseas gives the United States a first line of defense removed thousands of miles from the United States proper, a strategic situation which every country would like to have, for which many a war has been fought, and which is in fact at the root of the entire Russian satellite system. It could be said without exaggeration that Russia would gladly compensate the United States for its expenditures to countries on the rim of the Communist bloc, were the United States ready to withdraw its forces and liquidate its bases there. In fact, the problem of United States bases around the world is involved in every Russian move; it is at the root of the disarmament discussions; liquidation of bases is the central theme of all Russian propaganda.

It is, therefore, not hard to understand the statement made by Secretary of State Rusk at a hearing before the House Foreign Affairs Committee: "There is nothing that the Communists want more than to see the Yanks go home—not only from Western Europe, but from the Mediterranean, South Asia, the Far East, Latin America, Africa, everywhere. If we Yanks go home, the Communists will begin to take over. Why any American would want to cooperate with that global Communist strategy is beyond my understanding. But that is what shortcuts in our foreign aid programs would mean."

That is what is most amazing: that the extremes from right and left meet in this fervor to liquidate the first line of United States defense. The motives are of course diametrically opposed, but the results would be identical: exposure of the United States to a greater, growing danger.

In this concerted attack against foreign aid, the opponents of aid are greatly encouraged by what becomes, at times, a quite public clamor against United States involvement in certain areas around the world. South Vietnam is the latest example of such involvement. Aid to that country is used as a prime target of attack. But, in fact, aid to South Vietnam is no more than a consequence, a function of a policy, which aims at the preservation of a non-Communist Vietnam (even if it is not as free and democratic as America would like to see it) as a most vital condition for keeping the entire area of Southeast Asia out of the Communist orbit. Those who oppose giving foreign aid to Vietnam should rather take a firm stand against the policy of general support for that country, as similarly the derisive criticisms so often voiced about the "billions poured into Taiwan" (or South Korea) should be directed against foreign policy objectives as such, and not against the activities this policy requires, of which foreign aid is only one. It sometimes seems that opposition to foreign aid instead of being against certain policies is aimed at a kind of a shortcut to success in changing certain aspects of foreign policy—simply because the assaults on foreign aid are easier to make.

In this connection, mention should be made specifically of United States military base rights. The expenses related to such bases are included in the foreign aid appropriations. The Clay Report considers this practice incompatible with the objective truth about foreign aid. "Aid for such purposes," says the report, "should be viewed as defense costs." And though the report expresses the opinion that "no economic assistance should be provided as a consequence" of these base rights, it remains to be considered whether, on a practical basis, this aid is not a part of the deal the United States has to make to have these bases installed.

The findings of the Clay Committee on reductions in the foreign aid outlays should be considered in the same light. Reviewers of the report, even those who are not over-zealous in their support of foreign aid, have remarked that the recommendations of reductions are rather too vague in view of the fact that the report itself puts 91 per cent of the aid expenditures into the category of imperative, unavoidable expense. Taking this into consideration, President Kennedy delivered a rebuke to all who talk about sizable, decisive cuts in foreign aid when, at his press conference of August 20, 1963, he said, "One wonders which concrete actions critics would like to stop. Should we scrap the Alliance for Progress, which is our best answer to the threat of communism in this hemisphere? Should we deny help to India, the largest free power in Asia, as she seeks to strengthen herself against Communist China? Do we wish to dismantle our joint defenses in Korea, Taiwan, Pakistan, Iran, Turkey, and Greece, countries along the very rim of Communist power? Do we wish to weaken our friends in Southeast Asia?"

But with all this most eloquent defense of the foreign aid, the Administration did not find a completely convincing argument to justify the subjection of aid programs to blackmail tactics at the hands of certain countries. It seems that in this connection the Clay Report was speaking for a great segment of public opinion when it asserted that when "we accept promises in lieu of performance, respond to careful campaigns against our embassies, pay higher prices for base and other settlements if negotiations are long and unpleasant enough, and give unjustified aid in the hopes of precluding Soviet assistance in marginal cases, to that extent the firmness of United States negotiating positions loses credibility, our efforts to make aid more effective by getting local self-help are weakened, and United States Congressional and domestic backing for aid is undermined."

But these are marginal deficiencies which Congress tries to correct, which the Administration must strive to consider in its planning and which cannot affect the advisability or inadvisability of foreign aid. That all presidents, secretaries of State, secretaries of the Treasury and Defense, plus leading senators and representatives, have for seventeen years without interruption, supported and fought for effective foreign aid programs and that all fact-finding committees on foreign aid have found the assistance program advantageous to the United States, should at least be considered to be not less representative of American public opinion than the opinions of those who never were in a position of governmental responsibility. Senator Tom Connally of Texas gave clear expression to these opinions over a decade ago in 1952 when, opposing the attempts to cut the Mutual Security Program, he quoted General Dwight D. Eisenhower, Commander of NATO, who warned that any cut in the $7.9 billion foreign aid request "would be heavily and seriously felt" and warned that it would require "drastic revision of the whole program." Senator Connally's other remark, "who knows the most about the military situation—a trained soldier with a distinguished record, or some candidate for office?" did not lose its pertinence. As President, General Eisenhower did not change his opinion on foreign aid. He extended its underlying rationale, on the basis of his new experience in the more political office. In one of his messages he stated:

"We could be the wealthiest and the most mighty nation and still lose the battle of the world if we do not help our neighbors protect their freedom and advance their social and economic progress. It is not the goal of the American people that the United States should be the richest nation in the graveyard of history."

Years later, President Kennedy felt it imperative to make a place for the subject of foreign aid in his inaugural address when he said:

"To those peoples in the huts and villages of half the globe struggling to break the bonds of mass misery, we pledge our best efforts to help them to help themselves, for whatever period is required, not because the Communists may be doing it, not because we seek their votes, but be-

Colorful ceremony held at West Wharf, Karachi, on July 21, 1953, on the arrival of SS *Anchorage Victory* carrying first consignment of American wheat for Pakistan. The wheat was loaded on camel-carts for transportation.

cause it is right. If a free society cannot help the many who are poor, it cannot save the few who are rich."

This potpourri of appeals, this dovetailing of military security, political expediency, and lofty idealism which the proponents of foreign aid always find necessary to get into their arguments, can be found in many other pronouncements on foreign aid. Gordon Gray, a former Secretary of the Army who headed a committee appointed by President Eisenhower, commenting on underdeveloped areas, including overseas territories, said:

These countries no longer accept poverty as an inevitable fact of life. The contrast between their aspirations and their present state of unrelieved poverty makes them susceptible to domestic unrest and provides fertile ground for the growth of communist movements. . . . We must help bring about, in these areas, increased production and mutually beneficial exchange of material for civilian and defense use . . . [and] we must assist in bringing them increasingly into a network of international trade which will promote a more effective use of the economic resources of the free world and will enable the countries comprising it to achieve progress on a self-supporting basis.

These were words not of a nominal liberal, not of a "professional" internationalist but of a conservative member of a Republican Administration whose efforts bore the emblem of budgetary thrift and economy.

116

It is natural that such opinions should be eloquently supported by a man with first-hand knowledge of foreign aid problems, gained in direct contact with the nations which badly need this assistance for their proper development. In one of many statements on this subject Ambassador Chester Bowles said: "Ours is the age of rising expectations. More than a billion people in Asia and Africa have won their freedom since World War II. . . . Suddenly they have come to see that the ancient afflictions —disease, injustice, illiteracy, hunger, and poverty—are not a part of God's plan for the unfortunate, but evils to be fought and overcome."

If these afflictions be not overcome, it can advance the interest only of one factor—Communism. It was Stalin who said that the "backs of the British, the West, will be broken not on the River Thames, but on the Yangtse and the Ganges," thus repeating in fact what was said years before him by Lenin: "The road to Paris leads through Calcutta and Peking."

And though these prophecies taken literally have not been fulfilled in reality, the motive for their utterance and their potential is clear: to turn the poverty-stricken, undeveloped nations into a mighty instrument against the West, whether that be symbolized by London on the Thames, Paris on the Seine, or Washington on the Potomac.

It was, therefore, inevitable but shocking for many members that Congress was called upon in 1950 to approve a relief program for Communist Yugoslavia. Later Communist Poland was added to the list of beneficiaries of some limited forms of foreign aid, and the Administration has since had annually to run the same gantlet of attacks in Congress against aiding Communist nations, or, as it is usually called in Congress, "helping the Communist regimes in their aggrandizement."

The controversy over "assisting Communist countries" has never lost its intensity. Year after year, for seventeen years in a row, attempts have been made to terminate this assistance. But fortunately enough, its defenders have come, in strength disproportionate to their numbers, from the very circles that pride themselves on their unassailable anti-Communism. Senate Minority leader Everett M. Dirksen and former Secretary of State Christian A. Herter have supported in the strongest words the continuation of this assistance. They fought with the most convincing arguments against such votes of the Senate as the one which resolved to "ban any assistance to countries known to be dominated by Communism or Marxism." Stated Herter: "Yugoslavia's break with Moscow and its pursuit of an independent course produced significant political and stragetic advantages for the United States and the rest of the non-Communist world. Soviet power was rolled back from the Adriatic Sea and from Italy's northeastern border. Austria's southern boundary was freed from Moscow's control. The closing of Yugoslavia's borders to Greek Communists sounded the death knoll for the latter's effort to win over Greece."

117

Herter's words were written before the rift between Russia and China became visible. The importance of that first breach in the monolithic Communist bloc, the Yugoslav break, was its influence in strengthening heterogeneous tendencies in the Communist world. The rift between Russia and China can be directly traced to that first rift in the Communist camp. The history of the relations between the Communist parties in the last decade indicates clearly that the Yugoslavian schism was the turning point in the Communist world's ideological struggles. The attitudes towards this schism very early assumed decisive dimensions in inter-Communist relations. The first expressions of misunderstandings between Russia and China were related to just this problem of how to treat, from the point of view of Communist theory, the outlaw, Tito's Yugoslavia. Thanks to the United States, Yugoslavia had the ability to withstand, first economically, and then to a great extent politically and militarily, the pressure of Stalin, who understood full well that this schism foretold much greater disturbances in the Communist world. And, it would seem obvious that even the most undiscriminating opponent of the spread of Communism would be compelled to admit that the Russian-Chinese rupture, even if it be assumed that it will for a time remain patched up, is a development of historical dimensions, completely changing the world scene, now and in the future.

It would be no exaggeration to say that when practical security considerations are at stake there is almost no limit to the cost we are willing to pay. Those who initiated and preserved the assistance programs for Yugoslavia (and Poland) could well say to themselves that they had served well this Republic, the cause of freedom, and the independence of nations, while not neglecting considerations of thrift in national expenditures. But on this problem as on many other problems of foreign aid, many members of Congress have not been eager to support the Administrations. Almost every year attempts have been made to attach to the appropriations bill reservations which would limit the freedom of the Administration in operating foreign aid programs. Once it was an amendment barring aid to some country, the next time an amendment to add some country to the list of recipient nations, or it was a transfer of some funds from economic to military aid, or vice versa. Though some of the amendments limited considerably the freedom of the Administration, they nevertheless represented the commendable view that United States aid should not be used as a support for repressive policies in countries leaning heavily on United States aid. But perhaps the most representative of the general mood concerning foreign aid often prevailing in Congress is the Dworshak amendment (named after the Republican Senator from Idaho), which prohibited the use of funds within the United States to publicize aid programs, thus prohibiting in fact any effort of the Administration to explain to the taxpayers, who pay for this aid, how their money is being used.

118

The generally unfavorable and often capricious moods of members of Congress concerning foreign aid are expressed in opinions which members of Congress have delivered there and elsewhere on this subject. There have been statements such as that of Representative Charles A. Eaton (Republican, New Jersey): "We are regarded generally as a milk cow with everybody invited to bring their bucket and help themselves." Senator Taft (Republican from Ohio) in 1953 said: "Unless there is a big change in the world, this Congress is through with foreign aid." Representative Passman (Democrat from Louisiana): "It has been my purpose to help contain the foreign aid program." There have also been statements like that of Robert B. Chiperfield (Republican, Illinois): "We must strengthen the hand of the President and Secretary Dulles at these [Big Four] meetings. The best way to do it is to pass the [Mutual Security] bill intact."

Though the opponents of foreign aid have been outspoken much more often than its supporters, the House has always voted by an overwhelming majority for the foreign aid bills. Typical proportions of the vote have been 252–130, 258–153, 260–132 (of course, always with fluctuations). These proportions were sharply altered for the first time in 1963, not as far as foreign aid as such is concerned, but in terms of its dimensions, as compared with the Administration's proposals.

In appraising the stand taken by the House of Representatives, we should not overlook that the Senate has more often and more clearly manifested support for foreign aid and even taken legislative initiative as in the suggestion from the chairman of the Senate Foreign Relations Committee, Senator Fulbright (Democrat from Arkansas), backed by Senator Humphrey (Democrat from Minnesota) and Senator John F. Kennedy (Democrat from Massachusetts), for giving the Development Loan Fund $1.5 billion a year for five years. In this connection it is pertinent to note Fulbright scholarships (bearing the name of their initiator), and Senator Humphrey's association with the Food for Peace programs.

In the great dispute on foreign aid, the most frequent and obviously most convincing objection has been that to the big "giveaway." This argument is very often supported by facts which if not supporting the charge of a straight "giveaway," carry their own conviction. Per se these facts about domestic American needs are persuasive indeed: for $7 billion we could add 56,000,000 acres to our farmland through drainage, clear 42,000,000 acres of brush and lumber, place them in cultivation, and develop the remaining forest lands; for $15 billion, the United States could sextuple its hydroelectric power; for $3 billion, pollution of streams could be reduced to a point of reasonable safety; for $23 billion, 7,000 miles of waterways for ocean-going vessels could be added and the list could grow by adding school and road building and other worthy domestic projects. But, as military men have many times retorted to such assertions, these

Senator Allen J. Ellender of Louisiana with Wyman R. Stone, Director of U.S. Operations Mission in Costa Rica, inspecting coffee processing plant, one of the projects of U.S. assistance for raising the efficiency of coffee production.

goals could be much more easily and quickly reached if it were possible to reduce the national defense budget, a goal very much desired, not only for the direct saving in government expenditures, but also for the reduction of tensions and encouragement to the cause of freedom the world over.

There is another, more material, rebuttal to the "giveaway" or "handout" charge. Secretary of State Dulles, who certainly could not be considered an ardent promoter of "hand-outs" of American wealth, addressed to this nation one of his many outspoken and convincing statements when he said:

"There seems to be an idea in some quarters that the money appropriated for Mutual Security is in some way taken abroad and spent there.

Of course, this is not the fact. Actually, nearly 80 per cent of Mutual Security funds are spent right here in the United States to buy farm products, machinery, materials, and military hardware, which in turn are sent abroad to aid the recipient country. Thus, these dollars perform a double duty. Six-hundred thousand Americans in factories and farms owe their jobs to Mutual Security Programs." On another occasion, Secretary Dulles was even more outspoken when he stated that those who talk so much about "hand-outs" seem to forget that these hand-outs "land in American" hands. (By the way, the 80 per cent mentioned by Dulles grew last year to 90 per cent.)

Of course, there are people to whom even the retention of most of the aid outlays within the United States economy (for example in the form of the assistance to the shipping industry as 50 per cent of the goods must by regulation be shipped in United States ships) does not mitigate, in their view, the inherent wrongness of foreign assistance programs. But, people close to the Administration have often pointed out that they never have heard from those who charge "hand-outs" that other "hand-outs" ought to be terminated as well—for example, subsidies for domestic agriculture, subsidies for the expansion of exports, special privileges for certain investments, and the less obvious subsidies which are part of the complicated network of financial arrangements of a modern state. The functioning of the national economy is unavoidably conditioned by various forms of government intervention and subsidies, even if these are seen (with alarm) to constitute departures from the classical tenets of free enterprise.

But the promotion of United States production, and therefore of high employment is only part of the reflexive effect of foreign aid on the United States national economy. Foreign aid exports are paving the way for the extension of American business exports. It suffices for an example to point to the 500 per cent increase of United States exports to Marshall Plan countries, from $1,678,000,000 (exclusive of government-financed exports) in 1948 to $8,855,000,000 in 1960. Similar, though not less spectacular, figures could be quoted in relation to all other countries receiving United States aid. In the years 1953–1958, United States foreign trade expanded 68 per cent while domestic trade expanded by only 18 per cent. By 1958, foreign trade provided 4.5 million jobs, more than the automobile, textile, chemical, and steel industries combined. "Goods financed by the foreign aid program had made a significant contribution to the United States export drive to reduce the balance-of-payment deficit," stated David E. Bell, director of the Agency for International Development, on September 18, 1963. Bell added, "Statistics assessed the value of such goods at $2.3 billion; or 11 per cent of the total exports in 1962. The goods financed by the foreign aid program included one-third of all fertilizers exported, 25 per cent of the locomotives shipped abroad, and 21 per cent of all iron and steel products sold to foreign customers."

It is also pertinent to mention that total United States exports have roared upwards from the very beginning years of the "giveaways" (in various forms and under various titles): from $3 billion in 1937 to over $20 billion in 1963. And, as far as the sapping of the American wealth by foreign aid is concerned, another set of figures deserves to be examined: in 1914 the United States was still a debtor nation to the extent of $3,686,000,000, and in 1963 it was a creditor in tens of billions of dollars, with the gross national product surpassing $500 billion.

There has been no miracle-working in the growth of American prosperity. Market preparation, the creation of demand, and the development of special tastes are old merchandising techniques. Countries which use United States goods become in time the best United States customers. Countries which have to provide spare parts to the machinery they received as foreign aid become clients of United States industry. The growth of United States exports is also stimulated by the natural development of a country's economy. A prosperous country is clearly a more eager importer of foreign goods. For example, the per capita exports to developed countries in 1959 were $22.80, compared with $4.79 to less developed countries. If the per capita exports to the less developed areas had been even half what they were to the developed countries, United States exports to underdeveloped areas in 1959 would have been $15.4 billion—nearly 2.5 times what they actually were ($6.4 billion).

But the most potent weapon in the arsenal of foreign-aid opponents is the balance of payments problem. Their charge seems to be most convincing: Because the United States has an adverse balance of payments (more dollars going out of the country than coming in), something has to be done to prevent the concomitant deterioration of the United States dollar in the economy of the world. And what could sound more convincing than the assertion that the simple solution is to terminate foreign aid? Because the balance-of-payment deficit is about $3 billion annually, it would seem that the problem could be solved by reducing foreign aid by that amount. If it were that simple, perhaps even some in the Administration would consider serious cuts in the foreign aid for that reason. Unfortunately, there is very little causal relationship between foreign aid and the balance of payments, for the reason that 90 per cent of the foreign aid dollars are being spent inside the United States.

David E. Bell, administrator of AID stated on July 22, 1963, in a letter to the New York *Times*:

Recognizing the difficulty of estimating precisely the effects of a change in a single factor in the balance of payments, it can be said as a rough approximation that a one-billion cut in "economic aid" would reduce United States exports by $900 million. (If the hypothetical cut were assumed to affect what is ordinarily called foreign aid—and not affect Public Law 480 and the Export-Import Bank—the proportions would be about an $800 million reduction in United States exports, and a $200 million reduction in the United States balance of payments deficits.) The conclusion is clear. Under present policies,

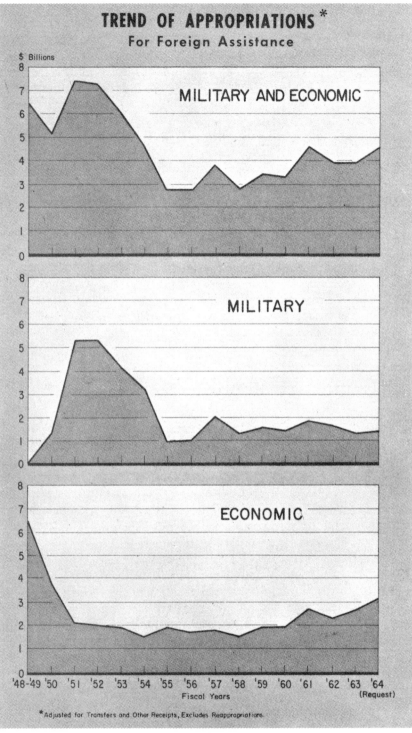

TREND OF APPROPRIATIONS *
For Foreign Assistance

$ Billions

MILITARY AND ECONOMIC

MILITARY

ECONOMIC

'48-'49 '50 '51 '52 '53 '54 '55 '56 '57 '58 '59 '60 '61 '62 '63 '64

Fiscal Years

(Request)

*Adjusted for Transfers and Other Receipts, Excludes Reappropriations.

123

with economic and military assistance to other countries almost entirely taking the form of United States goods and services, almost no gain to the balance of payments deficit can be achieved by reducing our foreign aid programs.

While many point at foreign aid as the alleged culprit in the balance-of-payment deficit, few mention foreign investments in this context. Whether purchases of foreign securities or more direct activities in foreign countries, these investments directly influence the balance of payments. They are so large that at times they are almost equivalent to the balance-of-payment deficit. In 1960 and in 1961 for example, United States investments abroad amounted to $3.8 billion each year.

As it is, with all their advantages and limitations, the foreign aid programs are in a constant process of diminution. From almost 2 per cent of the gross national product in 1949, foreign aid expenditures went down to less than .7 per cent of G.N.P. in 1963. As a share of the Federal budget, foreign aid declined from 11.5 per cent in 1949 to 4.1 per cent in 1963. Even if we were to add to the expenditures for economic and military assistance the contributions to the five international financial institutions and the shipment abroad of agricultural products under the Food for Peace program, both absolute and relative costs have been reduced from a peak of 28 per cent of Federal expenditures in 1947 to 5 per cent in fiscal 1962.

This continuous process of gradual reduction of foreign aid expenditures appears even more sizable if the so-called "pipeline" appropriations are considered. "Pipeline," says a publication for the Agency for International Development, "is the term used for those funds appropriated to a government agency committed by the agency for specific purposes but not all spent by the end of a fiscal year." Such "pipelines" build up when a project for which funds were appropriated has to take more than a year to implement as, for instance, the building of a hydroelectric dam or the acquisition of some complicated weapons system. The foreign aid "pipeline," including military assistance, reached $6.9 billion as of June 30, 1962, as compared with $38.5 billion for the Department of Defense "pipeline" and the general "pipeline" of $76.7 billion for all U.S. government agencies on the same date.

In the annual battle of appropriations in Congress, this "pipeline" plays a considerable role. Representative Passman uses the foreign aid "pipeline" in his annual quest for reductions in the foreign aid appropriations for that year. He says that even if there were no appropriation whatever for foreign aid, the Agency for International Development could still run its programs for another two years, an assertion as illusory as that on which the balance of payment argument is based. Appropriations which remain in the "pipeline" are appropriations already committed; and no added activity, no new program, can be undertaken with that "pipeline" money.

Misunderstandings about foreign aid are also attributed to those who assume that it keeps entire nations going and exerts considerable influence on the immediate standard of living in the countries to which it is supplied. Unfortunately, that is not so. United States aid may, for example, supply the marginal difference, often a very small difference, between one and another point on a particular nation's curve of economic development, but as far as individuals are concerned it does not mean very much. According to United Nations figures on international economic aid per capita to selected underdeveloped countries during the fiscal years 1954–1958, the variations were enormous even among countries with similar per capita income levels. Among sixteen countries in each of which annual income is less than $100 per person, aid received during the five-year period from American and non-American sources combined ranged from less than $1 per person in Indonesia, Saudi Arabia, Sudan, and Yemen to more than $60 per person in Jordan and Korea. The average in India was $1.3, in Nepal $2.6, and in Pakistan $6. It is only among countries with small populations that aid in the given period reaches considerable per capita amounts: $100 in Libya, $115 in Israel, $50 in Taiwan, $30 in Costa Rica.

These figures are being used against arguments that aid deprives nations of their sense of economic responsibility by making them rely on Uncle Sam. That is far from the truth. Aid creates the basis for some hope that an effort makes sense, that there is a prospect of change for the better. That such hope is not in vain is being proven daily by the steady progress the assisted countries make in the increases in their power resources, in income, and in the standard of living.

These improvements would be much more rapid were it not for the population explosion. In terms of standard of living many countries have to run very fast in their economic development in order just to stand still. And the poorer the country, the greater is the rate of population increase. Thus assistance to foreign countries is closely linked to the population problem.

Formally and officially the aid agency is not supposed to take this problem into account, but it is perforce one of the main concerns of the entire program. Statisticians have computed, for instance, that if India's death rate could be reduced to that of Puerto Rico, India, with her present birth rate, could fill five earths like ours in a single century. It is therefore no exaggeration when some sociologists point at the population explosion as no less a danger than nuclear warfare. Rising standards of living, including standards of education, appear to be among the best ways to overcome this problem, and are no less important than birth control and family planning. The rise in standards of living seems to be of decisive importance. Paul Hoffman said in a conversation with the author on these matters that as long as a big family remains the only means of social security in countries like India, no amount of persuasion and government intervention will change the rate of increase, which at present endangers not only the well-being of developing nations but, in the same degree, that of the entire world.

Foreign aid is, therefore, instrumental in combatting the special danger of uncontrolled population increases, of which so few are aware and even fewer are ready to talk about. To perform effectively in assisting foreign countries in developing their economies, United States aid must help carry out development plans in these countries. In the existing system of annual appropriations, no Administration has been able to commit itself to support development plans that would take years to carry out. With the exception of some small undertakings, each project needs years for its accomplishment. A dam or an irrigation system cannot be built in one year. It was, therefore, natural after some years of experience, for the Administration to ask Congress to approve long-range financing of development projects.

President Eisenhower tried to convince Congress that authority to plan such projects, if given to the Administration, would assure the best possible utilization of United States aid funds. Congress opposed the proposal, seeing it as an attempt to undermine and curtail the legislative prerogatives. The argument was that the control of federal allocations was granted Congress by the Constitution. On March 22, 1961, President Kennedy proposed that Congress approve a five-year authorization for development loans, totaling $8.8 billion, of which $7.3 billion was to be financed directly by the Treasury by creating a directly related public debt, rather than by the usual annual appropriations of Congress. Congress refused to accept the President's proposal as it was. Instead it "authorized" $7.2 billion for development loans over five years with the provision that the amount authorized be appropriated annually in five equal parts, reserving implicitly to itself the option of veto.

As it has turned out, in the light of political reality, foreign aid appropriations have a major and, some think, a most important, role in the continuing concern of Congress with the extension of its influence over the conduct of American foreign policy. It is, of course, not only through voting on foreign aid appropriations that Congress exercises its influence over the most important and sensitive areas of United States foreign policy. The hearings which precede authorization and appropriation in the House Foreign Affairs Committee, in the Subcommittee on Foreign Operations Appropriations, and in the committees of the Senate provide ample opportunity to prove that the Administration is not the only and final judge of what is good and useful for United States policy. So do the debates on the House and Senate floor. The hearings at which representatives of the Administration appear last for months and cover thousands of pages (3,189 pages for the hearings before the Subcommittee on Foreign Operations Appropriations for 1963). In these hearings, congressmen question every detail of United States foreign policy, including matters not necessarily connected with foreign aid operations.

And at these hearings statements are often made (sometimes even about foreign governments and their leaders) that are not exactly consistent with prevailing foreign policy objectives, or tactics. Sometimes such statements annul major political achievements or put an end to hopes for such achievements.

One of the most frequent charges made in these hearings is against western European countries and Japan for what is called insufficient participation in efforts to assist developing countries. Some of these charges are made in the most vehement language, as if United States insistence could make these countries increase their share in foreign aid efforts of the free world. It is true that much in these charges is justified. Western European countries could and should do more, but it is hard to see how the Administration could be made responsible for the behavior of foreign countries, even if those are nations linked with the United States in an alliance. Even acknowledging that these countries should do more to share the burden of foreign assistance, representatives of the Administration can point to the growing participation of western Europe and Japan in aid programs in recent years. Between 1956 and 1959, the volume of their aid to the less developed countries increased by 77 per cent— from $900 million to $1.6 billion. These figures do not include the private lending from these countries, which amounted to $1.6 billion of the $28 billion of free-world private lending in 1959. In 1961, their aid reached $2.5 billion. Aid from the free industrialized nations took a greater percentage of their gross national product than that which the United States allocates for its foreign aid. Aid to African countries is largely supplied by France and to a lesser extent by Great Britain; United States aid there plays a minor role.

The eleven countries (Belgium, Canada, Denmark, France, West Germany, Italy, Japan, Netherlands, Norway, Portugal, and the United Kingdom) which joined with the United States in the Development Assistance Committee (DAC) of the Organization for Economic Cooperation and Development (OECD) already carry a considerable part of the burden of foreign aid and keep on increasing their share, though every one of them has a lower per capita national product and lower per capita income than the United States. As for the tax burden, while in the United States in 1960, taxes amounted to 26.2 per cent of the total United States output, comparable figures for the others are: United Kingdom 29.7 per cent, Italy 30 per cent, Netherlands 30.3 per cent, West Germany 32.6 per cent, and France 35.4 per cent.

Recognition of these facts does not change the basic, justified demand that these countries increase their aid programs. Among the many foreign aid programs of America's western allies, special mention should be made of the so-called "Colombo Plan." It had its origin in a meeting of foreign ministers of the British Commonwealth in 1950 in Colombo, Ceylon. Its original members—Great Britain, Canada, Australia, New

Zealand, Malaya, India, Ceylon, and Pakistan—agreed to work together to attack poverty. The joint action would include surveying the needs of the area, assessing resources of capital and manpower, and providing workers with technical skills to assist the countries of South and Southeast Asia in raising their people's standard of living. The United States later joined the Colombo Plan Consultative Committee as did non-Commonwealth countries of that area.

In spite of what could appear to be an inexhaustible arsenal of merely practical arguments that have the effect of divorcing foreign aid programs from the ideas in which they originated, the moral and humanitarian aspect of this aid has never completely escaped the attention of the United States Administrations and legislators. Even the Clay Report, in which a great effort was made to stress the practical, "the business-like" considerations in foreign aid, does not neglect this basically human element in the motivations for foreign aid. In its last paragraph this report states:

> Our examination of U.S. foreign assistance programs and consideration of them in this report have been based upon the sharp criterion of their value to the security of our country and of the free world. We would not express ourselves adequately, however, if we failed to note the further interests of our country and of our people in the purpose and effect of these programs. For this reason, we would point out that the need for development assistance and an U.S. interest in providing it would continue even if the cold war and all our outstanding political differences with the communists were to be resolved tomorrow. This is not merely because it is part of the American tradition to be concerned with the plight of those less fortunate than ourselves. This is not merely because it is our national self-interest to assure expanding markets for our production and reliable sources of supply of necessary raw materials. It is because the people of the United States hope to see a world which is prosperous and at peace that we believe those nations which are seriously striving to promote their own development should be helped by us and by our partners to create and maintain the conditions conducive to steady economic progress and improved social well-being within the framework of political freedom.

And even this paragraph could not satisfy one of the members of the Clay Committee—George Meany, the president of the AFL-CIO, who attached to the report a dissenting statement in which he demanded an increase in U.S. assistance to foreign nations and stressed even more the moral obligation of the have's to support the have-not's. Meany rightly points out that "the many millions of dollars that are contributed each year by the American people to private voluntary agencies engaged in helping people all over the world amply testify to their willingness to have our government continue full-scale foreign aid."

At every occasion, these motifs of U.S. foreign aid appear and reappear. The harsh facts of political life, of the cold war, sometimes make these pronouncements sound unreal, but the fact stands out that the U.S. was the first country in the world to assist foreign nations not only in disaster, but in their struggle for progress as well. Sceptics among America's adversaries, and even friends who cannot admit that there is anything more than selfish interest behind U.S. foreign aid, cannot deny that even if this is allegedly a "new form of imperialism," it is a somewhat sublimated form, one which has replaced the kind of political subjugation and military conquests with which they are familiar.

Among the many expressions of support for foreign aid, the voice of religion is heard quite often. Archbishop Fulton J. Sheen, a leading member of the Roman Catholic hierarchy in the United States, has placed foreign aid in a different dimension than that to be found in the usual arguments. Speaking at a conference in support of foreign aid in Washington, he said:

> We need to justify our wealth by sharing it. Therefore with humility and not with pride and superiority we extend our hands to the needy; theirs is the burden of being under-privileged; ours is the burden of being over-privileged. It is their stomachs that are empty—it could be our hearts that are empty.

President Lyndon B. Johnson like his predecessors, sees in the foreign aid programs an indispensable component of the American foreign policy, and even more, a moral obligation of the United States towards the less fortunate nations. In one of his statements on foreign aid, President Johnson said: "No nation can long enjoy great affluence when all the other nations are impoverished." On another occasion when he was Vice President, he stated: "The United States wishes to use its resources for aiding peoples of underdeveloped countries."

This moral approach, as important as it is, represents only one aspect of the problem. Foreign aid has also another dimension—we could call it a social one on a global scale. It is the same dimension in which, on a national scale, the common care to eradicate poverty and want grew and gave birth to social legislation. Paraphrasing a saying of President Kennedy, that the world cannot remain "half free and half slave," it may be said that the world cannot remain half prosperous and half hungry. Whether we like it or not, "one world" is a reality. Even the remote corner of such a world affects all of us everywhere. The U.S. government slogan that the war against poverty, illness, and illiteracy is "the only war we want" stems in fact from the awareness of the objective imperatives of our age. Paul Hoffman calls it "waging of peace with an investment of $25 billion." Others call it the waging of progress. But, whatever the definition, the aim is the same: to help nations achieve a stage of development at which aid will never again be necessary. And it is no exaggeration to state that the American public basically understands the issues involved in foreign aid.

At a conference on foreign aid organized by the Eisenhower Administration, a report was delivered by two members of Congress who had returned the day before from a joint speaking tour of thirty-two cities in twenty-one states. According to their report, their audiences were interested in the aid program, eager to learn about it, and, they said, "We found that once the benefits of the program are understood and the program explained, there was enthusiastic support." A similar appraisal of public sentiment regarding foreign aid was reported by Governor Gaylord Nelson of Wisconsin at the National Conference on International Economic and Social Development held in December, 1961. Governor Nelson said:

Most people, I have found in my politicking, are decent and generous. They want to extend a helping hand to the underdeveloped countries of the world, but they don't want to be played for fools or suckers. Their wrath is aroused, especially come tax time, when they read in their papers stories of waste and corruption among officials of recipient countries and inefficiency and mismanagement on the part of our own representatives in the foreign aid program.

The average American has no way of knowing on his own that these stories are grossly exaggerated, or that even when true, they represent exceptions rather than the rule. This, it seems to me, represents in part a failure of communication—in the past—a failure on the part of responsible authorities to keep the people informed on the wide-ranging positive achievements that have marked our foreign assistance programs over the years. . . . The great and stirring human drama that lies behind the cold statistics of foreign aid has yet to reach people who pay for it.

And, as has been pointed out before, it was the Continental Congress, and no other ideology, that lit the fuse of today's revolution of rising expectations. It was not the men in the Kremlin, but Thomas Jefferson, Patrick Henry, Tom Paine, and Abraham Lincoln who gave life to the bold words that have stirred the hearts of millions in Asia, Africa, and Latin America.

If Gallup polls are of any consequence, the one in 1963 on foreign aid proved that the majority believes that foreign aid is an obligation which the United States should continue to fulfill. The question, "In general, how do you feel about foreign aid—are you for it or against it?" brought the following answers: For—58%; against—30%; no opinion—12%. And this in the face of an all-out attack against foreign aid in Congress and the press. Supporters of foreign aid as such, as distinguished from those whose support is dictated by expediency, can certainly find encouragement in this poll on one of the most criticized programs of contemporary Administrations.

6

$$$

Military Aid—the Conduit of Foreign Aid

Although the names of the agencies that administered the foreign aid program frequently changed, the over-all name of the program remained the same for over a decade—the Mutual Security Program. The connotation of this name was clear: "security" is generally understood to mean soldiers, equipment, and military installations.

The authors of the Mutual Security Program were well aware that national "security" has bi-partisan support and is above political dealings. They knew that whatever was wrapped in the mantle of "security" was assured a safe passage, even in an otherwise hostile Congress.

The name, therefore, was adopted to a great extent as a matter of political convenience and parliamentary tactics, for there was always a question of obtaining Congressional approval for the program. Thus, the most diversified tasks of the aid programs have come under the name of "security": e.g., delivering medicine to eradicate trachoma in a North African country, along with equipment for a combat division of NATO, or supplying hybrid seeds, together with a torpedo boat to defend the Vietnamese coast from Communist infiltration.

But the system worked, despite expressions of discontent, with this method of presentation of the foreign-aid programs to the Congress and public. Senator Mansfield spoke for many in voicing his objections to the catch-all program in a Senate speech in 1959: "We shall never know which is which, and what is what, so long as all the parts are hopelessly intermingled, as is now the case." There have been other reasons as well for the unhappiness with the system of lumping all forms of assistance together under the title of "security." Foremost among them was the fact that whatever within the framework of foreign aid programs was directed at relieving human sufferings was said to be done in the interest of American national security. Preserving the national security is certainly nothing to be ashamed of, but it hardly improves the image of the United States to brand every effort to relieve the sufferings of others as not humanitarian. This was and is so often the case with many of the American foreign-aid programs. Not only was it hardly in the best interests of the United States, it was not true. Portrayed as "security" measures, the United States policies thus seemed to bear out the slogans of

General Eisenhower, Supreme Commander of NATO, greets Harriman and other western leaders who arrived in Paris for conference.

anti-American propagandists who claimed that American assistance was really given with ulterior motives.

But the name of the program, although something of a misnomer, may be better understood as deriving from the events of the first postwar years. The idyll of postwar cooperation between the wartime allies was very soon shattered. The first shock came with the Russian refusal to remove its troops from Iran, in 1946. In 1947 came the Communist attempt at a takeover in Greece. And then in succession there was the Berlin blockade and the Korean war.

The billions which the United States poured into many countries around the globe to relieve suffering and to assist in reconstruction efforts seemed to be unconnected to developments in the changing international situation. The fact that out of $263 billion distributed between 1945 and 1950, $25 billion was economic assistance, seemed remote from the realities of the renewed threats to peace. The Truman Doctrine—the decision to give economic as well as military aid to Greece and Turkey—signaled the oncoming change in the evaluation of aid purposes and forms.

But it still was only a signal, and, it seemed, only an isolated one. Economic assistance, as exemplified in the Marshall Plan, continued to be the first order of the day, and the Economic Cooperation Administration was the formal implementation of this general American policy.

But the rapidly deteriorating relations with the Soviet Union brought about and hastened the change. The United States for the first time, while not at war, became a member of a defensive alliance. The North Atlantic Treaty Organization (NATO) came into being in the middle of 1949. Funds had to be supplied. Europe had not yet started on the road to recovery from the devastation of war, and, therefore, the United States had to undertake a great deal of the burden of the alliance. This was in addition to the contributions for the European Recovery Program (ERP). The President asked for $5.6 billion for the ERP in 1949. The $1.5 billion for military aid was over and above this amount and could not have caused much enthusiasm among the members of the Eighty-first Congress. Their reservations were quite understandable. It was hard to harmonize the idea of giving billions for economic recovery while attention had to be paid to military preparedness. In addition, many Congressmen thought that Asia should occupy a much more important place in military preparations than Europe. The news that the Russians had exploded an atomic bomb in September, 1949, put an end to the discussion. Congress appropriated $1,314,010,000 for military aid: $1 billion for NATO; $211,370,000 to Greece and Turkey, which had not yet joined NATO; $75 million to the "general area" of China; and $27,640,000 for Iran, South Korea, and the Philippines.

The Ninth Marines disembarking from attack transport USS *Bayfield* at Yokosuka, Japan, on way to Thailand to participate in exercise "Firm Link" of SEATO.

Berlin children watch from a hillside as a U.S. airlift plane approaches Tempelhof airport during Berlin blockade in 1948 which initiated decisive change in aid policies and resulted in the establishment of NATO, April, 1949.

The trend was unmistakable. Military aid was increasing along with expenditures for building up American military forces. The outbreak of war in Korea justified this new trend. It hastened the tempo of military preparations. From the start of the military assistance program in 1949 to June 30, 1952, funds allocated to the Department of Defense for use in Europe totaled $9.2 billion.

After the Berlin blockade, defense requirements were thoroughly re-examined. On July 26, 1949, Congress amended the Mutual Defense Assistance Act of 1949 and authorized $1.25 billion for continued expansion of the existing military programs. In September, another $4 billion was appropriated. By the end of 1950, the preponderance of economic pro-

United States armored signal corps sergeant explains operation of special camera to members of the Belgian army, part of exchange of technical information and military ideas among member nations of NATO.

grams was definitely on its way out. Of the $8.5 billion appropriated during that year, $5.7 billion went to rearm American allies who were facing the growing menace of Russia and Communist China.

The changing situation was reflected in the organizational setup of the foreign aid administration. The Mutual Security Act of 1951 abolished the agency which symbolized the economic aspect of American foreign aid, the Economic Cooperation Administration, and put in its place a new agency, the Mutual Security Agency. The date was December 30, 1951.

Thus the changeover from economic aid to military assistance was accomplished. The continuing Korean War drew more and more American resources toward the military aspects of the foreign aid program, and expenditures for the military assistance programs continued to grow. The Mutual Security Act of 1951 demonstrated the completeness of the change: of the $7,483,400,000 authorized, $5,028,000,000 was allocated in the form of military aid to the NATO countries. And this amount did not include the military aid to Greece, Turkey, and Iran which came to $396,250,000. This ratio between economic and military aid programs continued for the next few years. The areas of concentration of aid changed, with Asia receiving a larger share in the military assistance programs (in 1953 $1.1 billion), but the general trend was continued.

The reasons for this change were also continuously changing. After the first shock of Communist aggression was absorbed and some basic defense structures established, the United States began to fashion a most intricate system of alliances all over the world. These alliances assumed a position of central importance in the formulation of the foreign aid programs. Secretary of State Dulles emphasized many times that in his opinion economic assistance was no more than an adjunct of the military aid directed to those countries which have joined with the United States in the various defense alliances in Europe, Central Asia, Southeast Asia. "Economic aid was essential," stated Dulles, "to the construction of the alliance system. It served first as an incentive to join our side—and second as a means of helping those countries to meet the additional burden imposed by maintenance of armies."

The priority of security considerations in foreign aid programs could most clearly be seen year by year in the official documents dealing with foreign aid. The "letters of transmittal" signed by the President, which accompanied the semi-annual reports of the Administration to the Congress on the Mutual Security Program, used to repeat, in different phrases, the same approach: "The mutual security programs, as carried out

U.S. army sergeant instructs Ethiopian soldiers in use of a machine gun.

M-8 armored cars, provided under the Mutual Assistance Program, pass a camel train along a road near Teheran, Iran.

through the Mutual Security Agency, are effectively advancing the security of the United States, and of our cooperating partners in the free world." These "letters of transmittal" contained no mention of the non-military aspects of American aid, though in the reports themselves the non-military aid programs took up much more space than the military aspects because helping people to live, develop, and raise their standards of living makes a much more absorbing story than military training or the supplying of war materials.

But the military aspects and security considerations of the foreign aid programs were only part of the story. The strengthening of the United States defenses through the system of alliances was also only part of the general argument in favor of foreign aid. As the military aid programs evolved and as the impact they had on the defense posture of the non-Communist world became evident, there arose many new questions of their importance for the United States.

The partisans of foreign aid used to quote an interesting argument: The figures about the cost of two World Wars, which the United States had fought. World War I cost $186 billion and World War II $1,352,-

Two Berbers guarding U.S. Air Force planes at base in Morocco.

000,000,000, nearly seven times as much. To pay two or three billion dollars annually for the preservation of peace must, according to this line
of reasoning, today appear as quite a sound proposition, from the economic point of view.

But there was no need to go that far back into history. There were and
are much more persuasive arguments for the justification of the military
assistance programs. The government has handy a mass of figures to prove
that each dollar spent for military assistance saves many more dollars
which the United States would have had to spend to reach its present
defense position, had there never been any military aid. At a meeting
called in 1958 in Washington to get support for the foreign-assistance pro-

Rocket "Honest John" being prepared for field demonstration at Asiage, Italy.

grams, Secretary of Defense Neil H. McElroy and other members of the
Eisenhower Administration drew heavily on this arsenal of figures, which
are most convincing. "Since 1950," said McElroy, "our allies have spent
$5 of their own money on mutual defense for every $1 contributed by
the United States." He continued: "What has this mutual effort produced: a worldwide network of over 250 major land, sea, and air installations outside the United States. Our allies have also 34 per cent more
ground forces (better trained and equipped) than in 1950, 108 per cent
more combatant vessels, 12.5 per cent more conventional aircraft, and
23 times as many jets."

Vice President Nixon went even further, stating: "If we should attempt

DEFENSE EXPENDITURES AND U.S. MILITARY ASSISTANCE
EUROPEAN NATO COUNTRIES *
(Billions of Dollars)

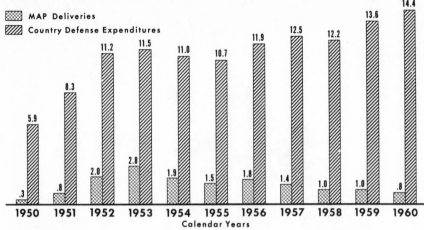

MAP Deliveries
Country Defense Expenditures

Calendar Years

* Includes Greece and Turkey.

to do the whole task ourselves, the number of young men inducted into our armed forces would be sharply increased. . . . If these forces weren't maintained by the Koreans, Formosans, South Vietnamese, Turks, and our friends in western Europe with our help, we should have to do the job. On the average, it would cost us in dollars, purely apart from the manpower, five times as much, at least, to maintain the same level of military strength abroad that we currently have." And for those for whom these arguments were not convincing enough, another set of figures was produced: the annual cost of maintenance of an American soldier was $3,515, of a French soldier $1,440, a Pakistani $484, a Greek $424, and a Nationalist Chinese $147.

The report to Congress on the Mutual Security Program of the Kennedy Administration, dated June 11, 1962, presents equally revealing details about the scope of military aid. The Kennedy Administration, the report said, made "a complete re-evaluation of the role of military assistance in support of the total national defense effort," which fully validated the importance of the program. In this re-evaluation effort long-range planning methods occupied a most important position. The report continued: "These methods, established in 1960, involve the formulation of 'military assistance plans'—five-year, time-phased schedules of action by areas and countries—intended to assure that military assistance conforms to a consistent purpose and directly promotes the military and foreign policy objectives of the United States."

Equipped with such general principles of guidance, the military-assistance programs continued to operate as before, although there was a growing tendency to separate military aid from economic aid. The reduction of military-assistance expenditures in Europe and the growing

MILITARY ASSISTANCE DELIVERIES*
By Region

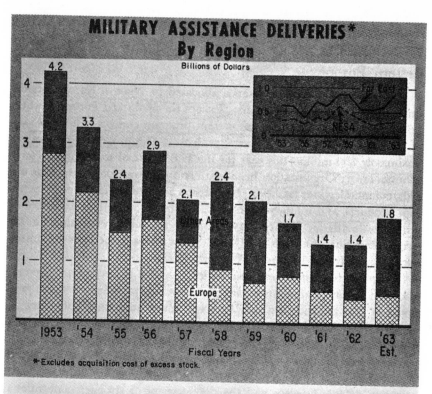

Billions of Dollars

* Excludes acquisition cost of excess stock.

Fiscal Years

DEFENSE EXPENDITURES OF EUROPEAN NATO COUNTRIES*
AND U.S. MILITARY ASSISTANCE

Billions of Dollars

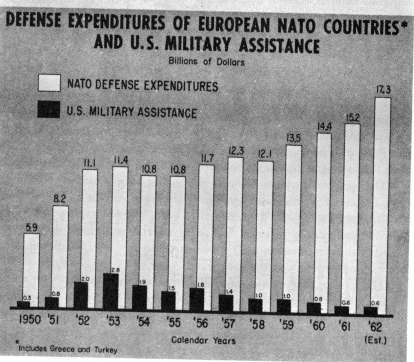

☐ NATO DEFENSE EXPENDITURES

■ U.S. MILITARY ASSISTANCE

* Includes Greece and Turkey

Calendar Years

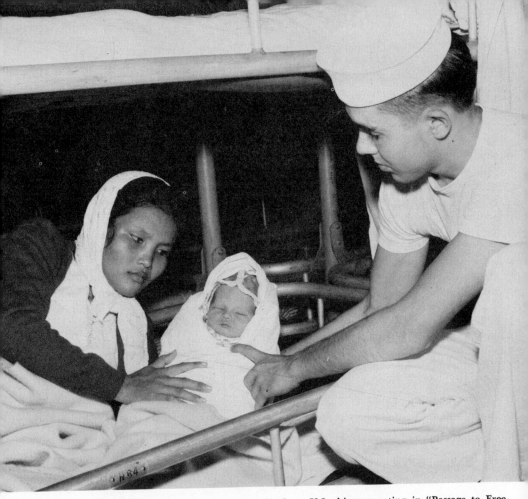

Hospital corpsman, aboard one of the forty U.S. ships operating in "Passage to Freedom," the evacuation of Vietnamese escaping Communism in Northern Indo-China, holding a little girl he helped bring into the world.

concentration on the Far East have continued. Out of the $1.93 billion of military-assistance funds, Europe (including the NATO countries and Spain) received $544 million while the allocation for the Far East was $782 million; Near East and South Asia $448 million; Latin America $54 million; Africa $25 million; and non-regional military assistance $76 million.

This diminishing defense assistance in Europe symbolizes the closing of an era in the American-European defense alliance, as far as the financial burden is concerned. The value of military assistance in materials and training provided by the United States to European NATO countries since the beginning of the alliance totaled approximately $15.9 billion while during the same period the NATO countries expended $123.8 billion of their own resources for defense. In 1960, the United States military assistance to NATO under the Mutual Security Program amounted to approximately 5 per cent of the total defense expenditure of the European NATO countries. Though over fifty countries are among the recipients of some forms of military assistance, more than two-thirds of these funds go to countries on the immediate periphery of the Soviet Union and China: Korea, Vietnam, Turkey, the Republic of China, Greece, Thailand, Iran, Pakistan, and, most recently, India. A surprisingly large number of countries are registered as recipients of military assistance. This is because a country is listed among the recipients of military aid even if its entire share of U.S. military assistance consists of the maintenance expenses of only a few of its officers in training in an American military school.

The officer-training program represents a very interesting part of military-assistance activity. Tens of thousands of officers of many foreign nations spend months, and even years, training in American military establishments. Since the beginning of the program approximately 175,-000 foreign nationals have participated in this program—in itself an army of American-educated men, whose importance and influence in their respective countries, with corresponding benefit to American interests,

"Concrete leaflet" that Communist guerillas in Vietnam set up on roads for propaganda purposes.

cannot be overestimated. In addition to these, another 50,000 have been trained at overseas installations of the United States, and many thousands in their own countries by U.S. teams.

These figures, however, do not tell the entire story. The fact that the eligible countries (there are sixty-six such countries) are also buying, for cash, American military equipment, that such equipment makes them dependent on U.S. spare parts, and that these cash purchases for dollars have amounted (through the middle of 1961) to $2.4 billion, is certainly another fact which should not be overlooked in an appraisal of U.S. military-assistance programs.

In these programs a special place is occupied by what is called in official language "defense support." This rather vague term is in fact the name for special appropriations for economic purposes. As the words indicate, this form of aid is supposed to alleviate the special burdens which certain countries incur in the interests of mutual defense—theirs and that of the United States. Large military establishments, sizable standing armies, and a state of permanent military alertness maintained by certain countries often constitute a disproportionately large drain on their economic resources. The "supporting assistance" is supposed to help such countries by increasing the economic aid they receive by means of special allocations from military-assistance appropriations. The extent of this assistance may be illustrated by the Kennedy Administration's proposals to Congress for 1964. Out of a requested appropriation for what now is called the "Strategic Assistance Program" of $2,140,000,000, $435 million is to be channeled to "supporting assistance" programs. In this category, economic assistance is to be given to "four countries on the fringe of the Communist bloc," and to six countries "which either are passing through periods of basic political and economic instability or have economies which simply are not viable at this stage"; and to "provide an alternative to excessive dependence on Communist bloc aid," as well as to "assure access to important U.S. military bases." The countries which are to receive this form of "military" assistance are Vietnam, Korea, Turkey, Thailand, Congo, Laos, and Jordan, while supporting assistance has been in the past two years discontinued in China, Greece, Pakistan, Iran, and Tunisia.

This economic aid, placed within the military-assistance programs, includes another kind of non-military activity, which has succeeded past all expectations. Under the title "civic action" programs are being carried out which give special meaning to the real aims of the military assistance.

"Civic action" covers many projects of the greatest importance not only to the security or to the military needs of a country, but also to the well-being of its population. Sometimes it means using military personnel and equipment, including rations, in meeting some kind of an emergency; sometimes it means building an access road for a remote village; sometimes it means the use of military equipment to build a

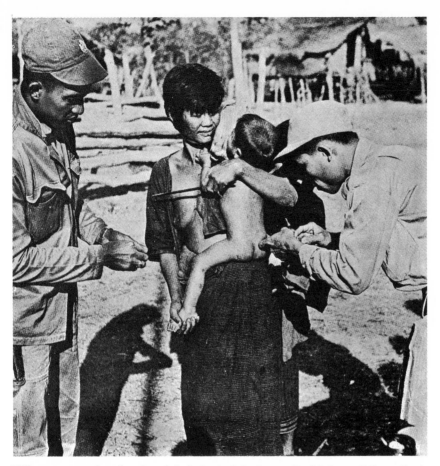

Military personnel performing civil duties in bringing medical help to E-Kav tribe in Thailand.

school; and sometimes the use of military personnel as teachers, instructors, or medical help.

The success of this effort in many countries has induced Congress to give it its formal blessing. Section 5056 of the Foreign Assistance Act of 1961 states that to an "extent feasible and consistent with the other purposes of this part, the use of military forces in less developed countries in the construction of public works and other activities helpful to economic development shall be encouraged." The definition of "civic action" in the Military Assistance Program goes even further. "Civic action is a term for the use of military forces on projects useful to the populace at all levels in such fields as training, public works, agriculture, transportation, communications, health, and sanitation."

Thus, "civic action" becomes an excellent means for turning the army into a real people's army and for establishing a real link between army and nation. And when we remember that in many of these countries a

145

Russian instructor teaching use of mortars at Yemenite military camp.

need exists for giving the people the feelings and convictions of nation-hood, this direct action of the chief exponent of nationhood in these countries, the army, contributes greatly to the molding of a unified, integrated political unit, and is the best guarantee of political stability.

The same reason which motivated the inclusion of the many non-military programs under military assistance caused the contingency fund to be placed as well within the framework of the "strategic assistance" programs. In the 1964 Administration proposals, it amounted to about 15 per cent of the entire "strategic assistance" expenditure.

As its name indicates, this was an emergency fund to be used at the President's discretion. A relatively new addition to the foreign-aid pro-gram, in existence for only six years, it has proved its usefulness in many situations in which quick reaction was necessary. Under the existing system by which authorizations and appropriations must be made spe-cifically for each project, the contingency fund has become a means of overcoming the slowness of the legislative process unavoidable in a democracy. With the contingency fund the Administration is able to respond swiftly to political and military challenges presented by author-itarian regimes which need no appropriations, no committee hearings, and no witnesses to decide what is appropriate and advisable.

Within the history of American foreign aid, the contingency fund has helped many a government in overcoming external pressures or internal subversion. The most striking example of this was the Congo crisis, when the ability of the American Administration to extend as-sistance quickly to the United Nations forces made the entire U.N. Congo operation possible—and prevented a situation fraught with the greatest danger. The contingency fund also made quick action possible when the new, liberal government of the Dominican Republic needed help to survive. Even acute balance-of-payment problems of nations which are recipients of U.S. aid have been solved with funds from the contingency fund. When, in 1962, Egypt (the United Arab Republic) and Syria faced a serious payment crisis, loans were extended to them from the contingency fund as part of a stabilization agreement with the International Monetary Fund. It goes without saying that in sudden disaster situations demanding immediate relief action, the contingency fund makes possible America's most immediate response. Earthquakes in Iran, Morocco, Libya, Chile, or in the summer of 1963, in Yugoslavia, typhoons and floods in Pakistan—such emergencies have always been met in time by American assistance in materials, personnel, and money.

During the years between 1951 and 1961, in what might be termed the "decade of mutual security" in U.S. foreign-assistance programs, military assistance assumed the leading role in the over-all aid activity. Even the most ardent critics of foreign aid seldom dared to extend their criticism to this aspect of aid. For even a non-military man can easily understand that the establishment of a first line of defense as far as possible from the borders of this country is an imperative which no party and no American can dispute. The outlays for military assistance have amounted to about 3 per cent of the U.S. defense budget. The Clay Report of 1963, which did not spare criticism of some aspects of the foreign-aid programs, stated though that "dollar for dollar these programs contribute more to the security of the free world than corresponding expenditures in our defense appropriations. . . . These countries are providing more than two million armed men ready, for the most part, for any emergency."

Thus, the approximately $30 billion appropriated for military-assistance programs between 1949 and 1962—about one-third of the general appropriations for foreign aid—has undoubtedly served a most vital interest of the United States, while fulfilling a mission of assisting other nations in the preservation of their territorial integrity and national independence. Viewed from this point of view, military-aid programs seem to have fully justified the adjective in their title—"mutual"—because they have clearly proved to be beneficial to both partners in the military-assistance programs.

But the defense advantages in these programs have not for one minute obscured the real issues for the leaders of the U.S. Government. In the midst of the arms race, when the military-assistance programs soared towards the $6 billion mark annually, President Truman stated emphatically: "Now what can we hope from all these weapons—all these billions of dollars we must spend for defenses? The most we can hope to gain from them is a stalemate—all we can do with them is to buy

147

View of entrance of hospital built with Russian aid at Phnom Penh, Cambodia.

time. . . . One of our best hopes is economic assistance for other nations. This is a chance to move forward, to do something affirmative toward breaking the stalemate."

President Eisenhower expressed similar thoughts some years later: "To maintain America's military strength during the next five years, we shall spend more than $200 billion. This almost unimaginable sum will, together with similar but smaller expenditures of our allies, keep us in a strong security posture. But these sums, great as they are, cannot produce a single constructive, useful thing for human beings."

These were not statements made at pacifists' meetings. They were made at various official occasions, including a conference in Washington in 1958 called for the purpose of mobilizing public support for the foreign-assistance programs. And this was still the "decade of mutual security programs."

This decade seems to be drawing to a close. The foreign-assistance programs of recent years seem to show a new trend in de-emphasizing military aid, with a consequent upsurge in aid for economic development. This new tendency did not start suddenly. It has been growing gradually. The establishment in 1957 of the Development Loan Fund was one aspect of this new tendency. It manifested the formulation in the Administration of a modern philosophy of economic development, based on a better understanding of the forces which are rising all over the world and yearning for change. President Kennedy gave clear expression to these changing attitudes when he stated in his "Presidential Letter of Transmittal" to the Congress, on June 11, 1962: "This report marks the end of one decade in our aid programs and the beginning of another; the transition from what was primarily a decade of defense to a Decade of Development."

The name of the agency entrusted with the implementation of these "old-new" objectives of American foreign aid, the Agency for International Development, is a fitting symbol of this new era.

148

7

$$$

Russia Follows the American Example

The changes occasionally forced in American foreign-aid programs by Russian pressures in various parts of the world, supported the already existing public belief in the alleged forcefulness and success of Russian foreign policy. The statement that the "Russians were acting while the Americans were only reacting" seemed to become true, and many disputed it only at the expense of provoking some doubts about the soundness of their political judgment. Even when, in January, 1954, the Russians first allocated aid to Afghanistan, and thereby followed America's lead, very few in the United States thought of the change as an indication of an American success in the contest with Soviet Russia. Long before Premier Khrushchev challenged the United States to a peaceful competition, the United States' aid programs were challenging the Soviet Union to match American generosity in assisting nations on their road to development, economic progress, and higher standards of living.

This challenge could not have been ignored. The Russians had to do something about it.

As early as 1952, at the Moscow Economic Conference, Russian spokesmen began to make statements about achieving "international cooperation" and "rapid industrialization" in less developed countries. These statements were followed by offers of technical assistance and even of "whole factories." But two years were still to pass, with Stalin's death acting to change Russian policies, before any practical steps were taken to help in the industrialization of undeveloped countries.

With the growing number of newly independent nations, it became obvious that the coming contest between the two political systems would, at least partly, be fought over the allegiance of the "uncommitted" third of the world's population. It was Chester Bowles, one of the earliest and most active supporters of aid to foreign countries, who foresaw that Russia could not afford to remain passive in view of the American aid programs. "With the Communist emphasis on economics as a basis for politics," he said, "it is unlikely that the Soviet Union will long sit idly by, once our efforts show signs of success. I can testify to the extraordinary interest and concern which Soviet representatives show in Point Four."

149

Cartoon in propaganda publication for underdeveloped countries showing big Russian space ships compared with the small American-manned satellites.

But before this interest was translated into deeds, Russia and the other Communist countries continued to do their best to fight the impact of American aid programs around the world. The vehement campaign against the Marshall Plan, and later against other aid programs, was initially entrusted, to a great extent, to the local Communist parties. The campaign against American aid in the Russian press served as an indicator of Russian concern with the American assistance programs, and as a guide for the Communist parties all over the world. This antagonism was soon manifested in the United Nations as well. In the early fifties, at one of the meetings of the U.N. Economic and Social Council, the representative of Poland, Katz-Suchy, stated that the United States engaged in foreign aid programs "because Wall Street bankers, not content with 3 per cent interest on International Bank Bonds, want the 20 per cent and more which can be derived from direct control of the resources of the underdeveloped countries."

Concern with the results of American foreign aid programs must have been growing constantly if Premier Khrushchev himself had to join the chorus of Communists who criticized it. In one of his speeches, intended to woo underdeveloped countries, he stated: "If the capitalist gentlemen wish to help backward nations as they constantly and clamorously declare, they are welcome to do this. . . . The underdeveloped nations, however, must bear in mind that the capitalists never give anything gratuitously because this contradicts the very essence of capitalism."

Thus, the ground was fully prepared, both politically and propagandistically, when Russia began her own foreign-aid programs to countries outside the Communist bloc. The beginnings were characterized by caution; they carefully probed the ground. Aid started in 1954 with an allocation of $11 million and progressed through the years, until, in 1961 it reached well over $1 billion. The aid commitments made by the Soviet Union and her Communist allies to countries outside the Communist bloc (excluding Cuba) totaled $7.1 billion of which Russia contributed 70 per cent, the eastern European Communist countries 22 per cent, and Communist China the rest.

Even in the choice of the recipient countries Russia followed, to a great extent, America's lead. Thirty countries, on all continents, were included in the Russian aid programs. And these thirty countries (Argentina, Bolivia, and Brazil in Latin America; Cyprus, Iran, Iraq, Syria, Turkey, Egypt, and Yemen in the Middle East; Algeria, Ethiopia, Ghana, Guinea, Kenya, Mali, Morocco, Somalia, Sudan, and Tunisia in Africa; Afghanistan, Burma, Cambodia, Ceylon, India, Indonesia, Nepal, and Pakistan in Asia; Iceland and Yugoslavia in Europe) do not include those of the Communist bloc (including Cuba), as every enumeration of beneficiaries of American foreign aid includes the countries of NATO and other political and military alliances in which the United States was a founding partner. According to Allen Dulles, the former head of the Central Intelligence Agency, Russian aid to China alone amounted to $1.6 billion worth of military credits and hardware, and $500 million in outright grants. Other Communist bloc countries received $3,700,-000,000 in aid. For instance, Russian aid to North Korea is $73 per capita, an amount which exceeds American economic assistance to South Korea.

Although this Soviet foreign aid program originated from the desire to compete with the United States, Russia, nevertheless, maintained different methods of offering and paying the amounts committed. There is good reason to believe that no more than 30 per cent of the Soviet economic aid commitments have actually been disbursed thus far. This situation results, to a great extent, from the special method Russia and the eastern European countries use in their aid agreements. First they agree to furnish aid, then they set the figures. Only later do they work out specific projects for which the aid is to be used, and last of all are methods of payment settled. It is clear that with such a method, there must be a difference between commitments and actual outlay of funds or their equivalent. Russian assistance has as well another characteristic:

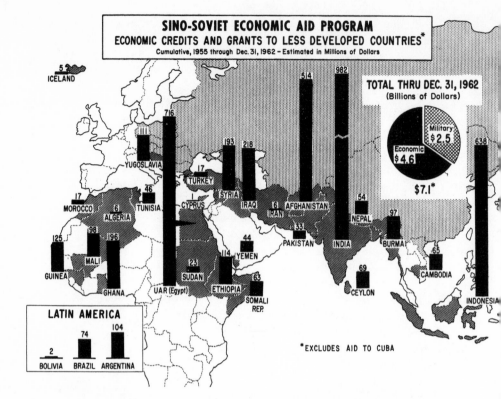

SINO-SOVIET ECONOMIC AID PROGRAM
ECONOMIC CREDITS AND GRANTS TO LESS DEVELOPED COUNTRIES*
Cumulative, 1955 through Dec. 31, 1962 – Estimated in Millions of Dollars

TOTAL THRU DEC. 31, 1962
(Billions of Dollars)

Military $2.5
Economic $4.6
$7.1*

*EXCLUDES AID TO CUBA

LATIN AMERICA

it is given in the form of large lines of credit. Outright grants constitute only a small fraction of Russian foreign aid. Interest rates, which Russian and Communist propaganda publicizes as being the lowest possible, reach 2.5 per cent, although there have been some interest-free loans, as well as some with interest rates as high as 5 per cent.

Russian aid shows a general tendency to concentrate its major effort in the few areas which are considered crucial in the contest with the West. These countries are Afghanistan, Yugoslavia, Indonesia, Egypt, India, and, until recent months, Iraq, although the emphasis continues to change along with new changes in the international scene. In some countries, Russian aid has exceeded that given by the United States. The United Arab Republic, Indonesia, and Afghanistan, besides India, have been the largest recipients of Russian aid.

This Soviet economic aid should be clearly distinguished from aid given for military purposes. Such aid, which is being given in billions of dollars to a number of countries—primarily to Indonesia, Egypt, Syria, recently to India, and in growing quantities to Yemen—represents a completely different and separate aspect of Russian support for non-aligned nations, and it is not included in the figures just mentioned.

The fact that some of this Russian war material has not been of the latest vintage has given rise to the assumption that these arms deliveries are of no consequence, as far as the Russian treasury is concerned, because these arms are obsolete and therefore play no part in the Russian defense program. Recent appraisals of Russian arms deliveries have proved that this supposition is not completely correct. Among the arms delivered to Egypt and to Indonesia have been the most modern types of tanks, planes ("MIG-21"), submarines, and even the most sophisticated and recent types of rockets.

Arms shipments, of course, furnish the easiest means of public demonstration of Russian aid and power. But it would be erroneous to assume that only "showcase" investments are of basic or primary concern for Russia. Though there have been some examples of Russian aid for the building of stadiums, luxury hotels, and highways, in general it is given to develop the basic conditions for the economic progress of the recipient nations. According to a State Department appraisal, Soviet bloc economic assistance is divided as follows, according to its uses: 57 per cent, manufacturing; 12 per cent, multi-purpose projects and agriculture (including reclamation, irrigation, and hydroelectric power projects); 12 per cent, transport and communications; 11 per cent, mineral surveys and exploitation; 3 per cent, health, education, and municipal services; 3 per cent, commodity credits; and 2 per cent, gold, foreign exchange, and funded trade deficits.

Among the projects built with Russian aid are many at which the Russians point with pride, such as the Bhilai steel mill in India, which produces one million tons of steel a year, cement plants, textile mills, sugar refineries, assembly plants, machine-tool factories, fruit canneries; such projects as the Aswan Dam in Egypt, and mineral exploration and exploitation in Afghanistan, India, and Pakistan.

In this general survey of Russian foreign aid, the problem of technical personnel deserves special mention. The number of Russian technical advisers by far exceeds that of the United States. It is estimated that about 10,000 Russian technicians are working all over the world. Two thousand of them are in Afghanistan, seven hundred in Egypt, over five hundred in India, and large numbers in Guinea, Yemen, Syria, Iraq, Indonesia, and Somalia.

This "export" of Russian personnel to non-Communist countries is supplemented by a most generous policy of scholarships for students from the developing countries. A special university has even been established for these students, the Friendship University in Moscow, dedicated to the late Congolese leader, Patrice Lumumba, and the Russian authorities are doing their best to afford the foreign students conditions superior to those in which Russian students themselves are living.

This program of aid has obvious political objectives. In setting these objectives Russia has been rather modest. In many areas where for centuries there had been no trace of Russian influence, Russia was ready to extend aid if only to establish its presence. In doing this, the Russians

New flour mill in Sukhe, Outer Mongolia, built with Russian assistance.

Soviet construction engineer Sokolov and his Ethiopian trainee Yezu.

try to manifest the selflessness of their aid. As opposed to the United States, the Russians do not ask too many questions, do not demand prior planning, and do not examine the feasibility of a nation's development project. Their first concern is to respond to the desires, if not the needs, of the recipient nation. And, of course, having extended aid, they have a channel for contact with the country in question. Agreements for trade, cultural exchange, education, and training usually follow an aid agreement. Once this is done, a base of contacts is established with leading labor union leaders, key officials, student groups, and trade circles.

An attempt to re-orient the development of the recipient country to a "socialistic" pattern is a natural followup of these efforts. In this attempt, the Russians use the much advertised argument of "the short-cut to success." They point at the development of the Soviet economy since the revolution as a proof that this is feasible. Lack of knowledge of the real conditions which prevailed in Russia before the revolution is an important factor in this argument. The Soviet officials do their best to present pre-revolutionary Russia as an undeveloped country, whose economy was as backward as those, for instance, of India, Burma, or Ghana before they started on their way to economic progress.

Few of those with whom the Russians discuss these matters know that Russia was an important supplier of agricultural goods to western Europe before World War I, that Russian industry had the capacity to arm armies numbering in the millions, that Russian literature was among the greatest literatures of the world, and that Russian scientists had achieved prominence in certain fields for many decades.

These arguments for the "short-cut" or "great leap forward," as the Chinese Communists have called their accelerated "socialist" development, are augmented by another factor of paramount importance: Soviet Russia and other Communist bloc countries are able to absorb many commodities which the United States cannot because she herself pro-

154

duces an abundance of these goods. A striking example of this is the Egyptian cotton delivered to Russia in exchange for various forms of aid.

Aid to Communist countries is of course in a completely different category. But this aid as well has been and is being used as a political instrument for the preservation of Russian leadership in the Communist camp. The discontinuance of Russian aid to China is a most vivid example of this. The mutual recriminations in the most recent chapter of the Russian-Chinese rift were very much related to the extent of Russian aid to China. In dealing with this matter, the Central Committee of the Russian Communist Party in its open letter of July, 1963, stated:

> World history has known no example of one country's rendering such extensive aid to other countries in developing their economy, science and technology. . . .
> With the active assistance of the Soviet Union, People's China has built 198 industrial enterprises, shops, and other projects equipped with up-to-date machinery. With the assistance of our country such new branches of industry as the automobile, the tractor, aircraft manufacturing, and others were created in China. The Soviet Union handed over to the People's Republic of China more than 21,000 sets of scientific-technical documentation, including more than 1,400 blueprints of big enterprises. We have invariably assisted China in consolidating the defense of the country and the creation of a modern defense industry. Thousands of Chinese specialists and workers were trained in Soviet establishments of higher education and our enterprises.

This quotation is only one section of a full chapter this letter devotes to the problem of aid to a Communist country, indicating not only its extent, but also the important role it plays in the relations between the members of the Communist bloc.

An interesting aspect of Russian aid to non-bloc countries is that the volume of this aid increased steadily until 1962 when it took a sharp drop. The first time aid was given to a non-Communist country was to Afghanistan in 1954; the amount allocated was $11 million. As the number of countries to which aid was granted grew larger, the sums granted also increased. In 1955 the allocation was $152 million; in 1956, $592 million; in 1959, $890 million; in 1960, $1.176 billion; and in 1961, $1,013,000,000. However, in 1962 there was a sudden reverse in policy and Russian aid was cut to only $519 million.

The reasons which prompted this drastic cut have never been officially revealed. Speculation by experts on Russian affairs ascribes the change to internal as well as external circumstances. In the first category would be the state of the Russian economy and the growing commitments to Cuba. Russia's appraisals of the economic achievements she had made in the last two years had to be drastically revised. The Russian official press admitted that lack of capital had caused the curtailment of many new investment projects. And, in recent months, the shortcomings of Russian agricultural progress have been a constant theme in Premier Khrushchev's speeches. It is obvious that with her national economy in

Dr. Mohammed Anas, Afghanistán Deputy Minister of Education, talking to the Czechoslovak Ambassador, Dr. Jan Czech, at reception given on occasion of the anniversary of signing of a cultural agreement between the two countries.

such a state Russia could not continue to give billions of dollars to countries which were not linked with the Communist bloc.

Among the external causes for this reconsideration in extending of foreign aid programs was the unsatisfactory experiences the Russians had had with them. The dividends Russia had expected were slow in coming. The recipient countries maintained their cautious neutrality between East and West, and in some of them the foreign aid outlays appeared to be a direct hit on a rathole. The political upheaval in Iraq, an aid-receiving country where Communists became a target of persecution, was, to Russia, a shocking experience. It is hard to avoid facing political conclusions from a situation whereby this country, which had long been on the edge of the Russian camp, turned violently anti-Communist overnight.

And Iraq was not the only example of such an unexpected negative turn of events. The expected political reward in Africa was also slow in coming. Developments in Guinea, which was expected to be the first Communist bloc country in Africa, have shown that such expectations, though not unfounded, were to be completely defeated. Russian diplomats were caught red-handed in attempts at subversion. It was this which precipitated the deterioration of relations, deterioration which affected not only Guinea but other African countries as well. This was only one of the many setbacks suffered by Russia in her pursuit of foreign aid objectives.

Officials in recipient countries quite often became disenchanted with the quality of Russian aid. Instead of promoting propaganda aims by proving Russian efficiency and development, Russian aid goods often had a completely opposite effect. Stories were commonly told about the deficiencies in Russian materials: of 4,000 jeeps sent to Indonesia with defective windshields and steering gears; of Soviet aircraft more expensive to operate and maintain than comparable Western planes; of such planes having faulty cabin pressurization, take-off speeds which were too slow, and landing speeds which were too fast; of antiquated and heavy drilling rigs; of diesel locomotives which proved inoperable because of faulty assembly, inadequate inspection, and damage in transit; of cement factories which turned out cement which could not be used; of highways which dissolved during a rainstorm.

Nor did the "new Russian man" prove his advantage over the American technician as an expert, comrade, or human being. The much criticized behavior of American technicians in foreign countries—tendencies to live luxuriously, show off, and ignore local customs—was also manifested by the Russian technicians. What is more, the Russians did not have that special American ability to mix with people easily, and they preferred living in self-contained communities, keeping their own schools, and shying away from social invitations. Their much-touted knowledge of local customs and languages has proved to be more myth than reality.

Of course, mere cognizance of these facts cannot alone provide the basis for complete understanding of the recent trends in Russian foreign aid policies. In spite of the obvious decrease in Russian aid, in July, 1963, the Council of Mutual Economic Assistance (Comecon), an organization for economic cooperation among Russia, Bulgaria, Czechoslovakia, Hungary, Rumania, Poland, East Germany, and Outer Mongolia (Albania was excluded after she sided with Communist China in the recent ideological dispute) decided to "continue and expand" economic aid to countries in Asia, Africa, and Latin America in response to the desire of these nations "to develop their national economies and to strengthen their national independence."

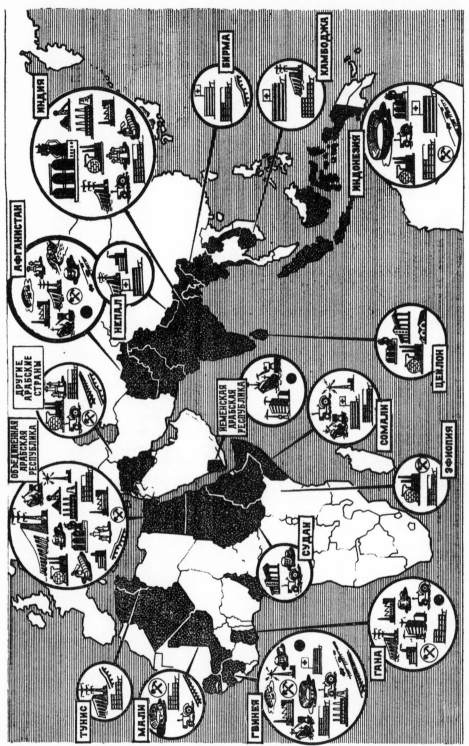

Экономическое сотрудничество СССР со странами Азии и Африки.

Map in Russia's Communist Party organ *Pravda* showing the extent of Russian aid. The caption reads "Economic Cooperation of U.S.S.R. with Countries of Asia and Africa." This map was part of a two-page report (out of eight

It is hard to imagine that this was only a formal declaration for the benefit of propaganda. As Russian publications of 1963 prove, the concern with foreign aid problems is growing. The official newspaper *Pravda* carried on August 7, 1963, two full pages (out of the six pages that made up the entire issue) of information about Russian aid to non-bloc countries. The headline over the whole page said: "The Soviet Union—friend and brother of nations." This presentation was accompanied by extremely critical remarks about the motives and impact of the American foreign aid. This too could hardly indicate a desire to discontinue Russian foreign aid.

Other Soviet publications, in Russian and other languages (including English), continue to carry extensive reports on Russian foreign aid. A letter from Colombo, Ceylon, in the Russian *New Times* of July 31, 1963, under the title "Friendly Assistance," reports:

Soviet machines and Soviet technicians are one of the main talking points here in the Ceylonese capital. People come to the port to watch the unloading of Soviet tankers and ships with building materials and equipment for Ceylon's first steel mill. In various parts of the country children are being inoculated with Soviet polio vaccine under the supervision of Dr. Drozdov from Moscow. The papers report plans for the construction, with Soviet assistance, of a tire factory and flour mill, and the organization of several big rice estates. Some of these projects are already under construction. . . .

A new feature on Ceylonese roads are filling stations bearing the emblem of the Ceylon Petroleum Corporation—a man carrying a torch. The corporation was inaugurated on April 28, 1962, when the Prime Minister, Mrs. Sirimavo Bandaranaike, handed its directors the keys to fifty oil trucks, formerly belonging to the American Esso and Caltex companies and the British Shell concern. . . . The three concerns rejected the Ceylonese offer of compensation. They tried to turn nationalization into a world issue. They even threatened to cut off all supplies of oil. Such blackmail tactics might have worked before, but not now. Ceylon is buying oil products from the U.S.S.R., Rumania, and the United Arab Republic at fair prices. The national Petroleum Corporation gets 80 per cent of its supply from the U.S.S.R. But the West is keeping up its economic and political pressure. The U.S. government's reply to oil nationalization was to cut off all economic assistance. That move by Washington is tantamount to an admission that American aid is a coercive weapon, a means of exerting political pressure. The disinterested assistance rendered by the Soviet Union stands out in sharp contrast against that background. . . .

The other paragraphs of the long letter continue the description of the multifaceted Russian aid which has reached into every corner of Ceylon. And at no place does the writer let the reader forget that this aid is part of the great struggle against "American imperialism and neo-colonialism."

From the point of view of practical politics, the impact (though at the moment hypothetical), of a basic change in Russian foreign aid policy, cannot be discounted. On the international scene it could be the kiss of death to many a political game which turned, as one political observer has said, a "local Communist minority into a kind of a natural resource,

Cartoon published in Russian publications for Africa and Asia showing the African rhino throwing off European colonizer.

like oil or uranium exchangeable for dollars of the U.S. Treasury." And nationally, because of the continuous American dialogue on the pros and cons of foreign aid, a Russian decision to start the phasing out of its aid programs is bound to strengthen the hands of those who want to see the demise of American foreign aid and the tradition out of which it comes. Such people see foreign aid, not as an investment which benefits America as well as the recipient nations, but purely as an instrument of the cold war. To them aid would become superfluous, once Russian competition in this field had ceased.

Such a Russian decision could also invalidate a favorite slogan of these opponents of foreign aid, a slogan based on the suggestion that in order to neutralize the impact of Russian competition in the field of foreign aid, a new basis for this competition should be promulgated: "Let's match the equivalent of a Swiss franc in American goods or money for the equivalent of each Swiss franc in Russian goods or money given in the form of foreign aid." There would be no need for an equivalent in Swiss francs of Russian foreign aid outlays as there would be no Russian aid.

But these are hypotheses and not realities. American aid started long before the birth of the Communist state, and it will not be Communism which will decide its fate. The problem of Russian aid programs influencing American programs in this field should rather be viewed in the light of a statement made by a man whose business is to represent and present daily the United States not to one country, but to all countries, including the many nations which are the main beneficiaries of American foreign aid—the United States Ambassador to the United Nations, Adlai Stevenson. Some five years before assuming that post, at a Washington conference on the problems of foreign aid, Stevenson made some remarks which are as pertinent today as they were in February, 1958:

This isn't just a contest with communism. Our interest in the independence of these vast areas would be just as vital if Russia and China were still governed by imperial Czars and Emperors. . . . Even if communism were to call off its campaign of economic and political penetration, the need for our effort to help these emerging nations make the transition to modern, viable economies would remain. For so long as a billion people in this shrinking world see no hope of fulfilling their impatient demands for a better life, the threat of disorder, desperate measures, and dictatorships remains, and there can be no real hope for the secure peace the world is yearning for.

8

$$

Alliance for Progress—*Alianza para el Progreso*

Jivaro is the only language members of the Indian Jivaro tribe speak. Hidden in the jungles of Ecuador's Oriente Province, they jealously guard the traditions of their past. Oil prospectors who dare to penetrate the dense vegetation to put up oil rigs have to be accompanied by armed guards. The Jivaro have no special love for the white intruders. They are part of the Indian population which amounts to more than half of the five million inhabitants of Ecuador, and they live as if nothing had happened between 1526, when Bartholemé Ruiz, the Spanish conquistador, set foot in this country, and 1963, with its complex technological civilization.

The Jivaro men live a rather leisurely life. While the women do the work, the men rest under the trees, or busy themselves making war on other tribes, or hunt. In their hunting expeditions they sometimes stalk a special kind of game: men whom they have some reason to hate. For those individuals they do not always use a poisoned arrow. They have a kind of lasso which helps them not only to catch the wanted man, but, by a quick and sharp pull, to sever his head. This is not all. The head then must be turned into a war trophy, one which has to be preserved. The Jivaros have their own way of doing it. The head is kept for some weeks in a special container with some liquid which causes the complete softening of the bones, while the skin is not harmed. After this process of bone-softening is over, the head is buried under hot sand and left again for some weeks of "processing." When the prescribed period is over, the final product is ready: a shrunken head the size of an apple, to be worn proudly within a string of beads. To possess such a head is a distinction which only few can achieve.

The Jivaros are not the only primitive Indians in South America. The Quechuas of Bolivia speak only their own language—Quechua. Their men wear their hair in pony tails, and only their headgear shows some traces of the Spanish conquest: it is modeled after Spanish helmets.

In their highland homes, they grow some sixty varieties of potatoes. They need neither storage facilities nor refrigeration equipment to preserve their potatoes. After harvesting the potatoes in March, the *chuno* processing starts. The potatoes are spread on the ground and left to

A Chacobo household, Indians living on Brazilian and Bolivian border, who don't speak Spanish and don't even know the name of the country they live in.

freeze in the cold winter nights of the mountains. The hot sunshine of the day, in this equatorial country, thaws the frozen potatoes, and then follows the next step: the potatoes are trampled under dancing bare feet, to squeeze the water out. The potatoes thus dehydrated are left to dry in the sun, to be stored away for months and even years.

Jivaros, Quechuas, Calchas, Ayamaras—scores of tribes spread all over Latin America. Some are as primitive as the Jivaros, who hardly know the name of the country they live in, and some are in much more advanced stages of civilization. But all are responding to the call of rising expectations. A few visits to a town shake off centuries of tradition; an agitator who speaks about changes finds attentive ears. Their primitivism is a challenge; it is the hardest task a civilizing effort has ever faced.

And they are not alone in longing for a change. The peasants, the workers in the cities, and the students in the schools are growing impatient with their poverty and disease. As the former President of Costa Rica, Jose Figueres, said: "Once dormant peoples are struggling upward toward the sun, toward a better life."

There is much that has to be bettered. The laborer whose income is no more than $200 a year, for whom scavenging in the garbage dumps

163

is part of what he gets to keep his family half-dressed and half-nourished; the peasant who has to farm handkerchief-sized plots while more than half of his country's land belongs to 1.5% of the population who are absentee landlords; the millions who must live in shacks made of cardboard or tin cans in the city slums—all of these have long ago stopped thinking that theirs is a God-given lot with which they must be content. They are longing for a change—and a quick one. What kind of change this will be depends on the action taken by those who lead their countries. As Milton Eisenhower, in his book on Latin America, *The Wine Is Bitter,* grimly warns, "Revolution in Latin America is inevitable. Only the form it takes is uncertain."

The Alliance for Progress has to supply the answer to the question of what kind of a revolution is going to take place. It is neither the first nor the only attempt at inter-American cooperation for lifting Latin America into the twentieth century, in terms of standards of living and education. However, the Alliance is certainly the first massive attempt at achieving these goals, the first far-sighted and adequately conceived program for the advancement of Latin America. It comes after several smaller-scale United

Indian girl selling bread.

164

American expert in soil conservation proudly inspects success in corn growing after modern methods of cultivation have been applied.

States efforts to assist her neighbors in the Western Hemisphere. We can see the Alliance in its proper perspective if we first review the aid efforts that have preceded it.

The Congressional authorization of September 26, 1940, which empowered the Export-Import Bank to loan up to $500 million to the Latin-American republics, would have been an impressive beginning had the money been given for economic development and had it marked the beginning of a program of continuous assistance. In fact, only about one-fifth of this amount was allocated for economic purposes, with the rest going for purchases of military equipment. Though the war served as an explanation and justification for this concentration on military aid, the fact remained that there was not much money for economic development. And, in view of the billions which started to flow only a few months later in the direction of Europe and Asia, this was a rather meager manifestation of United States concern with the well-being of its sister republics south of the Rio Grande. What was even worse, it was to be more than two decades before the United States awakened to its obligations and challenges in Latin America.

Of course, it would be an exaggeration to say that Latin America became a forgotten continent for United States planners for a better world. Undersecretary of State Sumner Welles, in speaking about development loans for foreign countries, made clear that "they were premised on the conviction that social progress and political stability in the hemisphere were contingent upon higher living standards and that the growth of true democracy was also contingent upon better nutrition, sanitation, and communications. It was believed that the measures of financial and economic cooperation that were undertaken would not only increase the probability of political and military security, but also provide a greater demand and increased purchasing power of U.S. exports." And the Institute of Inter-American Affairs, under Nelson Rockefeller, established in the forties the "Servicios," in the framework of which United States technicians worked with those of the host country, mainly on educational, agricultural, and public health projects. Technical aid to Latin-American countries preceded the formal establishment of the Point Four Technical Assistance programs. This aid was, in the forties, the most successful instrument of U.S. governmental cooperation with Latin America. The assistance program of the Department of Agriculture has cost this country less than $4 million in ten years. Yet by 1949 it had resulted in research and demonstrational projects in fifteen Latin-American countries. Latin-American governments were so satisfied with the results in the form of increased production of better crops that they increased their financial support for the program from $500,000 to an estimated $1,178,000, an average of about three dollars for every dollar put up by the United States. The entire operating costs of the Institute of Inter-American Affairs, a U.S. Government-owned corporation since 1947, were

Indian women striving for progress. Drive against illiteracy is one of the objects of the Alliance for Progress.

kept at a $5 million-a-year level and employed about 300, two-thirds of whom spent their time in Latin America helping some 10,000 Latin American technicians on several hundred projects.

When in February, 1949, President Truman asked Congress for the extension of the life of the Institute of Inter-American Affairs, with a budget of $10 million, he stated: "By continuing international cooperation for raising the standard of living for all peoples in the Americas, the U.S. can give further practical form to the high purposes of our policy." Though this was a far cry from being a serious implementation of a U.S. promise (given at the Inter-American Conference of 1945 in Mexico City) to help Latin America shift its economy from a wartime to a peacetime basis and to aid industrialization and improvement of agricultural methods, the Institute did, nevertheless, constitute proof of a growing concern with Latin American affairs. Compared with the days of direct intervention and so-called "Marine Corps diplomacy," and even with the "good neighbor" policy proclaimed in 1933 by President Roosevelt, these decisions and modest steps towards economic assistance indicate a new trend in United States policy.

The Charter of the Organization of American States, signed by representatives of twenty-one American nations on April 30, 1948, became the constitution of the OAS. It included in its provisions the establishment of the Inter-American Economic and Social Council, whose chief purpose would be "the promotion of economic and social welfare of the American nations." Within this framework, specialized organizations of teachers, doctors, engineers, and agronomists from all American countries are pooling their knowledge and experience. In addition, the Inter-American Institute of Agricultural Sciences at Turralba, Costa Rica, aids the member countries with research and teaching in all branches of agriculture, and the Council's analyses of inter-American economic problems provide the basic data necessary for any constructive plan for the development of the Latin-American economies.

But the greatest surge of inter-American economic cooperation was still to come. The initiative came in 1958 from the President of Brazil, Juscelino Kubitschek, who called on President Eisenhower to give practical meaning to the announced desire to strengthen the economic cooperation between the American republics. Kubitschek had a name for his program: "Operation Pan-America." This was not a mere slogan; it was a detailed, constructive plan. It envisaged seven areas of study. These areas were the control of inflationary pressure so as to strengthen the economy; increased private investment; establishment of a regional development bank; price stabilization of Latin America's basic export commodities, such as coffee, zinc, lead, tin, and copper; the eventual establishment of a Latin American common market; increased technical assistance; and appraisal of the impact of the European Common Market on the economy of Latin America.

The United States responded quickly. On April 8, 1959, representatives of the American republics signed in Washington the charter of a $1 billion Inter-American Bank to promote economic development in Latin America. Two agencies were established by the charter—the Inter-American Development Bank, with an authorized capital stock of $850 million; and the Special Operations Fund, with a total capitalization of $150 million.

The impetus, once given, was not abandoned. In September, 1960, the United States joined with eighteen other American republics in adopting the Act of Bogota, which stated that the signatories considered it advisable to "launch a program for social development, in which emphasis should be given to those measures that meet social needs and also promote increases in productivity and strengthen economic development."

The pace of development in recent years made it clear that the new development bank and increased technical assistance programs were not enough. It became evident that the "revolution of rising expectations" demanded revolutionary measures. Though the United States could point to assistance to Latin America amounting to more than $5.4 billion in the period from 1946 through 1961, including loans (with $275 million of this amount for technical assistance), and to private investments in these countries totaling more than $9 billion, the conviction grew that something dramatic was necessary to keep Latin America from stagnating. The first mention of this new approach in efforts to bring about Latin American progress, for an alliance of American republics, was made in President Kennedy's Inaugural Address of January, 1961. Two months later, on March 13, 1961, it resulted in the form of a definite proposal. At a White House reception for Latin-American diplomats,

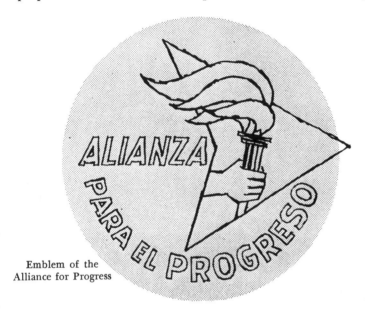

Emblem of the
Alliance for Progress

members of Congress and members of the Organization of American States, President Kennedy presented a ten-point program. Its revolutionary meaning and aim were strongly emphasized. "The revolution which began in Philadelphia in 1776 and in Caracas in 1811 is not yet finished," said the President. President Kennedy immediately made clear what kind of revolution he had in mind:

Throughout Latin America—a continent rich in resources and in spiritual and cultural achievements of its people—millions of men and women suffer the daily degradations of hunger and poverty. They lack decent shelter or protection from disease. Their children are deprived of the education or the jobs which are the gateway to a better life. And each day the problems grow more urgent. Population growth is outpacing economic growth, for living standards are even further endangered, and discontent—the discontent of a people who know that abundance and the tools of progress are at last within their reach—that discontent is growing. . . . If we are to meet a problem so staggering in its dimensions, our approach must itself be equally bold, an approach consistent with the majestic concept of Operation Pan-America.

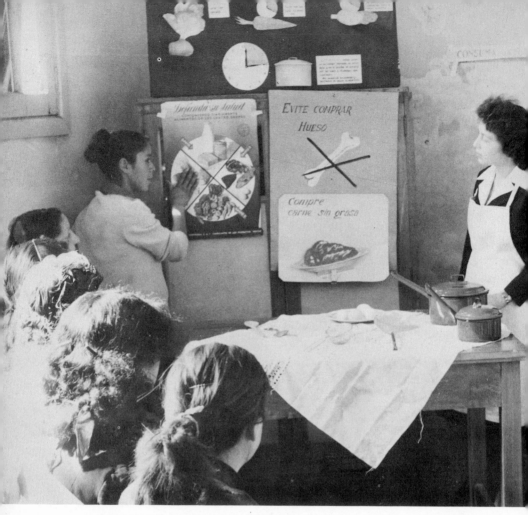

Home nutrition, sewing, and hygiene courses are some of the many activities carried out by the economists of the Agricultural Extension Division of USOM, Chile.

Therefore, I have called on all the people of the hemisphere to join in a new Alliance for Progress, *Alianza para el Progreso*—a vast cooperative effort, unparalleled in magnitude and nobility of purpose, to satisfy the basic needs of the American people for homes, work and land, health and schools—*techo, trabajo y tierra, salud y escuela*.

A plan of action followed these ringing words. It was a plan of ten years of continuous effort. In this effort, said President Kennedy, the Latin-American nations must play the decisive part. "They and they alone can mobilize their resources, enlist the energies of their people, and modify the social patterns, so that all, and not just a privileged few, share in the fruits of growth." Only after the Latin-American countries are ready to do their part, the President said, will the United States be ready to "provide resources of a scope and magnitude sufficient to make this bold development plan a success, just as we helped to provide against nearly equal odds, the resources adequate to help rebuild the economies of western Europe. For only an effort of towering dimensions can insure fulfillment of our plan for a decade of progress."

After making this basic point, President Kennedy spoke about long-range development plans, lowering of social barriers, creation of larger markets, examination of prices of commodities, stepping up the Food-for-Peace Emergency Program, exchange of scientists, training of experts, defense of those whose independence is endangered, and cultural exchanges.

People who participated in this White House gathering say that the impression the statement made was overwhelming. All present felt that such a program was long overdue. It was inspiring. It even inspired somebody to write a poem on the Alliance, which has been set to music: *Alianza para el Progreso/ Cada Hombre y nino/ Una gran hermandad merchando/ Esperanza en cada corazon.* ("Alliance for Progress/ For every man and child/ A great brotherhood marching/ With hope in every heart.")

But hope per se could not suffice—to keep hope alive, action had to follow. And it did. On May 8, 1961, the United States proposed that the Council of the OAS hold an economic meeting on the ministerial level to approve a general blueprint for cooperative action. On August 5, 1961, the Inter-American Economic and Social Council was convened in the Uruguayan resort town of Punta del Este. This was the first Alliance for Progress conference. The United States delegation of forty members was

Exhibits of posters are an important part of education of Latin American masses.

led by Secretary of the Treasury Douglas Dillon to emphasize the importance the U.S. ascribed to the conference.

The United States came with a plan of action. Secretary Dillon informed the delegations that the "U.S. development loans would be on a long-range basis, for periods up to fifty years, with the bulk of the loans at very low or zero rates of interest." As for the size of this assistance, Secretary Dillon made it clear that if the Latin-American countries would take the necessary steps toward economic development, an inflow of foreign capital of at least $20 billion could be expected.

The United States made its position clear: the foreign assistance of $20 billion within a decade, to come "from international institutions, from Europe and Japan as well as from North America, from private investment, as well as from public funds," would be forthcoming only when and if Latin America could show that it was moving towards the eradication of age-old ills. These necessary changes were clearly defined: tax reforms, to make the rich carry an appropriate part of their nation's development; land reforms, to give land to the peasant who works the soil; changes in labor policies, to assure fair wages and satisfactory working conditions for all workers; eradication of illiteracy; and monetary stability. After eleven days of deliberations, conducted in an atmosphere of cooperation, disrupted only occasionally by the obstructionist tactics of Ernesto Guevara, Cuba's minister of the economy—whose participation in the conference was the last Cuban appearance at an Inter-American gathering—the Punta del Este conference gave the Alliance for Progress idea an organizational form, and turned it into a program of action. A "Declaration to the Peoples of America" preceded the "Charter of Punta del Este—establishing an Alliance for Progress within the framework of Operation Pan-America," and Titles I, II, III, and IV dealt respectively with "Objectives of the Alliance for Progress," "Economic and Social Development," "Economic Integration of Latin America," and "Basic Export Commodities."

The goals of the Alliance were defined: improvement and strengthening of democratic institutions, acceleration of social and economic development, rural and urban housing programs, agrarian reform, eradication of illiteracy, improvement of health and sanitation conditions, fair wages, tax law reforms, monetary policies which would protect the purchasing power of the masses, stimulation of private enterprise, stabilization of prices for the commodities which are the basic Latin exports, and acceleration of economic integration of Latin America.

Faced with problems and tasks of this magnitude, the authors of the Charter of Punta del Este quite properly did not concern themselves with detail. Instead, they enunciated their vision of a new Latin America which the detailed plan was to bring about. The lofty aims of the Alliance for Progress were set forth in the Preamble to the Charter, which proclaims:

We, the American Republics, hereby proclaim our decision to unite in a common effort to bring our people accelerated economic progress and broader social justice within the framework of personal dignity and political liberty.

Almost two hundred years ago we began in this hemisphere the long struggle for freedom which now inspires people in all parts of the world. Today in ancient lands, men moved to hope by the revolutions of our young nations, search for liberty. Now we must give a new meaning to that revolutionary heritage. For America stands at a turning point in history. The men and women of our hemisphere are reaching for a better life which today's skills have placed within their grasp. They are determined for themselves and their children to have decent and ever-abundant lives, to gain access to knowledge and equal opportunity for all, to end those conditions which benefit the few at the expense of the needs and dignity of the many. It is our inescapable task to fulfill these just desires—to demonstrate to the poor and forsaken of our countries, and of all lands, that the creative powers of free men hold the key to their progress and to the progress of future generations. And our certainty of ultimate success rests not alone on our faith in ourselves and our nations, but on the indomitable spirit of free men which has been the heritage of the American civilization.

Inspired by these principles, and by the principles of Operation Pan-America and the Act of Bogota, the American Republics hereby resolve to adopt the following program of action to establish and carry forward an Alliance for Progress.

The real meaning of such a program was clear: it is to be a program for social revolution, implemented by democratic means. It is to be a social revolution with exact goals set in advance. Moreover, it is supposed

Distribution of free textbooks is part of Alliance program.

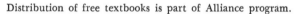

Work on health and sanitation sewer installation in Quito, Ecuador. Women work along with the men at slightly lower wages.

to be a social revolution with a timetable. Every single problem facing Latin America was to be solved within a decade. The language of the Punta del Este resolutions and decisions is precise and definite. A ten-year period was set to reduce "the present mortality rate of children under five years of age by one-half"; to "supply potable water and sewage disposal for at least 70 per cent of the urban population and 50 per cent of the rural population"; to provide "at least six years of elementary education, free and compulsory for the entire school population"; and to ensure that "the rate of economic growth in any Latin American country should be not less than 2.5 per cent per capita per year." In each and every field absolute goals were established. Compared with the methods of violent social revolutions, this must be considered an extraordinary and challenging approach.

174

Communism has never given dates for the achievement of specific goals in the betterment of the human life. In fact, there has been a definite reluctance and even outspoken opposition to the setting of such goals. The question of whether it should be done, whether this should be part of Communist thinking and planning, served for a time as a major subject of theoretical discussion in the camp of revolutionary socialism, with the majority opinion and official policy absolutely opposed to binding the revolution to an exact timetable of progress toward its goals. The five- and seven-year plans for economic development, which began at a later stage of the Russian revolution, should not be mistaken for schedules for the achievement of improvements for the benefit of the mass of the people.

The Alliance for Progress made a bold departure from this approach. It did so in spite of the fact that, unlike violent social revolutions, it lacks the main instrument of revolution—coercion. Its instrument is good will; its inducement for action is the reward of human well-being; its chief motive, the idea of mutual responsibility of men.

Like any social revolution, the Alliance for Progress must chafe against the well-established rights of many people, clash with interests preserved through centuries, and press for changes which must impinge on the privileges of the mighty. In Latin America this is the case even much more in evidence than in any other area of the world. The differences between the standards of living of the privileged few and the wretched masses are more striking than nearly any place else. Similarly, the deliberate detachment of the upper classes from the problems of their countries is much greater than is usual elsewhere. Senator Mike Mansfield has called those circles "the beachhead societies." They exist in each Latin American country, and they differ only in the degree of their detachment and the numbers of people they represent. They live on the luxurious fringes of their national economies as strangers in their own lands. And they are the people who usually constitute the elite from whom the country's political leadership is drawn.

Tax reform—taxation of the income of people who have never paid income taxes, or where income taxes are on the books, never to be implemented—and land reform—in a country where 1.5 per cent of the population owns more than half of the cultivated land—constitute a social revolution of unprecedented magnitude if they are to be accomplished by peaceful means. Seldom, if ever, have people given up power and privilege voluntarily—even when it becomes daily more evident that to save the few, care must be taken for the many.

This, however, is only part of the problem. It is easy to speak of the Alliance for Progress as a sequel to the Marshall Plan, the "Marshall Plan for Latin America." But this, while easy, is also deceptive. It deceives those for whom the Marshall Plan analogy will constitute a kind of guarantee that the Alliance will be a success.

Inspector Lamino of the anti-malaria campaign supervising the spraying with DDT of family homes in the province of Esmeraldas, Ecuador.

In fact, there is nothing in the conditions in which the Alliance has to work that even remotely resembles those which prevailed in western Europe after the Second World War. Europe was devastated, its factories bombed out, its production rate pushed back by decades. But the plants were there, the physical resources—and the human as well. Factories were repaired—and they were able to resume production. Human skill was abundant and only waiting to be put back to work. There were no millions—tens of millions—who could not read and write, as there are in

AID Administrator David Bell emerges from a school and is greeted by a group of young Colombians after he accompanied John V. Docherty, CARE Director of Colombia, and Charles P. Fossum, AID Mission Director, in an inspection of a school lunch.

Latin America. There were no tribes that have not yet emerged from prehistoric times. There was no hidden serfdom and landless peasantry. There was no city population which was without homes, schools, work, income. The social fabric for economic reconstruction was definitely there. But, unfortunately, it does not exist in most of Latin America; it has to be built, so to speak, from scratch. The Alliance for Progress is not only, as the Marshall Plan was, a plan for economic development. It is—it should be—largely a plan for social development and the development of human resources, a plan in which tens of millions of people have to be catapulted, in a span of a few years, into a stage which other nations took centuries to achieve.

And to achieve such a change in a decade, as the Alliance for Progress planners have decided to do, needs not only financial means; it needs enthusiasm as well. It requires that those who are to be helped will sincerely desire to lift themselves. Such desire and enthusiasm come mainly from one thing—hope. And this hope will only spring when facts prove that there is a good chance of dreams being turned into realities. This means preference for immediate, tangible improvements in living conditions for great masses of people: improvements in housing, sanitary conditions, education, communication, nutrition. It means that economic development programs have a real chance to work only after this hope starts to rise in every corner of the lands of the Alliance.

This truth was understood by the planners of the Alliance for Progress. Those responsible for the implementation of the Alliance acknowledged frankly that "to lift the standards of living of more than 200 million people, even to the minimum goals established by the Alliance for Progress, is not the work for one year, or even a few. . . ." Nevertheless, some immediate steps for the improvement of the lot of the masses were taken before development plans were worked out and approved. The fund which has to deal with such matters of immediate action, the Social Progress Trust Fund, went immediately into action, and within the first eighteen months of the Alliance, ending December 31, 1963, commitments for Latin America from the Agency for International Development, the Social Progress Fund, the Export-Import Bank, Food for Peace, and the Peace Corps have totaled $1.5 billion. Five hundred million dollars were appropriated by Congress in 1961 for the social progress program alone.

What has all this money accomplished? In absolute figures it sounds most impressive: 160,000 new dwellings; 18,000 new classrooms; 4,000,000 textbooks printed and distributed; 160,000 agricultural loans given to farmers; 700 community water systems and wells installed, and 900 hospitals and health centers set up. In the two years of the Alliance, the United States has committed $2,180,000,000 and actually disbursed $1,508,000,000.

Of course, whether the pace is quick enough does not depend solely on the United States. The well-known motto of all foreign-aid programs—"to help people to help themselves"—must apply to the Latin-American countries as well—and perhaps even more to them.

The Communists have not failed to seize the opportunities that the launching of the Alliance has created for them. They understand well that success of the Alliance will mean a death blow to their hopes of a takeover in Latin America. Soviet publications in Russian—and especially in Spanish, Portuguese, and English—miss no occasion to point at the Alliance as a plot of "Yankee imperialism." This line is typified in the following remarks from *New Times* of July 31, 1963:

The Clay Committee and also the President have made it amply clear that American aid will be granted to those Latin American countries that remain loyal to the Punta del Este declaration and fall in with America's anti-Cuban policy. . . .

What U.S. economic aid tries to do is to maintain pro-American elements in power and preserve the agrarian and raw material structure of developing nations. That is the real purpose, and no amount of propaganda can conceal the fact that Washington aid plays the same part, and pursues the same aims, as old-fashioned colonialist methods and techniques.

For obvious reasons, no mention is made of the social changes the Alliance hopes to bring about. But what for the Communists is too little

Iron foundry in eastern range of the Andes Mountains in Colombia built with American assistance.

and too late is too much and too soon for their counterparts on the Right. Nevertheless, this is a social, peaceful revolution and one that cannot become successful only by the actions of foreigners. It is primarily a task for the people and for the government of each Latin-American nation. It is not only national pride that is involved in the exclusion of foreigners from such far-reaching goals as those of the Alliance. Should it ever happen that those nations welcome direct United States involvement in their revolution, such involvement would bring no results for the simple objective reason that what is necessary in the Alliance for Progress is not only outside help, but, much more, internal revolutionary changes in all fields of life, and this can be accomplished only by a national government.

Even in the present circumstances, when the United States representatives are doing their best to avoid direct involvement in internal affairs, the other alliance of the extreme Left and extreme Right brandishes the Alliance for Progress as a "Yankee imperialist plot to take over Latin America." Both reactionaries and Communists have rightly understood the scope and task of the Alliance: a threat to the privileges of the few and a deprivation of the raison d'être of the extreme Left.

However, the record of the Alliance's achievements, when seen against the background of the needs it must satisfy, loses much of its impressiveness. Skeptics can easily find ground for saying "I told you so," and enthusiasts can hardly find comfort in what has been accomplished. The standard of living of the South American masses has not changed—yet; the reforms have not been implemented—yet. For such a profound revolution, even the decade as set forth by the Alliance could be no more than a jumping-off point in the march toward the changes the Alliance hopes to bring about. This fact, however, is not convincing where ill will or impatience prevail. But besides critics of the Alliance, or its pace, there are men of the highest standing who find many aspects of the Alliance in need of change. In a report on the problems of the Alliance, former Brazilian President Kubitschek said: "I have observed that mistaken appraisals within certain circles of the North American Administration, with respect to other countries of the continent, continue to make them short-sighted in vision and to influence their conduct. What is required is a revolution in the field of development."

Dr. Kubitschek also had some definite grievances: he accused the Congress of cutting 40 per cent from what he considered President Kennedy's promise of $1 billion worth of aid to Latin America in 1962; he objected to the Alliance taking credit for aid given under Public Law 480, which allows the sale of surplus food for local currency, and for the operations of The Export-Import Bank. Another report on the same subject, prepared by Dr. Alberto Lleras Camargo, former President of Colombia, contained an equal measure of blame for the Latin-American countries, because "one cannot see anywhere in Latin America the spirit of enthusiasm that should precede and go along with such a formidable adventure, and that the preparatory stage is proceeding with deceptive slowness."

Both former Presidents arrived at the same conclusion: The Alliance needs a new coordinating body, a new policy and implementation instrument, which would give a completely new outlook to the working methods of the Alliance. The existing situation has developed into a system of handouts by the U.S., a kind of a frustrating monologue, which cannot mobilize the energies of Latin America to the degree needed to accelerate the pace of the Alliance. To bring about a change in these conditions, the two former Presidents proposed an Inter-American Development Committee, which would run the Alliance.

The essence of their proposal was aimed at an arrangement which would be similar to that which prevailed under the Marshall Plan. In that Plan, the Organization of European Economic Development, representing all countries participating in the European Recovery Program, played the major role in distributing United States aid, with the heads of Economic Cooperation Administration doing their best to "under-supervise" and "under-guide," in the words of former ECA Administrator Paul G. Hoffman.

The basic idea for what was tentatively named the Committee for Inter-American Development was accepted by the American government. Ironically enough, it marks a return to a proposal made by the United States at Punta del Este to empower a committee of nine distinguished economists, seven of them Latin Americans, to determine which countries had undertaken meaningful economic and social reforms within the concepts of the Alliance, and thus deserved aid. However, Argentina, Brazil, and Mexico opposed the plan on the grounds that it would subordinate to an international committee a country's sovereign power to determine its international policies. And thus, the "nine wise men" were turned into no more than an advisory body in the affairs of the Alliance.

The establishment of such a committee to administer the aid for Latin American countries is a new step forward in improving the affairs of the Alliance. The decision of the United States government to agree to such a change certainly assures an acceleration of the workings of the Alliance. Fortunately, today, after more than two years of the Alliance, many of the misgivings of President Kubitschek and President Camargo seem to be receding into the past. Since they made their critical remarks there has been a considerable change for the better in the affairs of the Alliance.

In a memorandum to his staff on the second anniversary of the Alliance, its administrator within the Agency for International Development, Teodoro Moscoso, wrote: "Today the brick and mortar of construction under the Alliance can be seen in many cities and villages along the highways of Latin America" and, what is even more important, the objectives

Slum dwellings in urban centers in Latin America.

182

and principles of the Alliance are beginning to make an impact on the thinking of the people. He continued: "We have reason to observe our anniversary this year—not with the hoopla that marks a triumph, but with the satisfaction of builders who have dug the foundation and begun to pour the footings." Compared with Moscoso's message on the first anniversary of the Alliance, when he confined himself only to "marking" the date, these words confirmed that hope for success is now coming from tangible realities. The Council of the Organization of American States, also celebrating the second anniversary of the Alliance, praised it highly. It has made "a good beginning," in the words of the chairman of the Council, Ambassador Gonzalo J. Facio of Costa Rica. From all over the hemisphere expressions of satisfaction were voiced. But there were also notes of caution and even of some pessimism. President Kennedy himself stated at a press conference on August 1, 1963: "In some ways the road seems longer than it was when the journey started."

While praising the record of the first two years of the Alliance, Ambassador Facio also stressed the great economic problems which the Alliance still faces: declines in the prices of Latin America's commodity exports and the rising costs of the prices of manufactured goods. These factors are in many instances almost completely nullifying the impact of the American aid. According to Senator Hubert Humphrey's appraisal, over the past ten years Latin-American countries have lost at least $10 billion in the sale of their commodities to the United States alone, as a result of the drop in export prices. In a calculation by the Pan-American Union, the United States import price of Latin-American coffee dropped from 51.85 cents a pound in 1957 to 35.14 cents in 1961. This represented losses of $600 million a year for the fifteen coffee-exporting countries.

But now the big question in Latin America remains: who will benefit from this stabilization of prices? The rich, the plantation owners, the mill owners, the exporters, and some politicians—or, in an equal degree, the men who work the coffee plantations, the masses of *campesinos?*

The share of the little man in the achievements of the development of his country is in fact the main problem in Latin America. The complaint that the aid money disappears somewhere on the way to the people is all too well known in many countries—and especially in Latin America. The flight of $9 billion of capital from Latin America since 1959 is a well-published fact. People whose imagination was fired by the Alliance and its slogans are asking why should it take two years to start preparing legislation for land reform, for tax reform, for giving some tangible meaning to the demands of social justice. What has been done is not enough. They would like to see the improvements and to share in them quickly.

The pace must, therefore, be hastened. We are in a race, which we must win, against the forces that see in the Alliance the greatest danger to their hopes of subverting Latin America. Awareness of these dangers is being

The 500 kilometer broad asphalt road from Cochabamba to Santa Cruz which changed the whole life in the area.

constantly urged by the United States. On his visit to Colombia, President Kennedy warned an assembly of industrialists, landowners, and political leaders:

"Unless all of us are willing to contribute resources to national development, unless all of us are prepared not merely to accept, but to initiate, basic reforms, unless all of us take the lead in improving the welfare of our people, then the leadership will be taken from us, and the heritage of centuries of Western civilization will be consumed in a few months of violence."

The pace must also be hastened for another reason. Latin America has the fastest-growing population in the world. The 200 million people now living in Latin America will grow to 600 million at the close of this century. It is estimated that no more than 20 million people lived in Latin America in 1820, and their economic importance was then even greater than that of the United States. Within a century and a half, the population grew tenfold; it is increasing at an even faster rate. And, with each new clinic built and each village sprayed with antimalarial chemicals, the death rate decreases, the birth rate increases, and more babies survive.

The national income has to increase accordingly to take these develop-

184

Diplomacy by "beisbol."

ments into account. The national income must not only be more justly
divided, but it has to grow constantly to outdistance the population
growth. The Alliance for Progress has made its plans with this situation
in mind. The 2.5 per cent annual per capita rate of economic growth provided for in the Punta del Este program is only a starting point from
which the march forward has to start. Growing industrialization and
productivity are supposed to be incorporated into the gradual integration
of the Latin-American economies. The present situation, in which 90
per cent of the foreign trade of the various Latin-American countries is
with the distant markets of the United States or Europe, and only 10 per
cent with each other, must change if economic progress south of the Rio
Grande is to become a reality. Similarly, an effort must be made to diver-
sify the economies of these countries, most of which concentrate exclusively on one export product—coffee, tin, or beef.

Europe presently is a good example of economic integration. The
American prodding, in the years of the Marshall Plan, for the economic
integration of western Europe came to fruition first in the European
Coal and Steel Community, which paved the way for the European Common Market. There are signs that the Latin-American nations are also
beginning to increase economic cooperation among themselves. Slowly
but surely the conviction is growing that bigger markets—in time, markets
with over 200 million consumers—offer the best direction for economic
development and for higher standards of living. In 1962, seven Latin-
American countries laid a foundation for a Latin-American Common
Market. Meeting in Uruguay in December, 1962, the representatives of
Argentina, Brazil, Chile, Mexico, Paraguay, Peru, and Uruguay cut their

185

tariffs by an average of 27 per cent on 2,500 trade items, ranging from lemons to razor blades. The Latin-American Free Trade Association has made a promising beginning. Of course, results in the form of improvements in the economic conditions in the countries of the Free Trade Association will not be visible overnight. It took Europe some years for the process of economic integration to make its impact on the national economies and on the well-being of individuals.

Central America is also consolidating its own Common Market. With a central planning program, the Central American countries are moving toward diversification of crops and are already enjoying economic progress unknown there for years.

As encouraging as these developments are, there is of course no guarantee that their impact will suffice to prevent revolutionary developments of the Castro type.

The objective conditions exist for economic progress in Latin America. The blueprints are now being prepared, the will for a change is universal, outside aid in amounts sufficient to make the plans work is supposed to continue to flow in a steady pace. The countries are rich—rich in natural resources, rich in fine soil for agriculture, rich in human skills which wait to be exploited. What was once said about Bolivia—"It is a beggar sitting on a sack of gold"—could well be said about the rest of the Latin-American countries. Whether their richness is based on gold or tin, or copper, coffee, or cattle makes little difference. It is up to the partners in the Alliance to use these abundant resources and to use them quickly and efficiently. Because in Latin America it is really "one minute to midnight."

9

Foreign Aid Through International Channels

Partnership with others in extending aid to developing countries is not limited to regional organizations, which arose either through American initiative or with American participation. America's leading share in the financing of international aid programs through the United Nations and its "family" of specialized agencies was only a logical consequence of the traditional American concern with the promotion of economic progress everywhere. President Roosevelt's State of the Union message of January, 1941, which requested the Lend-Lease legislation, also proclaimed long-term peace objectives, formulated in what has come to be known as the "four essential human freedoms." The "third freedom" is "freedom from want," which, translated into world terms, means economic arrangements which will "secure for every nation a healthy peacetime life for its inhabitants—everywhere in the world."

This was not meant to be a mere wartime propaganda slogan. Serious studies by government committees followed. In July, 1941, Undersecretary of State Welles included in his memorandum on the best way to prepare for the future a paragraph dealing with economic problems, which spelled out quite clearly the principle of sharing of wealth in the international community. Stated Welles: "No peace which may be made in the future would be valid or lasting, unless it established fully and adequately the natural rights of all peoples to equal economic enjoyment. So long as any one people or any one government possesses a monopoly over natural resources or new materials, which are needed by all peoples, there can be no basis for a world order based on justice and peace."

Thus the basis was laid for what was to become one of the most important documents on the organization of the postwar world—the Atlantic Charter. There appeared in a draft of this charter a most far-reaching statement of principle: an obligation on nations to share their wealth with other nations. The pertinent paragraph stated clearly: "They [the Allies] will strive to bring about a fair and equitable distribution of essential produce, not only within their territorial boundaries, but between nations of the world." Although this paragraph was somewhat rewritten in the final formulation of the Atlantic Charter, its basic ideas were preserved in the following words: ". . . they [the Allies] desire to bring

187

The assisted give assistance: Members of farming demonstration team from Taiwan pose with local farmers at a rice field in Liberia.

about the fullest collaboration between all nations in the economic field, with the object of securing for all improved labor standards, economic advancement, and social security."

Preparations for implementation of these principles followed. To understand what the authors had in mind in adopting these principles no deep study of official documents of those days is necessary. It is enough to read some of the memoranda on postwar aims to grasp fully that economic cooperation and the responsibility of developed nations for the welfare of the less fortunate were considered of prime importance for the attainment of a lasting world peace. Perhaps the most characteristic

Signing of documents of $74,628,000 loan by the International Bank for Reconstruction and Development for 12-year program of agricultural and industrial development of Southern Italy. Participants in signing ceremony, from left to right: Professor Gabriele Pescatore; Hon. Pietro Campilli; Eugene R. Black, President of the World Bank. Standing: Henry Ralph, Vice-President, Bank of America, which participated in loan.

pronouncement in this respect was made in 1942 by Milo Perkins, executive director of the U.S. Board of Economic Warfare:

We lost our battle to avoid war. It was lost primarily because the world was unable to distribute what it had learned how to produce. . . . The nightmare of underconsumption was the black plague of the prewar era. We put up with a civilization in which commodity rich and consumption poor lasted too long to avert the catastrophe. . . . The greatest production of raw materials, the greatest industrial plant and the greatest number of skilled workers in all history exist side by side with intense want in every land. The bridging of the gap will present the greatest challenge any generation of young people ever faced.

The steps taken by government agencies should be considered against this background. The Department of State initiated the preparation of plans for an international exchange and stabilization fund. The Treasury Department developed a proposal for an international bank for reconstruction financing, and a Conference on Food and Agriculture was convened in Hot Springs, Virginia, in May, 1943, to search for practical ways to carry out what had already become more than an idea—a "Program for Freedom from Want of Food."

The search for a solution to the basic economic problems among members of the international community was intensified with the preparations

A Public Health nurse demonstrating the preparation of UNICEF milk in a health center, Shiraz, Iran.

for the establishment of an international organization. In all these activities, the United States played a leading role. This role was soon to exceed that of planning and wording resolutions, or drafting charters and constitutions of international bodies. The plans for an institution to finance reconstruction and to stabilize currencies were put into final form. The United Nations Monetary and Financial Conference at Bretton Woods, New Hampshire, in July, 1944, brought into being the International Monetary Fund and the International Bank for Reconstruction and Development. The professions of good will then had to be matched with deeds. And these came without delay. Two billion seven hundred and fifty million dollars was the United States's subscription to the Fund, whose total assets were approximately $9,213,400,000. The $10 billion authorized as capital for the International Bank for Reconstruction and Development was divided into shares of $100,000 each, of which the United States took 31,750 shares, the largest subscription, by far, of any nation. One country subscribed to two shares only.

This financial backing given by the United States to these two international institutions gave to the world a most potent instrument for the development of basic economic conditions necessary for progress, as well as an instrument of monetary stability on which almost every one of the sixty-eight member nations has drawn in the course of the Fund's existence. Besides these two institutions, United States participation was the leading factor in the establishment of the International Development Association, the International Finance Corporation, and the Inter-American Development Bank—all additional institutions furthering international economic cooperation.

A check for $3,904,000 presented by U.S. Permanent Representative to the United Nations, Henry Cabot Lodge, Jr., left, to U.N. Secretary-General Dag Hammarskjoeld, center, in February, 1954, which was in turn passed to David Owen, Executive Chairman of the Technical Assistance Board (TAB), right. This was one of the installments of the U.S. share in the budget of this U.N. institution.

It might be added that the American contributions to these financial institutions, generous as they were and are, have always been administered according to the strictest banking principles, under the permanent scrutiny of the United States and through the American members of the administering bodies of these institutions. Also important is the fact that these were non-recurring contributions to the building of basic instruments of international economic stability and development. Once granted, the American share did not increase the annual appropriations for foreign aid.

These were not the only American aid programs operating through international channels. At a time when the United States was already well advanced in assisting foreign nations, with the Marshall Plan on its way, the major organ of the United Nations that had been conceived to serve the same purposes had hardly begun to act. This organization, the Economic and Social Council, was largely ineffectual in the aid field. The Council's resolution of October, 1946, asking the Secretary-General to recommend the transfer of UNRRA welfare activities to the United Nations, spoke also about "expert technical advisory services" which "presented the greatest need" in the fields of "public health, child care, child feeding, the training of social service personnel for child welfare," and

A loan from the International Bank for Reconstruction and Development helps Mexico to develop its hydroelectric power.

"expert advice which was also needed regarding the manufacture of artificial limbs, where the best methods of production should be put at the disposal of countries which had a large number of disabled persons as a result of the war."

The scope was, clearly, rather limited; the restricted character of these assistance programs was reflected in the budget adopted for this aid: $670,186. It was obvious that with such aims and such a budget the activities of the Economic and Social Council would never carry out its tasks as defined in the United Nations Charter—"to promote social progress and better standards of life in larger freedom." The direction toward which the Council needed to go was soon indicated by the United States Point Four technical assistance program. Only some months after the launching of Point Four by President Truman, the Economic and Social

Council, on U.S. initiative, began its study of a possible framework for an expanded program of technical assistance. The planning took into consideration the existence of the U.N. specialized agencies with which the Council was to cooperate. The comprehensive program, which was worked out by the summer of 1949, was unanimously approved by the U.N. General Assembly on November 16, 1949.

The blueprint existed, but the money needed for its implementation had to be supplied by U.N. member nations on a voluntary basis. The United States took the lead. It announced it would contribute 60 per cent of the sum pledged by all other nations. For 1952 the American pledge amounted to $11.4 million. With the passage of years, and with the increase in the number of contributing states, the United States has continued to increase its share to keep to the promised 60 per cent of the total. It has done so in spite of the fact that the Soviet Union refused to participate in the Fund until March, 1954, when it finally withdrew the restrictions it had originally attached to its pledges, and made a contribution of four million rubles, the equivalent of one million dollars. The many critics who linked U.S. aid only to East-West competition had to admit, because of these U.S. contributions, the sincerity of American intentions in promoting and financing U.N. programs of technical assistance.

The budget thus provided enabled the United Nations to carry out projects of technical assistance in seventy-six countries in the fields of health, agriculture, education, vocational training, and public administration. In addition to this important contribution to the welfare of so many nations, the U.N. Expanded Program of Technical Assistance has given rise to a new category of truly international civil servants, numbering thousands of experts from scores of countries. The magnitude of the tasks is best illustrated by the number of people engaged in this work. Dag Hammarskjold, the late U.N. Secretary-General, stated in 1959: "In ten years, more than 8,000 experts of seventy-seven different nationalities have served in the field as advisers and instructors; some 14,000 fellowships have been awarded by the U.N. and the related agencies; altogether 140 countries and territories have received assistance. . . . The program has provided a valuable leaven for economic and social development throughout the world."

This growing sense of responsibility for the welfare of less developed countries is clearly illustrated in another development in this field. The underdeveloped nations' share in all forms of U.N. assistance is constantly growing. In 1960 the distribution of project expenditures by region showed that Africa was the beneficiary of 15.4 per cent of this assistance, as compared with Europe, 6 per cent; Latin America, 25 per cent; the Middle East, 17.9 per cent; and Asia and the Far East, 33.3 per cent.

Thus the American 60 per cent in the financing costs of the many U.N.

Catholic school in Jacmel, Haiti, supported by UNESCO.

programs is being put to the best of use, as is the American share in many other programs of United Nations assistance and activities of the related Specialized Agencies. For UNICEF, the organization which provides the basic needs for over 70 million children in one hundred countries and territories, the United States has carried the bulk of the financial burden. In 1953, for instance, out of contributions of $14.4 million made by forty-six nations, the United States's share amounted to $9.8 million, 68 per cent of the total.

The immensely important part taken by America in these activities of the U.N. and its various agencies has not only made the many assistance programs possible, but it also has served as an outstanding example. Such generosity has caused other nations to increase their contributions to cover the costs of these U.N. activities. The other members of the U.N.

194

have had to acknowledge that the role taken by America has been disproportionately large; as a result they have had an obligation to help change this great inequity. It is obviously grossly unfair that programs conducted under the aegis of an international organization should be financed so overwhelmingly by the United States, which is only one member, having one vote. Through the years, the gradual increase of contributions by U.N. member nations has gradually reduced the American share from more than 60 per cent to 40 per cent. At this still extraordinarily high level of American participation, the U.N. assistance agencies are working today.

Compared with the large amounts of direct American foreign aid, the sums expended by the United States through international channels may perhaps seem rather insignificant. But in terms of rendering real help to people, in terms of concrete humanitarian accomplishment, the more than $100 million the U.S. appropriates annually is of vast importance. An examination of the way this money is spent affords a good indication of the scope of the problems to be solved. The proposed American contribution to the U.N. for the fiscal year 1964 comes to $136,050,000. This amount is to cover voluntary contributions to eight international programs: $55 million for the Technical Assistance and Special Fund; $5 million for economic assistance to the Congo (in addition to the many millions the United States has contributed to cover the costs of the U.N. Congo operations); $17.2 million for the Relief and Works Agency for Palestine Refugees; $12 million for UNICEF; $2 million for the Food and Agriculture Organization's world food program; $1,250,000 for the International Atomic Energy Agency operational program; $500,000 for World Health Organization special programs; and $43.1 million for the Indus Waters Fund.

A record of what these American dollars are accomplishing would fill volumes of the most dramatic stories about the alleviation of human distress, the raising of standards of health and living, the development of resources, and the easing of physical burdens on people. There would be the story of a survey of land and water resources and establishment of agricultural experimental stations in Afghanistan; of a mineral survey in Senegal; of the preparation of a water supply and sewage plan for Ghana; of long-range regional development of agriculture, forestry, and water resources in Turkey; of nation-building in the Congo; of the sustenance of hundreds of thousands of refugees; of efforts to control tuberculosis, yaws, and leprosy; of improvement of nutrition and education facilities; of sanitation, milk conservation, and improvement of primary education in Brazil; and of a survey to determine how food aid can be used on a multilateral basis in developing countries to stimulate economic and social development, assist in pre-school and school feeding, and meet emergency food needs.

These are not the only programs of assistance through international

A Bissa woman in Upper Volta on her way to the river for a supply of fresh water, one of the main problems in most of Africa.

channels which the United States supports to such a marked extent. The American contribution to the budgets of the other international agencies —the International Labor Organization, the Food and Agriculture Organization, the World Health Organization, the United Nations Educational, Scientific and Cultural Organization (UNESCO), the International Civil Aviation Organization, and the other members of the so-called "United Nations family" are included in the Department of State's budget, though in fact they come within the framework of the United States contribution to various assistance programs of the United Nations.

The success of these assistance programs has given rise to recurrent discussion about the merits of this form of aid, as compared with that given directly on a bilateral basis. While it is an open question whether assistance given through international channels is more or less efficient than bilateral aid, there is one argument in its favor which the American government plainly acknowledges. In the summary Presentation to the Congress of the Proposed Mutual Defense and Assistance Programs for 1964, in the chapter on "Contributions to International Organizations" it is clearly stated:

The use of these agencies supported by many nations, permits greater use of the financial resources of other developed countries and, of increasing importance, technical skills which are in short supply. Certain elements of development assistance, such as those designed to lead to administrative or financial reforms, are often more readily accepted by the less developed countries, and hence tend to be more effective if given by multilateral organizations of which they are members. Similarly, in certain acute circumstances, such as the recent Congo history demonstrates, there may be important U.S. political and security interests in avoiding risks of cold war rivalries inherent in a direct confrontation of bilateral programs.

Mother and child of Bobo-Niénégué descent in Upper Volta, before their "banco" (dirt bricks) home. One of the many areas in which U.N. agencies try to assist development.

197

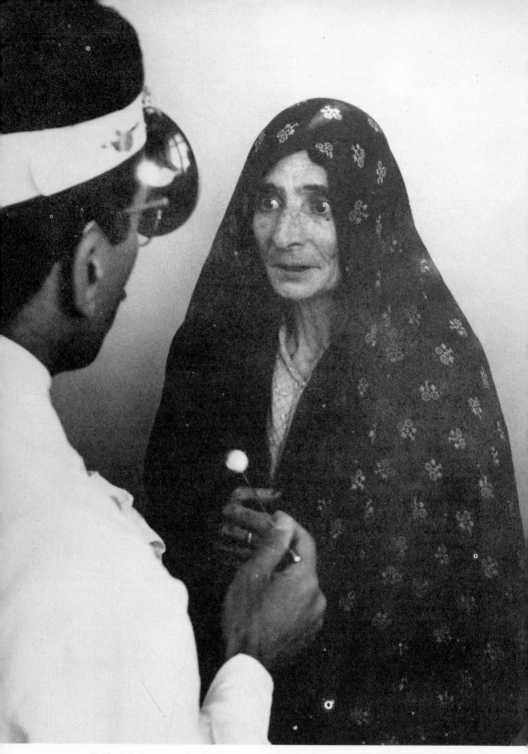

Patient being examined for a cancer of the larynx in the Teheran Cancer Institute organized by the World Health Organization.

198

The sensitivities of the recipient countries are largely related to the international situation, which makes these countries eager to preserve, or at least appear to preserve, their independence from the powers engaged in the cold-war struggle. Taking aid from an international body is considered to be completely free from any political obligation to any of the great powers. It is the international community of which the recipient nation is a member to which gratitude is due. It is possible that this characteristic of international aid may, by eliminating questions of cold war competition, put the entire aid policy on a much sounder basis than it has today. And, last but not least, there is the purely human matter of pride: when aid is given through an institution of which a nation is a member, it is much less likely that national self-respect will be lowered.

As of today, this form of aid remains a goal still to be realized in the future. However, its merits are continuously expounded by leaders in the foreign aid field. Eugene Black, who for many years headed the International Bank for Reconstruction and Development asserted only recently that "one obvious and enormous virtue of the international approach is that it can be objective. . . . Because we have no axe to grind, we can take on the jobs which are necessary, but unexciting. Because we have no political or commercial motives that might distort our effort, the underdeveloped countries can rely on us to help them find the very best experts, the cheapest supplies, the projects which will best meet the needs of their countries. . . ." In October, 1963, the Senate Foreign Relations Committee arrived at the conclusion that it is time for the United States to shift most of its aid away from the traditional bilateral approach to a multilateral basis.

America's positive approach to international assistance, which was demonstrated most concretely over the more than ten years since the U.S. delegation to the United Nations initiated the Expanded Program of Technical Assistance, was again demonstrated in the U.S. initiative in proclaiming the United Nations Development Decade. In his address before the United Nations General Assembly in 1961, President Kennedy announced that his "nation, which has freely shared its capital and its technology to help others help themselves, now proposes officially designating the decade of 1960 as the U.N. Decade of Development. Development can become a cooperative, not a competitive enterprise—to enable all nations, however diverse in their systems and beliefs, to become in fact as well as in law free and equal States."

The American challenge was accepted. On December 19, 1961, the U.N. General Assembly designated the current decade as "the United Nations Development Decade, in which Member States and their peoples will intensify their efforts to mobilize and to sustain support for the measures required on the part of both developed and developing countries to accelerate progress towards self-sustaining growth of the economy of the individual nations and their social advancement." The aim, con-

In Nov., 1962, U.S. Permanent Representative to the United Nations, Adlai Stevenson, received from then Acting Secretary-General U Thant a U.N. bond for $44,103,000 which U.S. purchased to match the equivalent of the total amount of U.N. bonds purchased by all other governments until the time the U.S. check was prepared.

tinues the resolution, would be "to attain in each under-developed country a substantial increase in the rate of growth, with each country setting its own target, taking as the objective a minimum annual rate of growth of aggregate national income of five per cent at the end of the Decade."

In all respects, therefore, each American dollar invested in international institutions of assistance is put to the best of use. The American experts working in the many countries receiving assistance through these institutions are doing their best to coordinate their efforts with those of the international experts. An American expert on health problems may be advising a country on the best methods of serving public health needs while at the same time a mission of the World Health Organization, in whose budget the United States participates considerably, tries, in the same country, to do exactly the same thing. Avoiding duplication as well as avoiding competition sometimes becomes not less important than the aid and advice itself.

This is only one side of the problem, though. The American government is putting growing pressure on other developed nations to give an appropriate share in aid programs. Special measures have been adopted to coordinate and increase the aid given by developed countries. In March, 1961, the Development Assistance Group was established in Paris. Ten nations have joined this new organization. The United States is a party to a treaty which established a new major organization of international cooperation and coordination in aid giving, known as the Organization for Economic Cooperation and Development (OECD), of which the Development Assistance Group became the Development Assistance Committee. In two resolutions adopted at a meeting of the Development Assistance Group the member nations acknowledged that rendering assistance to underdeveloped nations was a common task, to which each nation

"Reverse technical assistance"—Dr. Shao-wen Ling, a world authority on fish farming, advising the U.S. Fish and Wild Life Service on the establishment of a research laboratory and experimental station to be built in Arkansas, to study fish propagation in rice growing areas.

Mrs. Edna Kelly, member of Congress and of the U.S. delegation to the 18th U.N. General Assembly, signing for the United States pledge of U.S. contribution of $57 million to the $131,500,000 Expanded Program of Technical Assistance and the United Nations Special Fund.

should contribute in accordance with its ability. The major role the United States will play in this organization of the industrialized nations of the West and Japan is emphasized by the resolution, which provides for the appointment of a full-time chairman of the Development Assistance Group, the appointment of whom was to be an American prerogative.

This initiative of the United States government was fully endorsed in the foreign aid authorization bill for the 1963 fiscal year, in which the House Foreign Affairs Committee inserted a provision calling on advanced industrial nations of the non-Communist world to assume a larger share of the help for underdeveloped areas. The American government has suggested a simple, but nevertheless far-reaching formula for determining the extent of the foreign aid: the total foreign assistance by the industrialized nations should amount to about one per cent of their total gross national product—a principle which the U.S. had already used in setting the amount of its contributions to the UNRRA funds.

And not without importance is the fact that the United States has supplied, proportionately, the greatest number of experts who work on behalf of the international assistance organizations. Among them is the chief officer of all United Nations technical and development assistance programs, Paul G. Hoffman, who has served for years as the managing director of the United Nations Special Fund. This Fund, which was established on the proposal of the United States delegation at the twelfth session of the U.N. General Assembly, has become a major factor in international development assistance in the pre-investment stage of development of the recipient nations. There is no doubt that the experience Hoffman gained while heading the first major and most successful foreign-aid operation—the Marshall Plan—has been a most important asset. This, combined with his real and personal involvement in the efforts to help people help themselves to become self-supporting members of the international community, has turned the office of the managing director of this Fund into a center of world-wide planning, to which every nation turns with confidence and hope.

10

The Peace Corps—"The Revolution of Rising Esteem"

"Willing to serve abroad under conditions of hardship if necessary." The sentence was short, but its meaning was revolutionary. It announced a new mission for Americans to assume. It was one of the goals and conditions of service the Congress had established for members of the Peace Corps.

The idea was new in the affluent society that the volunteers came from. It was new in a nation where refrigerators, running hot water, and indoor plumbing are nearly universal, and a car a normal means of transportation for everybody. And it was new in a country which had tens of thousands of its people spread all over the world—as diplomats, technicians, and advisers—completely isolated behind their servants, air conditioners, cars, and tax-free liquor.

Nevertheless, the Peace Corps has passed the test. Its volunteers are spread over forty-five countries. From the peaks of the Andes to the peaks of the Himalayas, from the deserts of Iran to the lush plateaus of Brazil— the Peace Corps volunteers have been demonstrating to the world the existence of a new kind of Westerner, a new kind of American.

This new American is doing amazingly resourceful and diversified work. Somewhere north of New Delhi, in India, four volunteers stationed in Nabha on a mission to advise local people in small-scale industry, dairy farming, agricultural extension, and youth work decided they could do more. After investigating local methods of poultry raising, they decided to start there. The first problem was that of obtaining proper feed which would not be too expensive. The solution was not hard to find. A book on poultry raising in India by a specialist of the Agency for International Development (AID) had the answer. To get the necessary ingredients for this well-balanced chicken ration, they had to travel miles. They did so, and soon, with good-quality chickens and inexpensive, high-quality feed, excellent eggs and chickens appeared on the local market. Word about it got around. Indian farmers became interested in poultry farming. The volunteers continued on the job—they raised the feed themselves and sold it at low cost to the farmers.

204

Inquiries about the new industry began to flood their shack. They had no offices, no clerical help. So they decided to do what everyone does when he has special knowledge which should be shared with many: they wrote a handbook on raising poultry. And though they spoke Punjabi well enough to communicate with the local people, they did not trust themselves sufficiently with the new language to become authors in it. They wrote in English, a local man did the translation, and the volunteers had their handbook published. Instead of writing letters of advice on poultry growing, they sold their handbook. And so, from the poultry business, they entered the publishing field. However, it was a very special type of publishing, for they sold their books for one cent each.

Their initial success was encouraging. Now they felt they could do something more for the youth groups they were working with. They began to sell them day-old chicks on a pay-out-of-profits basis. The circle of chicken growers increased, consequently the protein content of the local diet improved, and the incomes of many farmers started growing as well.

The four volunteers were not alone. The AID and other agencies extended the fullest support for their initiative. In March, 1963, the Peace Corps representative in India wrote to Washington:

Eggs and poultry meat may well become a surplus commodity in 1963—at least in certain areas of the Punjab. We are beginning to experience the first problems of marketing, due to the fact that the first Punjab volunteers have now got running some seventy-five good poultry units, each of which is producing an average of fifty eggs per day. Transportation and marketing are looming as major problems.

But the volunteers had not run out of resourcefulness. A wealthy Indian had become sufficiently impressed to offer to back a chicken freezing and canning business and, when last heard from, he and the "Nabha Chicken Volunteers" were hunting for a technical expert to provide the necessary know-how.

In the Far East the experience has been different. While the nations of the Middle East and South Asia are mainly interested in promoting agricultural development, education is the most pressing need in the thousands of islands that form the Philippines. Here again, the work has to be done without fanfare—and almost without funds. The volunteer has to use all his resources and ingenuity. David Mulholland, 23, of Quincy, Massachusetts, used it magnanimously.

His assignment was in an elementary school in the town of Negros Occidental. When vacation time arrived, the children were turned loose with nothing to do. David and a group of other volunteers decided to do something about it. They organized Camp Brotherhood, the first free summer camp in the Philippines.

David was the moving spirit of the camp. He was known for taking a personal interest in his pupils. People told about a sixth grader in

R. Sargent Shriver, Director of the U.S. Peace Corps.

David's school who suddenly disappeared from classes for a week. David searched for the boy and found him at work at a sugar-cane field. "If I want to continue in school, I must work," the youngster told David. Though it was technically not his concern, David found an answer to this problem. He induced the villagers to establish a scholarship fund. It started a pattern. Other children received scholarships as well—one of them to a university. These small accomplishments added up to a beautiful testimony of one man's compassion for his fellow men. David wrote about it once to a Filipino friend: "Try some day to do some little thing that's immortal. Perhaps then everything will seem worthwhile." When David died at his post after contracting a liver ailment, Vice President

Emanuel Pelaez of the Philippines spoke this epitaph for David Mulholland: "He was a martyr to the cause of winning peace."

This cause of winning peace has brought a growing number of volunteers to the Latin American republics. These countries are primarily interested in community development. However, it must be remembered that this was not neutral territory as far as relations to *Norte Americanos* are concerned. "Yanqui imperialism" is a potent slogan in many of these countries. The Peace Corpsman had first to win confidence before he could prove his usefulness.

The volunteers did it by simple, down-to-earth work. In the *barrios,* the slums of Caracas, Venezuela, where 60 per cent of the population is between 14 and 19 years old, and, as one observer has put it, "out of school, out of work and out of patience," Peace Corpsmen are organizing neighborhood centers, playgrounds, and recreational programs. The volunteers mix daily with thousands of university students. They teach English, science, and library science.

In Chile, the volunteers are helping in the organization and development of the Institute of Rural Education. Emery L. Tomor, of Calabasas, California, is a case in point. Assigned to the Galvarino Farmers Cooperative, he helped plan the diversification of crops, conservation of resources, and vaccination of livestock. In a short time he became an integral part of the cooperative. Its members looked to him for initiative, advice, and help. Time passed quickly. Emery Tomor's tour of duty was nearing its end. The leaders of the cooperative found that losing Tomor would be a major blow to the cooperative. They decided to act; they wrote a petition to let Tomor stay with them.

We have now learned that our collaborator must return to his country, and we want you to know that our cooperative is in serious danger of remaining with unfinished work, the more so since we are at the preliminary stage and we lack leaders with the vision and spirit of enterprise which characterized our friend Emery. . . . The cooperative's directors consider that if our friend Emery could collaborate with us during six more months, then by the time he leaves us we would be in a position to carry on by ourselves and would get a great deal of experience. Therefore, we request and beg you to allow Mr. Emery Tomor to remain here for another half year, starting from the date on which he is supposed to return to his country.

Tomor is no exception. The Peace Corps "social technicians" are making their impact felt throughout the Latin-American continent. Laying the foundations for social organization and democratic action in the smallest Colombian settlements, the volunteers are giving a sense of purpose to the *campesino,* where previously there were only apathy, frustration, and bitterness. They taught them the big lesson of "do it yourself" for their own communities. Many a school, road, aqueduct, and bridge has been built this way. People learn to cooperate, to pool their resources, to present demands to the government not for an abstract improvement of their conditions of life, but for specific projects.

207

Engineer James Welcome discusses a brickmaking enterprise with workers on a Colombia redevelopment project.

In Peru another urgent task awaited the volunteers. The earthquakes of 1958 and 1960 had shattered cities and villages. Tradesmen, sanitation experts, and social workers were needed to help the people of the *barriadas*, the crowded sections of the cities, to build decent housing and improve their living conditions. The volunteers have been a vital part of this effort. They also teach carpentry, masonry, and electrical skills, and they disseminate technical knowledge among nonskilled workers. And, after a long day's work, the volunteers teach the Peruvians in their area to organize and run a credit cooperative for constructing new homes.

Honduras is a small Central American republic of two million population with the highest birth rate and lowest per capita income in Central America, where, according to that country's President, "70 per cent are illiterate, 70 per cent illegitimate, and 70 per cent die of preventable diseases." The twenty-five Peace Corps volunteers, nurses, and social workers who arrived in Honduras in September, 1962, have their hands full. In ten cities and towns they are working in hospitals, health centers, social welfare centers, and even in the homes of hundreds of Hondurans. They teach local social workers, arrange vaccination campaigns, and organize health education classes. And when the day's work is over, they continue with adult education to eradicate illiteracy, and they also teach English, sewing, and carpentry.

Teaching is the main occupation of the volunteers in Africa. In some countries the corpsmen teach up to 60 per cent of the school population. In some nations, the volunteers make up about half of the entire teacher staff. In Ethiopia, for instance, with only 470 secondary school teachers, the large contingent of 276 secondary school teachers of the Corps meant

Chilean laborer works with Peace Corps volunteer Elden Stang in repairing a machine.

a revolution in the teaching methods, as well as in the capacity, of the schools. In Nigeria, the largest and most advanced equatorial African country, 15 per cent of the nation's schools have Peace Corps teachers. In Ghana, Peace Corps teachers are the instructors of 60 per cent of all secondary school students. In Gabon, where school attendance is compulsory until the age of 15 and 80 per cent of this new nation's youngsters are in schools, the Peace Corps teachers are of primary importance.

The Peace Corps is already a familiar sight all over Africa. Thousands of African youth are learning from the volunteers not only English and science, but also a first-hand impression of America. This does not come only from the contact made in school. With the school day over, the volunteer's day starts again. His after-work activities depend on his situation and his initiative. It may take the form of an adult class in English, a school-building project, gardening, or animal husbandry advice. It might also be organizing a choir or a soccer team, or building a sports field out of the desert or tropical forest.

Miss Marion Elizabeth Frank of Pittsburgh is one of the five American Peace Corps teachers on the 11-man teacher staff of the Yaa Asantewa School for Girls at Kusami, Ghana.

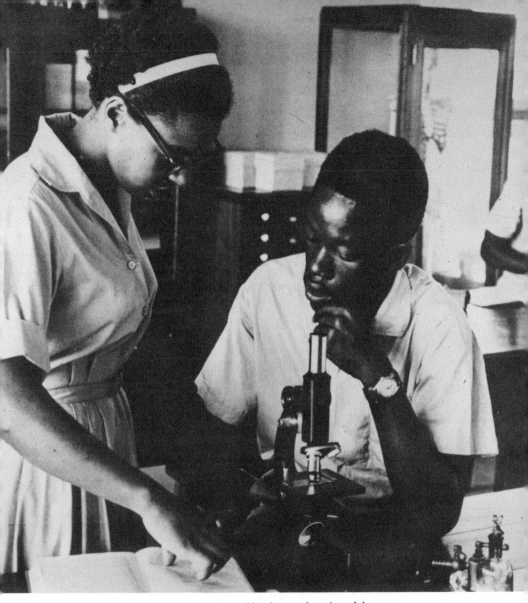

Member of U.S. Peace Corps, left, helps a Ghanian student in a laboratory.

But it is always something to do with people. And the people are not officials, but ordinary citizens living their ordinary lives. The corpsman's main effect may be simply in his hard work and personal example. In countries in which white-collar work has a very high status, the volunteer revives the honor of manual labor. "They are not afraid to soil their hands in physical effort," remarked an official in Asia, and he expressed what so many toiling people everywhere feel so often.

Not always are the accomplishments tangible. Not always are there opportunities for the corpsman to work on new chicken farms, school buildings, bridges, bricks, and dams. Very often there are "only" seeds which remain in people's minds and hearts. One of the volunteers, Carol Brynes of Duquesne, Pennsylvania, a teacher's aid, put it in these words:

> The important thing we are doing here is not that which can be measured with a camera. People in other projects can photograph a bridge they have designed, a road they helped to build, or a toilet they constructed. But who can photograph the mind of a child. . . . Our rewards in a project like this come from the satisfaction in seeing the child's face light up when he has learned. . . . We have had to learn, and must continue to learn, how to accept an intangible gratification. Only time and the future will tell whether our efforts have been successful. Many of us have had to grow up and mature to the point of doing a job where we sometimes can see no normal result in our efforts.

To become a member of the Peace Corps is not easy. First, the prospective volunteer must send in an application. Between April 1, 1961 (within a month after the Peace Corps was established by Executive Order of President Kennedy) and April 1, 1963, 47,000 adult Americans volunteered their services. Their number has been constantly growing. In January, 1962, 935 persons applied. In January, 1963, 4,515 sent in their applications. And these figures represent applications to join the Corps after the applicant has finally made up his mind. Letters of inquiry come in at the rate of 6,000 a week.

Corps members come from all fifty states of the Union, from the District of Columbia, the Commonwealth of Puerto Rico, and the Virgin Islands. Not all are youngsters fresh from college. Many come with a great deal of professional experience behind them. There is a 70-year-old heavy-equipment maintenance man who finished grammar school in 1907, and a young engineer of 21 from Yale, and an 18-year-old high school graduate with farm skills. The average age of the volunteers is 28.5 years for the 1,827 women, and 24.7 years for the 3,176 men in the Corps. Seventy-five men and 123 women are over 40. The greatest number of volunteers has come from California—743.

Speaking about the problems of selection of volunteers, in his October, 1963, testimony before the House Foreign Affairs Committee, the director of the Peace Corps, Sargent Shriver, informed the Committee that standards of acceptance have been raised: "We recently selected out a *magna cum laude* Phi Beta Kappa graduate of one of our major universities; he did not have the personality to match his intelligence. The best efforts of his supporters, which included some very distinguished names, failed to convince our selecting officers otherwise. The sons and daughters of people prominent in business, government, and communications have also been selected out in spite of the comfort it would have given the Peace Corps to acquiesce to the pressure of relatives and friends."

Skilled people are sought—sanitation experts, surveyors, well-drillers, heavy-duty-diesel mechanics, engineers, geologists, language teachers, science teachers, and farming experts. However, the mere possession of such

212

a skill is not sufficient. Innumerable tests still await the candidate before he can attend a Peace Corps training center. In 1962, only one out of six applicants completed the selection procedures, which include professional aptitude, knowledge of a foreign language, proper motivation, acceptable personality, high degree of idealism, ingenious creativity, moral stamina, emotional maturity, physical strength, and the passing of a security check.

The selection process continues during the training. In the training institute the volunteer is under scrutiny of the instructors virtually twenty-four hours a day. During the eight or twelve weeks of training, every weakness in a candidate is discovered. Fifteen per cent of prospective volunteers are eliminated within this period. For those who stay on, the training is most strenuous. It is a combination of a high-pressure university course, commando training, and hard living.

The program is remarkable in its planning and severity: ten to eleven hours daily, six days a week, with a minimum of sixty training hours per week. Language training takes the lion's share of the work week: twenty-eight hours per week, 336 hours during the entire course. Ninety-six hours are devoted to studying about the area to which the volunteer is to be assigned. Forty-eight hours are given to study of world affairs and Communism, thirty-six hours to health and medical training, and forty-eight hours to American studies. These are to give the trainee a deeper understanding of the intricacies of the American government, of the social system in the United States, and to advise him on how to interpret American foreign policy to foreigners.

Forty different languages are being taught in the Peace Corps training institutes, among them some that most people never heard of: Kannada, Ewe, Temne, Nyanja. Universities cooperating with the Peace Corps have had to formulate the courses and sometimes even prepare handbooks and grammars in those languages where such means of instruction did not exist. To make these courses more efficient, an effort is being made to have students who are native speakers of these languages live for some time with the volunteers, to allow them to practice the language while they are in training.

The volunteers are exposed to conditions so harsh that plain endurance is required simply to survive. They have to climb rocks, get through an obstacle course, and learn map reading and survival techniques. They have to be ready to live in a tropical jungle, in a desert climate, high up in the mountains, or on a remote island.

The administrative expenses of this entire operation are being held to a minimum. The 1963 appropriation for "administration and program support costs" provided for a maximum expense of $15.5 million. Administrative expenses have declined from about 33 per cent in 1962 to about 27 per cent in 1963 and 19 per cent in 1964. This figure would have been reduced much more were not "administrative expenses" to include such costs as direction of recruitment, selection, training of volunteers, and medical programs. If these were excluded, figures for administration for fiscal year 1963 and 1964 would be reduced to 17.1 per cent and 12.4 per cent, respectively. By the same token, the Peace Corps adminstration prides itself on the ratio of the Corps staff to members: in August, 1962, it was 1 to 4.4 (784 to 3,465); in March, 1963, 1 to 5.6 (898 to 5,003); in August, 1963, 1 to 8.6 (1,051 to 9,000).

It is noteworthy to stress the fact that all this work is done with practically no financial reward in sight, because the allowances the volunteer receives are, from any point of view, substandard. There is a $125 monthly living allowance, a $40 housing allowance, $10 for travel, and $13 leave allowance; all of which add up to $6,741 over a twenty-one-month period of service overseas. All in all the total cost of each volunteer is $9,000 per year, including the cost of training and of administration.

How much does it cost the taxpayer? Thirty million dollars in 1962, the first year of the functioning of the Peace Corps, $59 million in 1963, and an estimated $108 million in 1964. The increase is natural: it stems from the doubling and tripling of the numbers of volunteers.

Of course this kind of American in the underdeveloped countries has not found favor with America's adversaries on the international scene. Like the Marshall Plan in the 1940's and the Point Four and other foreign-aid programs in the fifties, so the Peace Corps has received the wrath of the Communists. Premier Khrushchev honored the Corps on May 30, 1962, by calling it a "tool of the imperialists." The cue having been given, the follow-up was not slow in coming; the Communists "appointed" Sargent Shriver, director of the Peace Corps, a member of the Central Intelligence Agency, and the volunteers its agents. The "cowboy imperialists" were also called "idle loungers in the cafés," whose only aim was the subversion of the new nationalism of African and Asian countries and to "serve the need of neo-colonialism, tamper with local women and prepare the raiding of local economies by the American monopolists."

This has been the official Communist line. Radio Moscow, in its French program to Africa, informed its African listeners: "It could be seen that the real aims of this corps had nothing to do with a peaceful mission. First of all, the recruiting was entrusted to the secret services." The Soviet journal *International Affairs* wrote in October, 1962: "American imperialism is searching for new forms and methods of oppression of the new states. The Peace Corps is one of the means. . . . Instead of a network of navigation canals, the members are laying the nets of plots and intrigue; instead of the seeds of high-yield corn, they are sowing the seeds of enmity. The Peace Corps leaders are the representatives of well-known American families who have made big fortunes through the exploitation of the African and Latin American peoples."

The lead having been given by Russia, the campaign was taken up by the Communist press all over the world. *El Siglo* in Santiago, Chile,

Games for girls at St. Joseph's School, Nicosia, occupy part of spare-time of Peace Corps volunteer Domenic Marine, who helps Physical Education Department of Greek schools in Cyprus.

wrote: "Twenty assorted spies belonging to that intelligence service of Yankee imperialism, the so-called Peace Corps, arrived in Santiago from the United States. They came as the representatives of the Alliance for Progress, which, instead of the longed-for dollars that the official decadent circles dream about, sends its well-trained servants. These individuals will perform their 'jobs' in the San Gregorio housing district, and this will undoubtedly aggravate the pollution of the air." Another Communist paper, *Haravghi*, thousands of miles away in Nicosia, Cyprus, wrote in the same vein: "The Cyprus government should cancel the visit here of the American Peace Corps because through them Cyprus will become a place for the activities of the Corps, well-known instruments of imperialism in the countries they have already visited. For this reason they have been expelled from many countries."

The truth, of course, is completely the opposite of these allegations. No country has asked to discontinue any of the Peace Corps programs initiated in it; rather, each has requested increases in the numbers of the volunteers. The requests have been limited only by the need for proper planning and other factors, of which budgetary considerations are not least.

Expressions of appreciation, often highly enthusiastic, are to be found all over the world in press editorials on the Corps, in official statements, and in declarations of city councils, school boards, PTA associations, and cooperatives. An editorial in *Siam Nikorn* read: "The coming of this American Peace Corps unit is practical proof of the ideal that all human beings, irrespective of nationality and language, are equal." Tunisia's biggest daily said: "The Peace Corps may be the first refutation of Khrushchev's claim that only socialism has created a new man." West Cameroon Prime Minister J. N. Foncha, summing up the volunteers' work, said: "The Peace Corps Teachers have become an educational influence of great importance in our country. . . . Americans are practical in their educational system. A young country like ours needs practical education." A most moving appraisal of the Peace Corps mission was recently given by a leading Turkish educator who said:

Rightly or wrongly, we think of ourselves as a people with a past, filled with accomplishments, but temporarily left far behind by many other nations. In our eagerness to catch up, we have to accept material aid: economic aid, military, and sometimes even food to eat. Our gratitude for such aid is diluted with a measure of shame that we have fallen into such a state that we must accept gifts and loans.

What these people [the Peace Corps] are doing is something infinitely more appreciated. It is aid acceptable without any sense of unfulfillable obligation. These people, of course, are giving something they alone can give. They are giving themselves. There is nothing like it in the world.

The Peace Corps volunteers can, therefore, justifiably report that they are fulfilling the Congressional mandate to the Corps to help "promote a better understanding of the American people on the part of the people served." And the American public has not failed to acknowledge the success of their mission. The Peace Corps Congressional presentation, submitted by the Peace Corps Agency in July, 1963, informed Congress that "here at home, the Peace Corps is receiving press support which is close to unanimity. More than 90 per cent of United States newspapers which wrote editorials on Peace Corps activities in 1962, wrote about the agency favorably—often enthusiastically."

Compliments were abundant. They came from every section of the country, from writers and newspapers which could not be suspected of excessive admiration for the Kennedy Administration. What some opponents of the plan tried at the beginning to label as a "juvenile experiment" became "an inspired American experiment in foreign affairs" (New York *World Telegram*); "a splendid expression of Americanism at its best—we wish it continued and spectacular success" (Los Angeles *Herald-Examiner*); and "by any reasonable standard a fine over-all success" (*Time*, July, 1963).

The *Journal Star* of Peoria, Illinois, took a slightly different point of view. Its editor wrote:

Thank Heavens we thought of it first! What if the Russians had teachers in thirty out of thirty-six high schools in Sierra Leone, a new African nation?

Bruce MacKenzie, center, International Peace Corps Secretariat Regional Director of European Programs, meets staff of Netherlands Young Volunteer Program.

And in four of its six colleges? With similar programs in most new African nations? What if in the oldest African nation, Ethiopia, we discovered that school attendance there has been more than doubled under the impact of hundreds of Russian school teachers? What if other hundreds were known to be working in the interior of Brazil at grass-roots levels and were scattered in villages and towns throughout Central America? In Colombia? Peru? Chile? These conditions do exist—but the people there are Americans—Volunteers of the Peace Corps.

More important than this great chorus of praise, perhaps, has been the fact that the Peace Corps idea has been adopted by twelve countries. In February, 1963, the Netherlands announced the establishment of a Dutch Peace Corps; Denmark has formed a volunteer organization to work in developing countries; Norway has established a Peace Corps; New Zealand has a Volunteer Service Abroad (VSA) with Sir Edmund Hillary, the first conqueror of Everest, as its president; West Germany's Bundestag has appropriated funds for the administrative costs of setting up a Peace Corps. In addition to these volunteer units to help foreign nations, Peace Corps organizations are springing up all over the world on the local level, to give help within countries where public effort is necessary to eradicate diseases, fight disasters, and comfort people.

This new development of international dimensions has resulted in the creation of an International Peace Corps Secretariat (*Voluntarios de la Paz, Voluntaires de la Paix*). A unanimous resolution to this effect has been adopted at the International Conference on Human Skills in the Decade of Development, held at San Juan, Puerto Rico, in October, 1962, in which forty-three countries participated. A small secretarial staff initially supplied by the United States will soon be supplemented by full-time workers from Israel and West Germany, to be financed by those governments. Eight governments have designated members of their embassies in Washington to serve as advisers.

217

Who can claim authorship of the Peace Corps idea? The opinions about this question are divided. In 1960, Wisconsin Democratic Representative Henry Heuss introduced a bill, which was passed, appropriating $10,000 to study the feasibility of a Peace Corps. But the Peace Corps as a living program was proclaimed by President Kennedy during his election campaign. Besides making many scattered references to it, he devoted an entire speech to the Peace Corps idea at the end of the campaign. From a slogan and a research project it grew into an integral part of the Kennedy program. And, finally, it became a campaign promise which President Kennedy fulfilled on March 1, 1961, only six weeks after his inauguration as President.

These are the facts about the inception of the Peace Corps. However, as an idea, it had another predecessor, much earlier than Representative Heuss: Walter Hines Page wanted something on the order of the Peace Corps to be included in President Wilson's peace program. Speaking about the moral obligation to invest Western skills to end misery and stagnation in backward areas, Page suggested, when the Armistice had been concluded, turning the "warring armies loose on the yellow fever and the hookworm of the tropics." The Peace Corps is to a certain extent the realization of this idea, in international dimensions.

The impact of the Peace Corps idea has not been confined to the international scene. A Peace Corps for ourselves for use within the United States is being considered by Congress, and scores of private organizations and institutions have been made partners in the many phases of Peace Corps operations. Some fifty universities serve as centers of education for volunteers, and private institutions and firms are supplying their know-how and sometimes their personnel, on a contractual basis. President Kennedy's statement, at the establishment of the Peace Corps, to "make full use of the resources and talents of private institutions and groups" is serving as a permanent guide for the Peace Corps Agency. The Heifer Project, the YMCA, the 4-H Foundation, the Experiment in International Living, the Tennessee Valley Authority, and the Caterpillar Tractor Company are but a few of the many institutions and groups on whom the Peace Corps draws for talent, advice, and cooperation.

The Peace Corps is, thus, not merely an isolated project on the part of the Administration. It is a new phenomenon in American life and, as developments have shown, even in international relations. Its influence even transcends the importance of the many projects the volunteers are working on, for the Peace Corps is now an *idea:* an idea which has an ever-growing number of supporters; an idea which creates new values in relationships between human beings and between nations; an idea which often transforms the personality of the volunteer himself. Said one volunteer on a project: "I am now more critical and afraid of nine-to-five existing. I can never be content doing a job to earn money

Jamaican pupils learn how to overhaul an engine from Peace Corps volunteer John Harvey.

without doing something of value. I am a better American, seeing more clearly the good and bad of my country."

Hardship ceases to be a burden—it becomes a challenge. The volunteers living in a remote mountain settlement in Peru, which can be reached only after a four-day jeep ride over barely passable mountains and roads and across unbridged rivers, or those on an island of the Indonesian archipelago which has no regular communication with the nearest settlement, who eat the local food and live in shacks and huts, come to assume a missionary zeal which elevates them and gives them a new sense of purpose in life. Young David Cozier of West Plains, Missouri,

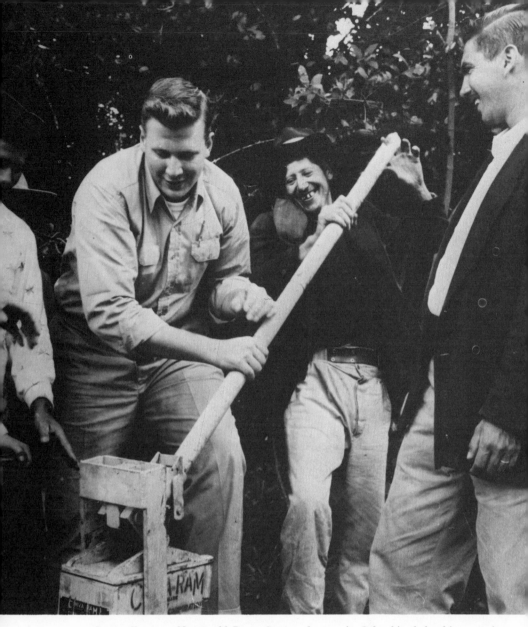

George Kroon, a 22-year-old Peace Corps volunteer in Colombia, helps his co-workers make bricks.

who worked at Jardin, a jungle-surrounded *barrio* in southern Colombia, wrote his parents some time before he died in an air accident: "Should it come to it, I had rather give my life trying to help someone than to give my life looking down a gunbarrel at them."

This new sense of a noble mission in life has created admiration for the Corps among the friends of the volunteers, their parents and the parents' friends. The father of Nancy Boyd of Martinez, California, who was one of the six volunteers who met death in the line of duty, expressed this attitude in the following words on his daughter's death: "I said to my wife this morning, 'So many citizens of the world have lost their children to wars, but we lost our daughter to something far more worthwhile. This is peace.' We feel her sacrifice worthwhile."

It is feelings like these which are the real motivation of those who decide to volunteer. A Corpsman in the Philippines, when asked why he had volunteered, said simply: "I am happy and still cannot answer the question. Whatever my original motivation was, it has long since been pushed aside by the Peace Corps experience itself, and not even hindsight can recover it. Every day I discover at least a dozen reasons why I should have volunteered."

"We as a nation," said Sargent Shriver, Peace Corps Director, "were in danger of losing our way among the television sets, the supermarkets, and the material abundance of a rich society. Our debt and gratitude to the developing and emerging nations of the world is that they have reminded us of our own traditions and given us a treasured opportunity to sacrifice and work once more for those principles which created our own nation. By letting us participate in their struggles, they have given us a chance to find ourselves."

Shriver expressed a similar idea when speaking before a group of 170 volunteers at the Columbia Teachers College in their last week of training. He quoted Yevgeny Yevtushenko, the young Russian poet who rebelled for greater freedom of expression. Mr. Shriver quoted a passage from Yevtushenko's *A Precocious Autobiography*, which says: "However prosperous, a man will always be dissatisfied if he has no high ideals. . . . But if even the rich feel burdened by the lack of an ideal, to those who suffer real deprivation, an ideal is a first necessity of life. Where there is plenty of bread and a shortage of ideals, bread is no substitute for an ideal. But where bread is short, ideals are bread." And Mr. Shriver commented: "The Peace Corps from my point of view is such an ideal."

In all fairness it must be said that the high ideals of the Peace Corps and the acceptance of its mission by over forty nations are not the entire story. There have been failures, there have been drop-outs, there have been volunteers who could not stand the physical and mental strains of their mission. A twenty-one-year-old volunteer had to be sent home "on sick leave" after he decided to marry a grandmother in Colombia; a girl had to discontinue her service because of an unhappy love affair; some volunteers have asked to be sent home because they could not stand the hardships. But these have been cases of personal maladjustment; they had nothing to do with the countries in which the volunteers worked. The case of Margery Michelmore, the Peace Corps girl who wrote home an open postcard with some critical remarks about conditions in Nigeria, which anti-American elements got hold of and turned into a campaign against the United States and the Peace Corps, was an isolated case that occurred during the first days of the Peace Corps and is already long forgotten.

What we have today is a real American success story. It is not all glamour and excitement, and it often has real hazards, mainly those the volunteers themselves call the hazards "of dysentery and boredom." But these hazards are being turned into challenges which thousands of Americans meet with responsibility and a high sense of duty and which bring only respect and appreciation from the host countries. The Philippines *Free Press* said on April 7, 1962: "If the hearts of Filipinos have been lost by exclusiveness and arrogance in the past, they are being won back by the nice, the truly wonderful people who have left their country to come here and be of help. . . .The Philippines is independent, but with the Peace Corps around, Filipinos and Americans have never been closer to each other. . . ."

Yes, to bring people close together, to make them feel what America stands for, is quite a mission in this turbulent world. And the Peace Corps volunteers are accomplishing this mission not by words, but by work, deeds, and outstanding example.

11

$$$

The "Ugly American" Performs
Around the World

Lawrence Cowper of California was away for weeks from his headquarters in Katmandu, capital city of the mountain kingdom of Nepal. He left behind him his attractive young wife, Constance, and their three blond young children. With his Nepalese antimalaria spray teams, he was on the mountain and jungle trails of Nepal. "Sahib Larry" walked as if he were on one of the streets of his hometown, far off in the States. Many people knew him here, perhaps as many as those who knew him in his little town in California.

It took some three and a half years to make these acquaintances. When Larry arrived at Katmandu, much of the hilly region was virtually closed for the officials of the Malaria Program. It was considered inaccessible. There were no roads, even those which might be considered "jeepable," no maps of the areas, no one to help. Larry was not discouraged. He set up a map-survey laboratory and prepared maps. He had his Nepalese assistants produce spare parts for sprayers out of locally obtainable materials. They cut up Nepalese rice paper and out of it made bags for DDT powder, which they sealed with glue obtained from the sticky pulp of the local *bel* fruit. Scales for weighing the DDT were improvised from cheap aluminum plates, and iron weights were used as balances. To mark houses which were sprayed, paint was prepared by boiling a weird mixture of local ink powder, raw sugar, and kerosene.

With the materials on hand, Cowper was ready to begin. The project demanded the skill and efficiency of a military operation: an organization had to be created, plans prepared, transportation chosen and assured, supply lines equipped, maps distributed. Even the paymaster could not be forgotten because the locally recruited people would not travel to Katmandu for the equivalent of the $10 per month they were paid.

In this way, 300,000 square miles of the hill areas were sprayed twice within a two-year period. Larry covered much of this territory on foot. His companions were often wild jungle animals, snakes, crocodiles, bloodsucking leeches, scorpions and insects—and sometimes gangs of *dacoits*, or highwaymen, who could hold their own against American gangsters.

223

Fresh purified water is one of the most important problems in the Philippines. This photo shows a well built there with U.S. dollars and technical advice.

Over 2,000 miles of such "walking" could not have been accomplished without special traits of character and extraordinary physical stamina. Larry lived off the country. He learned to eat the simple food of the Nepalese peasants, who competed among themselves in offering hospitality to this tall "sahib." But he always carried his own camping gear, a small amount of food, and a pressure cooker. He drank water he had treated chemically, and his first-aid kit helped many a villager. He made many a friend for America—and some enemies among people who feared that American methods were undermining the sources of their income. Thus it happened that Larry sometimes encountered the wrath of the *jhankri*, the witch doctor, who hates malaria eradication since it dries up the source of illnesses, and his business with it.

But Larry learned to overcome these difficulties. Generally, the villagers accorded him a most generous reception. The hundreds of thousands of villagers among whom Larry worked on the malaria eradication schemes have learned what this kind of progress means.

But, it was not always like this. The Nepalese well remember how they had opposed another mission of progress led by the Americans from Katmandu. These were the teams of Village Development workers. They greeted them with stones. They wanted nothing of their instruction about new ways of planting and double-cropping, about latrines, and about sickness coming from invisible worms and micro-organisms. They were not then ready to change their conviction that such matters are regulated by supernatural forces and that if the Village Development workers had a proper respect for their elders, they would rather hasten to make *pryas,* to propitiate themselves to the deities, lest they be punished for sacrilege.

However, with time, the Village Development workers succeeded, and, therefore, Larry had an easier job. Local people have begun to do things for themselves. The village councils, the *Panchayats,* organized with the assistance of the Village Development workers, are an excellent intermediary between the people and the various technical assistance teams. The establishment of a nine-man council in each of 3,400 communities with a population of 2,000 has helped the development of almost the entire rural population of nearly nine million of Nepal.

Only recently, representatives of various branches of the U.S. technical

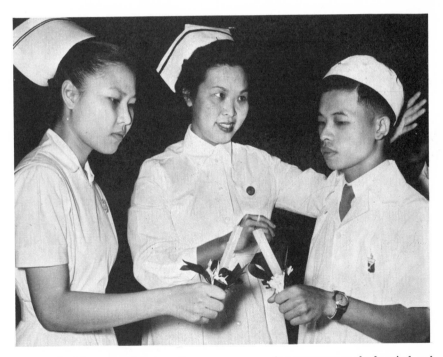

Care for health means education of nurses: nurse-capping ceremony at the hospital and nurses training school in Hue, South Vietnam. Training program is supported by U.S. aid.

mission attended a conference of thirty-eight *Pradhan Panches,* the senior
members of these councils. They were participating in a five-day training
seminar, supported by American aid. Some walked from distant villages
in order to attend. All brought their own rice to eat, for they were given
no pay and received no allowances. Although they were of many castes
and ethnic groups, they sat together to eat. As they sat down, one remarked: "After all, we are all brothers. Times are changing."

Times are indeed changing. Malaria, which used to take a toll of tens
of thousands annually has been completely eradicated. In the 1959–1960
season alone, 420,203 houses were sprayed. In 1958, there were no women
health workers—today, hundreds of them attend sick people in the modern health centers at Hitsura, at Bharatpur, and of course at Katmandu.
A 56-mile, two-lane gravel road has opened up nearly 1,200 square miles
of rich fertile land of the Rapti Valley for cultivation. Nearly fifty thousand people have been settled in the valley, and each settler has been
given a minimum of eight acres; eleven schools have been established for
the children of the new settlers. This new, settled area, often called "the
American Valley," is the best proof that there is no misunderstanding
as to the identity of those whose help made this development possible.

It is not always so easy to identify the source of assistance because
America is not alone in aiding Nepal. The Russians are working in the
Khabra district, building a hydroelectric power station, and the Chi-
nese are surveying a road through the area. How do these two types of

Fire-fighting equipment demonstrated by AID experts in Colombia.

assistance compare in the eyes of the people? A missionary who has lived and worked in the area for years is of the opinion that the Village Development approach, working through the village people on a self-help basis, is the most important and effective thing that has been done in the area. This is a program, says the missionary, in which the people participate themselves, in which they are able to do for themselves things that are meaningful to their lives—water supply, wells, schools, irrigation canals.

To express a preference for American aid takes some courage in Nepal, which borders on Communist China, and which has received aid from the Soviet Union as well. Though the period of ridiculing American efforts has passed, the spreading of suspicion about the motives of American aid remains a potent instrument in the Communist struggle against people like Larry, whose impact cannot easily be neutralized. Antimalaria schemes can no more be pictured as a device to spur American exports of DDT than can the building of a road with American assistance be easily represented as an attempt to extend American lines of communication into a strategically important area.

Nepal is only one of the examples of American technical aid in such sensitive areas. About a decade earlier, another American assistance team had to pave its way into another Asian country. Iran was the place, and the year was 1950. Iran was the first country to sign an agreement with the United States for technical assistance, the first Point Four agreement. United States Ambassador Henry F. Grady and Iran's Prime Minister, General Ali Razmara, agreed to establish an Iranian–United States Joint Commission for Rural Improvement. Under this agreement, American experts in agriculture, health, and education were to work with Iranians in training local peasants and villagers.

The allocation for this first "country agreement" was rather modest—$23,450,000. The task soon proved much harder than anybody had anticipated. When the time for implementing the program arrived, the Premier who signed the agreement was no longer in office. A violent revolution had taken place and the "crying Premier in pajamas," Dr. Mohammed Mossadegh, had taken over.

The Communists controlled the field. The activities of the American Point Four mission, under the enthusiastic, devoted, and experienced William E. Warne, were, in their opinion, a nuisance that they hoped at least to neutralize, if not liquidate completely. The character of the Point Four programs seemed to call for a special kind of opposition. There were no big projects, revolutionary programs, dams, mills, new ports, or cities; only simple down-to-earth efforts to improve health conditions, increase the yield of fields, and introduce new breeds of cattle and other domestic animals.

The occasion for an all-out attack of ridicule came very soon. In their efforts to improve the breeds of working animals, the livestock division

Mules sired by Cyprus Jacks which were supplied by U.S. aid for improving the breed of working animals—the target of Communist ridicule of U.S. aid programs in Iran.

of the Point Four mission, in cooperation with the Ministry of Agriculture, sent a man to Nicosia, Cyprus, to select ten jacks and ten jennies for improving the local Iranian breed. This is what the Communists were waiting for. Jackasses have a traditionally low standing in the Middle East. When an Iranian farmer is asked how much stock he has, he mentions the number of sheep, of oxen, and of cows, and then adds "and excuse me, one jackass." The Communist-influenced newspapers of the Tudeh party had a theme. A headline in these papers said: "Ah, the great United States comes to help Iran and what does Iran get? A few jackasses! The people are hungry, but what do the promises of the wealthy amount to? Jackasses!" Warnes's picture appeared all over in the company of . . . jackasses.

The Iranian officials became impatient. They too wanted something big, something which would make a noise and give jobs to thousands of people at some site. Cables from Washington demanded explanations about the jackasses. Weeks passed—and then the first break came. Ghaghghai tribesmen wired from Shiraz for four of the jacks. "We need to breed better pack animals for our migrations," explained the tribesmen in their request. Soon a request for the "new jacks" came from a village in central Iran; the Iranian army requested two dozen jackasses for its remount service; the *"giveh telegraph"* had brought the news about the special breed of asses to every corner of Iran. This proved to be the most efficient news and advertising agency available. A *giveh* is a moccasin-like shoe worn by Iranian country people, and *"giveh* telegraph" is the Iranian version of the American Indian "moccasin telegraph," our present-day "grapevine." The tables were now turned: The Communist propaganda had been an excellent advertising campaign for the jackass project. The

228

Turkish miners, whose daily production rose from half a ton to two tons daily with U.S.-supplied equipment.

mission could not fill the demands. The jackass became a symbol of honor for the U.S. mission, which gained praise from all over. And when Point Four technicians traveled around the country, they were received everywhere by the local people, who competed in the volume of their shouts: *"Yea, Yea, Yea, Asle Chahar!"* ("Hurray, hurray, hurray, Point Four!").

Another project, that of providing Iranian farmers with tractors, did not prove quite so successful in certain areas. The tractors worked for a year or two and suddenly were left idle in the villages. Marvin Cernik of Schulenburg, Texas, who left his 200-acre farm to join the U.S. Aid Mission in Iran as a vocational educator and adviser, was called upon to do something about it. When he opened his first course in a centrally located village, he asked what had happened to the tractors that now stood idle. The peasants were honest. "We used the tractors," they said, "for a year and we liked it, but now it doesn't work." In one of his classes with younger people, the students said: "We don't need a course in maintenance. What we need is a course in engineering principles." Cernik got the point: "engineering" carries prestige, "maintenance" does not. Within three years, he established thirteen Agricultural Training Centers with almost 2,000 graduates spread all over the country to keep the tractors going, thus increasing agricultural production and introducing new methods which assured growing yields.

Elephants moving logs in Burma forests have been replaced by tractors.

The entire economy was in need of an improved system of transportation in order to accelerate economic growth. In 1956 the United States helped to modernize the Iranian railway system. A $33 million loan from the Export-Import Bank enabled Iran to replace old steam engines with Diesel locomotives. Today the Iranian railroad is making money for the first time in its history, and all payments due on the loan are being met on schedule.

Lebanon, a small country on the eastern shores of the Mediterranean, also experienced the effects of Point Four. The story began on May 29, 1951, with the signing of the Assistance agreement. Within a few years a poultry industry had been established, providing additional protein food in a country where such food was very scarce. The income from poultry rose from less than $1 million to $7 million. The capital city was provided with daily deliveries of bottled, pasteurized milk. Vocational schools were established, better methods of agricultural production were introduced, and the Litani River waters were utilized.

In the case of Burma, the problem, which had existed for years, was how to increase the production of highly prized teak wood, one of the most important earners of foreign exchange for the country. The answer was mechanization. Until American assistance was given, in the form of a $600,000 loan for two complete extraction units, the work was done by elephants. They had been used for centuries. The elephants were used to haul the logs for miles to the nearest transportation center. But even the big animals could not compete with tractors. An elephant could move one log half a mile per day; a tractor moves two to five logs six miles per day. The cost of elephant extraction per ton is $7.06 and the cost by machinery is $5 per ton. The Burmese were quick to recognize the advantages of the mechanical process of extraction. With the American loan and American technicians, they managed in the 1958–59 season to double the timber output per unit from 10,000 to 20,000 tons.

In the largest nation in Africa, Nigeria, the most pressing problem is education. Trained personnel are needed to administer the newly independent country's government, business enterprises, and institutions, as well as to implement its development plans. The U.S. technical assistance program in Nigeria stepped in. In 1957, a teacher-training program was initiated. With the cooperation of an Ohio University contract group, teacher-training centers were established. A Federal Teacher-Training Center was organized. The Teacher-Training Center of Ibadan provides training for instructors who teach in sixty-seven teacher-training schools. Teachers in commercial and vocational schools received their certifications and helped to build new schools and to provide better curricula in existing schools. Commercial courses were developed and adapted by the Ministry of Education. Funds have been provided for a new Federal Teacher-Training Center at Lagos to accommodate 400 boarding students and 350 day students.

Sudan, the country where the White and the Blue Nile join their waters, experienced the fruits of American assistance in many different ways. The average annual export volume of ground nuts, sesame, and dura (millet) increased from 10 per cent of total exports in 1956 to 16 per cent in 1960. Two thousand tractors contributed markedly to farm mechanization, crop production has been diversified, water supplies have been explored, and water storage capacity expanded to 500 million gallons; a government highway organization is providing the country with all-weather roads where previously they had been practically nonexistent; new industries have been established, and geological surveys prepared for mineral exploitation.

Miss Olinda Croci, AID, Washington, D.C., introduces puppets made by a Bolivian which are being used as an educational tool in rural areas.

Here in the Western Hemisphere, many evidences of progress were achieved by American aid. In the first year of the Alliance for Progress, income tax revenues in San Salvador increased by 42 per cent, foreign exchange in the Central Bank rose by 10 per cent, industrial production went up by 19.6 per cent, and the value of agricultural production mounted by 15 per cent. By January, 1963, 228 classrooms had been completed, accommodating 10,120 children. A national literacy campaign has made efficient use of the radio. A Radio School of the Air has distributed single-channel receiving sets, and the five broadcasts a week, each one hour and forty minutes long, have become a hit with the rural population, as did the publication *Vida Campesina* (*Rural Life*) which started with 6,000 copies, rose to 16,000, and now has requests for 40,000 copies.

Santa Cruz, Bolivia, one of the oldest cities in this Hemisphere, founded in 1557 as a Spanish missionary outpost, has moved into the civilization of the twentieth century within the last few years. For centuries situated off the beaten paths of colonial commerce and later on the sidelines of economic development in Bolivia, Santa Cruz retained its beamed stucco houses, its dirt streets, its men wearing knitted wool stocking caps with flaps (against possible cold spells), and its women carrying their babies in colored ponchos.

In the mid-1950's, the winds of change reached these semitropical lowlands. It took several land-development programs of the United States Operations Mission (which is the official name of the U.S. Point Four missions abroad) before construction of the Santa Cruz-Cochabamba highway, financed to a great extent by a $33.4 million twenty-year loan from the U.S. Export Bank. The highway revolutionized the entire area and is now well on its way to bringing an economic revolution to the whole of Bolivia. The center of the nation's economy started shifting to the Santa Cruz area. Settlers have moved into the newly opened territory, and transportation facilities have turned the region into a major rice- and sugar-production center, with a decisive influence on the entire economy of the country. From 14,500 metric tons of rice in 1956, the production rose to 24,500 metric tons in 1961.

These are only some of the potentials which this area has for the Bolivian economy. The Gulf Oil Company drilled and found petroleum and natural gas. Bolivia's economic planners look with excitement at the prospects of industrialization, once fuel for power plants is available. And the relative proximity of the Brazilian industrial combine in São Paulo opens unlimited possibilities for the Bolivian gas, for new incomes, and for an escape from what became a curse of the Bolivian economy, the forced reliance on one major product—tin. As the economic importance of the area increases, its population, income, and literacy also increase. The signs of an economic boom are becoming visible. The population of Santa Cruz, the capital of this area, has risen from 15,000 in 1955 to 60,000 in 1963; the population of Montero, a town 27 miles north of Santa Cruz, rose from 1,500 to 14,000 during the same period.

The technicians officially entrusted with the task of assisting nations have often obtained supplementary aid for their efforts from Americans abroad whose missions are sometimes rather remote from technical-assistance programs. Technical-assistance people like to tell the story of General Douglas MacArthur's "intercession" in a technical-assistance problem. While serving as commander of the American occupation forces in Japan, MacArthur presented a representative of India with a little Japanese rice-thresher. Made up of galvanized iron and a few nails, it considerably speeds up the rice-threshing process. Until then rice had

233

been threshed in India by hand. The "MacArthur rice-thresher" revolutionized rice production in India, perhaps even more than the great Indian irrigation projects.

These are only a few of the many success stories which could be told about the impact of the American technical-assistance programs, as distinguished from the economic-assistance schemes spread all over the world. In more than one hundred countries, there is almost no field of human endeavor in which the United States Operation Missions have not tried at least to give a helping hand. Conceived as a program of people working with people, this program covers the efforts of almost 85 per cent of the employees of the Agency for International Development.

U.S. poultry advisor instructs local farmers in Liberia.

Before classrooms are built, education starts even in these primitive conditions.

Working currently with about fifty nations and dependent territories, almost 5,000 American technicians lend their know-how to people overseas.

They draw their enthusiasm from the same source which has inspired the initiators of technical assistance in high office. Frances Perkins, in *The Roosevelt I Knew,* recalls a flight over Saudi Arabia during which President Roosevelt said: "When I get through being President of the United States and this damn war is over I think Eleanor and I will go to the Near East and see if we can manage to put over an operation like the Tennessee Valley system that will really make something of that country. I would love to do it."

It is in this spirit that these American technicians assist, instruct, initiate, and cooperate in education and the eradication of illiteracy, reclamation, reforestation, water prospecting, business promotion, highway building, airline communication, new crop techniques, antimalaria projects, nurses' education, tractor operation and repair, public administration, village organization, banana-disease control, fishing, arid-areas reclamation, capitalization and savings, milk pasteurization, poultry raising, radio communication, power development, agricultural education, revamping of transportation systems, self-help home building—in hundreds of projects which have benefited hundreds of millions all over the globe.

There was and is no fanfare, no headlines, no propaganda—but rather a day-to-day effort which benefits the little man in the village, in the town, in the settlement. With little money per project, sometimes no more than a few tens of thosuands of dollars, progress is being demonstrated and implanted while new vistas open for struggling human beings.

In these efforts, the American technical advisers must always bear in mind that they cannot simply copy American standards in countries whose economies are substandard, in countries in which the annual per capita income is lower than the average American's yearly expenditure for health. They must understand that they must make nations adapt modern techniques to specific local conditions.

In carrying out this arduous task, there are no spectacular achievements, and there are no spectacular rewards. There is only the awareness that a start is being made, a foundation on which the superstructure of development has to be laid. The old Chinese proverb that the longest journey must begin with a first step has perhaps never before found such deep meaning as in the hundreds of technical-assistance programs pursued all over the world.

What have these technical-assistance and economic-aid programs accomplished? This is a question asked not only by the American taxpayer, but by all the nations in the world. The answer is to be found in the statistics of the growth in national incomes, in production indices, in average annual incomes, and in the daily intake of calories by people.

Examples of these changes in assisted countries are many. A typical case is Greece. A country completely devastated by the Second World War and by subsequent civil war waged by Communist guerrillas, Greece was a major beneficiary of UNRRA aid. The $416 million of UNRRA funds did little more than keep the people alive. Soon after UNRRA came direct American assistance under the Truman Doctrine. But much of this money still had to be channeled off to the war being waged with the Communist guerillas. It was only in 1950, with the restoration of peaceful conditions, that United States assistance was aimed toward economic stabilization and long-range development.

The effects were evident both immediately and gradually. Since 1950, Greece's gross national product has risen at an annual rate of 6 per cent. Per capita income has increased more than 5 per cent per year. Between 1950 and 1961 agricultural output rose 73 per cent and industrial production 150 per cent. The expanding economy has experienced a continuous increase of investment. By 1961, this investment reached 24 per cent of the gross national product. Though only half of this investment was financed by domestic savings, it greatly accelerated the rate of growth.

Obviously, American aid alone is not responsible for this growth. In the period 1950–1961, total U.S. aid to Greece equaled 18 per cent of the inflow of new foreign capital. In the years between 1949 and 1953, aid

A Star and Crescent club meeting in Pakistan. Organization of clubs is promoted by U.S. advisors.

from the United States averaged $140 million per year. In 1953, this sum began to be reduced until in 1962 both development grants and supporting assistance were terminated. If the present trend in domestic savings and external financing continue, there are good prospects that even development loans may soon be terminated. The fact that Greece was and is a recipient of military assistance in amounts equaling the economic assistance is certainly of importance, as such aid has helped release Greek resources for development rather than for defense.

Greece is not the only example. Foreign aid planners currently point to Israel as another example of good use of United States assistance. The rate of economic growth attained by Israel, 10 per cent, exceeds that of even Japan and of West Germany. This growth was achieved despite meager natural resources, great problems in absorbing massive waves of immigrants, and disproportionately high expenditures for defense, necessary in view of the threat of open conflict with the neighboring Arabian nations. The $700 million in American aid to Israel in the years 1950 to 1961 in the form of grants and loans (whose redemption has already started) were initially directed chiefly to maintaining financial stability and protecting the balance of payments. Later aid was aimed at support of Israel's economic development. About one-third of American aid was in the form of agricultural commodities, made available on a loan basis, another third was in the form of long-term loans at commercial interest

237

New well becoming major attraction in Ethiopian village.

rates; technical assistance and other forms of grant aid accounted for the balance. Israel has attained such development—in the growth of its exports, its rate of capital investment, and its annual per capita income—that the U.S. government has started gradually to decrease assistance to Israel. In 1962 the technical-assistance program was discontinued completely. The United States Operations Mission ended its activities with the statement: "Mission accomplished."

Taiwan (Formosa) has also made great strides forward in economic development in the estimation of the Agency for International Development. In appraising Taiwan's economic progress, the AID Summary Presentation to Congress for 1964 states that "within the current decade, Taiwan is expected to achieve the capability of financing its capital and external economic requirements by domestic savings and borrowing from normal world capital markets. Consequently U.S. assistance in the form of loans on concessional terms will be discontinued in three or four years, and the Food for Peace program will be gradually reduced."

How did the agency arrive at this conclusion? The following figures were at the roots of this appraisal: A 7.5 per cent average annual growth in gross national product, which has approximately doubled between 1950 and 1961; exports up from $93 million in 1950 to $196 million in

1961; over $2 billion dollars of capital investment in the same period. Of this $2 billion, American aid amounted to more than $1 billion and was nearly 90 per cent of the flow of external capital and donations. U.S. military assistance, in all its forms, contributed greatly in releasing for economic development resources which would have otherwise been absorbed in the defense effort. This economic picture is further brightened by the almost complete literacy of the population (90 per cent), elimination of epidemic diseases still common in most of Asia, and in an average life expectancy of 63 years, well above that of most Asian countries.

Though the "graduation" of these three countries from United States assistance programs may be considered a landmark for such programs, it must be remembered that the populations of these nations are relatively small compared with the masses of people that U.S. aid programs were designed to help. But these countries are not the only ones to which the United States can point as proof that aid makes sense, that it helps, and that the end is in sight for the need of this kind of assistance. Take India as a good example. The second most populous country in the world, with over 450 million inhabitants, India has none of the conditions prevailing in the three countries just mentioned. With only 24 per cent literacy rate, with a population whose average annual income is among the lowest in

In India wells built with U.S. assistance are encouraging the struggle against caste prejudices as well as meeting an important need for water.

the world and whose life expectancy is forty-two years, and with no class of skilled workers, India was not able to utilize most efficiently the aid which was flowing to her.

American economic aid for Israel, Taiwan, and Greece, with populations of two, six, and eight million people, respectively, amounted to considerable sums when computed on a per capita basis. But per capita aid to India has been rather small. It is clear that in such circumstances American aid has a much weaker impact than in smaller countries.

Aid to India has grown constantly over the years. Averaging $75 million per year from 1951 through 1956, it increased sharply to an average annual level of about $500 million for the years 1957 to 1962. Though this amounted to only 6 per cent of the gross investment in India, it was 53 per cent of the net inflow of foreign capital and donations. About half of the aid was given in the form of surplus agricultural commodities, thus freeing India's foreign exchange resources for the import of capital goods and essential raw materials.

Though U.S. aid can claim only part of the credit for India's economic progress, that progress nevertheless furnishes convincing arguments for further American aid to India. Seen against a population increase of 21 per cent within the decade ending in 1961, the pace of India's development must be considered most impressive. Here are some figures of growth for this ten-year period: national income increased 42 per cent; per capita income, 16 per cent; index of agricultural production, 41 per cent; index of industrial production, 94 per cent; installed electrical generating capacity, 148 per cent; and students in schools, 85 per cent.

These achievements notwithstanding, India still has a long way to go. But as a showcase for the potentialities of economic development and improvement of standards of living in an open society, under a democratic form of government, India has already demonstrated the superiority of this system over that of its neighbor, Communist China. Nobody can predict whether this encouraging beginning justifies the hopes of the Indian government for doubling of the per capita income by the end of the fifth five-year plan in 1975, and the elimination at that time of the need for foreign aid. But even if these plans are practicable, until they are realized India will have to count on a great deal of foreign assistance. For the third five-year plan alone, the Indian government estimated a need of a minimum of $6.7 billion in foreign assistance, including $1.2 billion in U.S. surplus food. These are enormous figures, as staggering as the tasks to be accomplished. But the results already achieved can give comfort to those who advocate aid to India as a great demonstration of international partnership in an effort to permit a growing number of people to benefit from the achievements of technology, while at the same time serving the American interest in the advancement of a world of free societies and democratic forms of government.

In this respect, another example deserves mention—that of a European

Malaria eradication is a major health project. Spraymen loading American-supplied materials for a spraying expedition in Vietnam.

country, one of the most backward among those which benefited from the Marshall Plan. That country is Italy—and the witness is none other than a Soviet publication. Writing about "Italy: The Boom and Its Effects," the June 19, 1963, issue of *New Times* acknowledges some most interesting facts:

From an agrarian industrial land, Italy has been turned into an industrial-agrarian country with a developed heavy industry, equipped with the latest plant. Between 1950 and 1958, the average growth of annual production was 5 per cent and in the three years from 1958 to 1961, 7 per cent. In 1961 industrial production increased by 9 per cent and the national income by 6.5 per cent. The country's balance of payments has improved and the gold and foreign exchange reserves have risen. From 1951 to 1961 the share of gainfully occupied population in agriculture dropped from 42 to 28.8 per cent. What is known as the third sector (trade and services) has grown considerably. The rapid growth of the economy determined the expansion of the country's exports. Between 1950 and 1960, the value of Italian exports nearly quadrupled, and their share in the national income rose from 9.7 per cent in 1950 to 17.8 per cent in 1960.

Of course this appraisal is not the whole picture of the Italian economy given by the publication. The Communist paper does its best to point

Home economics class in Peshawar, Pakistan. Standing: Miss Mae Everett, AID Economics Advisor.

to what it calls excessive concentration of capital in a few major concerns, monopolies, and big business. This is not the place to discuss the merits of the Russian contentions or their validity as negative factors in the Italian economic picture. There remains the fact of economic growth and development in one of the Marshall Plan beneficiaries, one which started its great upsurge at the termination of the European Recovery Program, which has created the foundation for what even the Russian journal calls "the Italian economic miracle."

The countries cited in this chapter by no means cover the entire spectrum of U.S. aid. Those mentioned are no more than "sample" countries. They are "samples" of what is being done, what is being achieved in scores of communities with commodities, grants, and loans. To describe all of them in full detail would require an entire library devoted to the effect of American foreign aid.

But it should be clear that even these few examples do not resemble the accounts given in such works as *A Nation of Sheep* and *The Ugly American,* which seem to reflect the present-day idea of the conduct of our foreign aid. Although it is true that waste, embezzlement, and corruption have occurred, it must be remembered that such things are to be found in every major undertaking, government, or private industry alike. There has been more of it as the foreign aid programs have spread all over the world and have had to work with people of all creeds, races, nations, on the most diversified levels of culture and civilized development. But soaring above the mistakes and the mismanagement our diversified foreign aid is in final account a great monument of a real and important American contribution to the well-being of hundreds of millions—of billions—of human beings. This story deserves to be told, at least as much as the incidents that figure in the wave of self-criticism which seems to have become an American national trait. Adlai Stevenson spoke the truth on this subject when he once said: "I hope we Americans will cease to be ashamed of generosity and magnanimity. No nation ever before approached what this one has done to help others to help themselves, and not by means of self-protection either. Why don't we glory in it? Why aren't we proud of it? Why do we ridicule our best instincts? I have said it before, and I repeat, that I haven't seen any repeal of the command to love your neighbor."

12

People to People Aid

The American people did not earn their "title to glory" only in the decade and a half of U.S. foreign aid programs. Neither is it a title which is theirs by virtue only of the actions of their government and their legislators. People, private individuals, are at the roots of the tradition of helping other lands. Banded into special organizations to help the people of foreign nations, they introduced into the realm of international relations a new element on which no other nation could pride itself: assistance to the needy on a grand scale which knows no boundary.

Long before anybody dreamed about foreign aid, such aid was flowing from the generous hands of Americans to almost every corner of the world. Wherever disaster struck, whenever pestilence felled human beings, "Uncle Sam" did not fail to appear at the right time—not with cables of condolence, avowing their participation in grief, but with deeds which meant rescue, which amounted very often to the difference between death from starvation or the means for persevering until the emergency was over.

"Uncle Sam"—the legendary distributor of bounty—did not, as we have said, come into being within the last two decades. The good deeds of over a century have accumulated to form this image of the United States of America. For over a century responses to the needs of their fellow men on the part of millions of Americans pronounced the message of a country which practices unhesitatingly the most essential tenets of humanitarianism.

This, the most amazing phenomena in the history of this country, appeared first in a form very much related to the religious fervor that is distinctly American. The country which produced almost two hundred religious denominations, popular evangelistic crusades, and preachers on the grand scale seems to have been a natural breeding ground for Good Samaritans on the world scene. The blueprint for humanitarian activities existed; all that was needed was that Americans discover foreign needs as well.

American missionaries began helping peoples in need and distress very early in the history of this Republic. Concentrating their activities at first in India, China, and Japan, and later in Latin America and Africa, the

Human scavenger scanning garbage box for food scraps in India.

missionaries were not only the first technical-assistance experts helping people to attain progress, they were as well the suppliers of material means of support for the people among whom they chose to work. In this respect, American missionaries—some of them simple lay people having no place in the ecclesiastical hierarchy—were more lucky than their counterparts from other Western nations: they had behind them a nation with open hands and open purses. American missionaries had not only their hearts, their experience, and their skills to offer; they were able to accompany their goodwill with tangible evidence of their concern with the fate of their fellow man. The superior material means at their disposal does not diminish the importance of the missionaries' work overseas. A nation which, from before its independence, observed the prin-

A household of an Indian farmer where voluntary agencies try their best to help.

ciple that the general welfare and cultural institutions are the responsibility of the individual citizen, as well as the government, was naturally responsive to calls to assist people who lived outside its boundaries.

Compared with present-day amounts, their efforts represented, of course, rather modest sums. But they have to be seen against the background of the material realities of their day—the U.S. population then, its industrial development, its national wealth. Compared with the expenditures for missions by other nations, America's contributions must be judged considerable (the expenditure of 1890, for instance, was $4,023,005).

But the early activities in foreign lands, often exotic, very remote, and rather obscure to the great majority of Americans, were limited in scope. Great as the assistance of the missionaries was, it involved comparatively small groups of people on the giving and receiving ends of the line. The first test of national dimensions (national at both ends—givers and recipients) came in the days of the great famine in Ireland (1845–1847). Relief on a grand scale started to reach the shores of Ireland from America. Dublin's newspaper *Freeman's Journal* wrote in glowing phrases of America's warm-hearted response to Ireland's needs: "We write with hearts of overflowing gratitude and love, gratitude and love not springing so much from the sense of benefits received as from a respect for the manner in which they have been rendered." This meant

246

more to the Irish than mere rhetoric. At one of the many meetings held in Ireland for expressing gratitude for America's help, one speaker was so overtaken by his enthusiasm that he even pledged Ireland's help to America when need be. Said he: "Should any calamity threaten America, we who have escaped the famine and pestilence produced by England, would assist her."

As things developed, some decades later Ireland needed American generosity again. Though the response was as generous as in the eighteen forties, some said that something should be done to terminate these recurring appeals to American magnanimity. Wrote the New York *Daily Tribune* in 1880: "Irish demands on U.S. charity must be met, but things in Ireland should be so managed that such demands end."

Characteristic though these remarks were for certain segments of the American citizenry, the tenor of public opinion as expressed in the press was rather very much on the side of those who felt it was their duty to share the wealth of their country with those in need. The New York *Herald* expressed this feeling, saying: "We think it important to be noted that the growth of wealth has not been attended with a growth of selfishness; that the character of our people has not degenerated; that habits of luxury have not dried up the fountains of generous human sympathy; that increase of riches is not accompanied by any signs of moral deterioration."

That the American people's social conscience was not put in danger of deteriorating through the growing abundance of material goods was proved again only some years later. If the magnificent response to the needs of Ireland could be ascribed, to some extent at least, to the considerable number of Americans of Irish origin, the response to the appeal of Russia for United States assistance could certainly not be linked to such ethnic motives. The response was generous, but somehow the donated articles had to reach Russia. Appeals that the U.S. Navy take over the responsibility for delivery were heard by Congress, which voted $100,000, in January, 1882, for the expenses of shipping relief materials to Russia. President Harrison supported the measure strongly in a message: "It is most appropriate that people whose store houses have been so lavishly filled with all the fruits of the earth by the gracious favor of God should manifest their gratitude by large gifts to His suffering children in other lands."

The decision in Congress and the debate preceding it gave rise to a fundamental dispute over whether Congress had the power to spend the taxpayers' money for shipping expenses incurred in the interests of foreign citizens. Influential members of Congress argued that Congress was elected on the promise to reduce taxes, and approving an appropriation to be spent for the benefit of foreign people would thus be deceitful.

Nevertheless, aid was flowing to the hungry Russians. The Russian government made no attempt to conceal the fact of need and the fact of

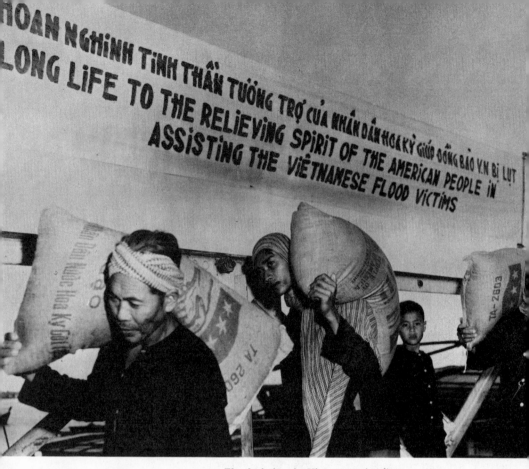

Flood victims in Vietnam assisted.

American aid. The Moscow *Gazette* greeted the shipments of U.S. grains and other articles, stating: "The gifts of America have been gratefully received. From the highest prince to the lowest peasant, all Russia is deeply touched by what has been done by the United States for Russia's hungry people." Tolstoy, Russia's leading writer and moral authority, spoke of the American assistance as of "a dawning universal brotherhood." A prominent Russian artist presented to the Corcoran Gallery in Washington his painting of a *troika* loaded with American supplies at a Russian dockside as a token of appreciation from the Russians for "the generous and timely assistance rendered by the United States during the recent famine in Russia."

To assume that American hearts have responded only to disaster would be more than erroneous. Early in the history of American private assistance efforts, schools and hospitals attained considerable importance in the over-all planning of assistance programs. Some of the finest institutions of learning have been established abroad with American money, and have been continuously supported with American money. In this connection it is enough to mention the American University in Beirut, an institution which rightly credits itself with remarkable achievements in the education of Western-oriented intellectuals, whose influence both in Lebanon and outside its borders has become more than considerable.

In these diversified aid programs, a growing role was being performed by voluntary private organizations whose entire existence was linked with aid to people in foreign countries. They carried this mission with pride. They developed elaborate forms of promotion under the clear banner of assistance to foreign citizens. So many U.S. citizens traced their origin to some foreign country that there arose a special form of organization of aid groups related directly to a particular country. Poles, Irish, Russians, Ukranians, Chinese—all have established their own organizations to give comfort in despair to people with whom they have had a natural affinity. And religious affiliations—Protestants, Catholics, and Jews—played a major role in American relief through private organizations.

But to assume that the entire voluntary assistance effort of the Americans was organized according to national or religious allegiances would be completely misleading. Non-sectarian, non-ethnic general giving for assistance by far outstripped anything any of the denominational organizations have done. During and after World War I, no fewer than 212 private charitable organizations collected funds and materials to assist people hit by the war. These separate organizations were sometimes organized on a most bizarre basis. Besides the many religious, ethnic, and professional organizations for assistance programs overseas, there were "Cognac Fund," "American Poet's Ambulance in Italy," "American Lee Flotilla Committee," "Army Girl's Transport Tobacco Fund," "War Babies Cradle" and the like. With all these different names, these organizations helped to mobilize American public opinion for the assistance effort and, in various degrees, helped those people affected either directly by military operations or by the consequences of war. To achieve some notion of the dimension of this assistance it would suffice to mention, for instance, the Near East Committee's relief appropriations which, from its inception in late 1915 until the Armistice in 1918, amounted to $13,033,437. And this was only one of the more than two hundred relief agencies operating at that time, some of which expended much bigger amounts than that mentioned above.

The form of this assistance was in itself a most remarkable feature of the operations of these agencies. The records of the Salvation Army show such relief activities as manning of motor ambulances, operating hotels, establishing and operating hospitals, caring for prisoners of war, assisting families whose breadwinners were with the armies, and even transmitting information between members of families separated from each other by front lines.

Among these many voluntary relief organizations the American Red Cross deserves special mention. Established in 1881 by Clara Barton, the

American Red Cross has since served as a most outstanding instrument of American compassion for people suffering everywhere. The outbreak of World War I was a major challenge to the Red Cross, which initially extended its many forms of assistance to belligerents on both sides. America's entrance into the war faced the American Red Cross with additional tasks. Up to September, 1918, a total of $108,532,516 was expended overseas by the American Red Cross.

People of the fighting nations appreciated the American assistance fully. France's President Raymond Poincaré spoke, in fact, for many nations when he stated:

Never will France forget the bounties she received in the gloomy hours of war from a multitude of American friends. The crusade of Charity preceded the military crusade, benevolence came to our aid even before the birth of our brotherhood of arms. In the first days of hostilities, the United States turned spontaneously to France, attacked and invaded: and never in the world, within memory of man, was there such outflow of sympathy and solidarity. Neither distance nor the ocean could prevent the hearts of our two peoples from feeling closely drawn together.

As political events unfolded, the period after World War I was one of prolonged armistice, rather than a period of peace. The U.S. aid given for the restoration of the shattered economies of the belligerents on a government-to-government basis was only part of U.S. assistance to foreign countries. Private voluntary organizations, which had done so much for many millions overseas, did not terminate their activities. Of course, those organizations which had been organized especially for war relief had no more purpose in being. But the great many voluntary organizations which had been engaged in foreign assistance programs before the war continued or resumed their work on a much broader basis. For the number of needy was greater: the world had become "bigger," as war made people aware of the existence of countries and nations they had never heard of before. The American Jewish Joint Distribution Committee, American Friends Service Committee, Catholic Relief Services, and many other voluntary organizations had to expand their activities considerably. Millions of people depended on their assistance—everywhere. And this assistance was not only in the form of funds, food, clothing—but also often in the form of Americans who volunteered for these services overseas and became, certainly, the best ambassadors of goodwill America ever had.

The extent of American concern for the welfare of people overseas and the degree of awareness of their plight was clearly indicated by the amount of money contributed by the voluntary agencies for people overseas: between the years 1919 and 1939, a total of $1,270,100,000 was expended by U.S. voluntary agencies for foreign aid programs. Almost half of this amount, $431,400,000, was collected on a non-sectarian basis and spent, mainly, in countries of the Middle and Near East and China;

250

The wife of an American aid official, one of many volunteer relief workers, distributes food to river-boat dwellers after floods in East Pakistan.

$599,800,000 was collected by Protestant agencies and spent on assistance programs in China, Japan, India, Latin America, and Africa; $89,600,000 was collected by Catholic agencies and spent mainly in Europe and China; the $149,300,000 collected by Jewish agencies was spent in Central and Eastern Europe and in Palestine.

Hardly had these operations gotten into the stride of peaceful activities when World War II again put them all on a "war footing." Legislation adopted by Congress at the beginning of the war brought limitations on the activities of the voluntary agencies overseas. The Neutrality Act of November 4, 1939, prohibited certain kinds of economic aid to nations which the President declared to be belligerents. This was not a final termination of assistance to belligerent countries. Assistance to them by private organizations for the relief of the sufferings of civilians was permitted, provided these agencies had registered with the Department of State. Though the registration was only a formality, it signalled the growing awareness by government of the role voluntary foreign assistance agencies were playing and could play in relations with foreign countries.

The request for registration did not limit the number of organizations which volunteered to assist foreign nationals in times of duress. Within a few short months, by February, 1940, 362 agencies had registered under

Food packages carried home.

the terms of the Neutrality Act. At one time their number reached 591—almost three times as many as during World War I. The private, voluntary relief effort was organized on a wide basis. People of the highest standing and experience in relief activities, such as former President Hoover, have publicly demanded that Congress appropriate considerable amounts for relief of the destitute. Testifying before the House Foreign Affairs Committee, Hoover spoke about the $400 to $500 million which was needed for the feeding of some seven million people, according to his estimate. Thousands of petitions, representing some twenty million Americans, were submitted to Congress, urging initiation of international negotiations for the solution of relief problems.

In this atmosphere of burgeoning humanitarian fervor, private agencies were encouraged in their efforts and the number of new agencies was growing. By early 1941, some seventy organizations were raising funds for British relief alone. Private initiative was abundant. People, masses of individuals, were drawn into action. "Bundles for Britain," for instance, which started on the initiative of one society matron, Mrs. Maud A. Latham in New York, could serve as an excellent example of the atmosphere prevailing then. From a shop in New York and a small supply of wool from which women volunteers knit sweaters and socks for refugees and soldiers, a whole movement developed which involved, in time, 975 branches all over the country, with almost a million people engaged in the operation. By the spring of 1941, "Bundles" had sent 40,000 sleeveless sweaters, 10,000 sweaters with sleeves, and hundreds of thousands of pairs of socks. "From your American Friends" (the inscription sewn on each such item) has transmitted the message of America's interest in the lot of the individual in need overseas more effectively than any official dispatches or statements of sympathy. Only one of these organizations, The British War Relief Society, collected $10 million by the summer of 1941.

In time, the voluntary assistance effort became an outpouring of goodwill. Even children were drawn into action. "Children's Crusade for Children"—though insignificant as far as amounts of money were concerned—collected 13,500,000 pennies, served as an excellent stimulus for the adults, and helped greatly to create the atmosphere of giving.

The massive response of people to the call for assistance overseas soon reached dimensions which made their regulation necessary, even from the point of view of the American war effort. In 1941, Secretary of State Cordell Hull suggested to President Roosevelt that he "examine the entire problem and make recommendations as to what steps might be taken to preserve local and essential welfare services and to maintain a balance between the facilities and resources available for foreign relief with particular regard to the financing of our new welfare activities in connection with national defense measures." Government concern with this problem found its expression in the appointment by the President on March 13, 1941, of a committee to examine the whole problem of foreign war relief.

The finding of that committee resulted in the establishment, by Executive Order of July 25, 1942, of the President's War Relief Control Board. The Board was entrusted with the regulation of overseas shipments of relief supplies collected by voluntary agencies. The scope of these relief supplies was immense: in 1939–1945 contributions to the voluntary agencies amounted to $504,700,000.

Government initiative in coordinating voluntary assistance was soon to be snatched by the voluntary agencies themselves in a similar organizational accomplishment. An American Council of Voluntary Agencies for Foreign Service was established in 1943. Seventeen voluntary assistance agencies were among the founders of the Council. Within four years, the number of agencies affiliated with the Council grew to fifty-five. The combined budget of those agencies for 1947 was $200 million.

Among the many agencies active in assisting war-ravaged countries facing serious problems in feeding their populations a new one appeared. Cooperative American Remittances to Europe (CARE) appeared on the public scene with an original idea: "personalized" giving. Giving through CARE was personalized on both ends: the giver, if he wished, would be identified to the recipient, whom the giver could choose.

This was something of a revolutionary idea in the field of private, voluntary assistance. Its appeal was natural and, therefore, immense. It showed how people desired to be identified with a good deed and it grew, therefore, at a rapid rate. In 1945, $500,000 was put at the disposal of CARE, and within one year this amount grew to $21 million (to $25.6 million in 1948).

The name of CARE had to be modified before long. CARE did not want to discriminate against the needy who happened not to live in Europe. "Europe" was replaced by "Everywhere." A new name was adopted, Cooperative for American Relief Everywhere, that preserved the acronym "CARE," which had already become a "trade-mark." CARE has scored another "first" as well: it was the first American voluntary agency to make significant use of agricultural surpluses. Following CARE's example, other voluntary agencies started to use such surpluses in their programs. By 1961, five billion pounds had been sent overseas by voluntary agencies. The relief agency for "everywhere" has won praises everywhere. Characteristic of the wide appreciation of CARE activities is a statement by Mrs. Vijaya Lakshmi Pandit, a leading political personality in India, who served as India's chief representative to the United Nations and president of one of the U.N. General Assemblies. Speaking of CARE, Mrs. Pandit said: "This is the kind of warm hearted and spontaneous gesture that spread honor and love to the American people throughout the free world."

CARE activities kept on expanding. By accepting amounts as small as a dollar, CARE made possible mass participation in giving. To food packages, another form of gift was added: tools for people overseas—tools

Needy Indian mothers with their children gather daily at Mexican Health Centers for supplementary rations of milk and other U.S. farm abundance sent by Americans through CARE's Food Crusade.

for an artisan, with which he could improve his professional equipment; tools for a farmer, so he could improve the yield of his fields. By 1962–63 CARE was sending $40 million worth of goods to people everywhere.

CARE is only one of the many voluntary agencies active in the field of foreign assistance. All of them together are responsible for the transmittal of an almost incredible amount of donations, especially if one remembers that these are voluntary agencies, receiving voluntary donations from private individuals. In 1946–1956 $6 billion was sent overseas by Americans in gifts of cash and kind. The amount in 1948 alone was $715 million.

CARE package of agricultural hand tools.

Giving did not slacken from the set pace. In 1960 and 1961, a total of $294,700,000 was sent overseas. This amount was made up of $124,400,-000 transmitted by Protestants, $39,700,000 by Catholics, $75,800,000 by Jews, and $54,800,000 by non-sectarian agencies. To the amounts collected and transmitted through voluntary agencies, a separate, explicitly individual form of aid to people overseas should be added: gifts sent by individuals, without the intercession of agencies or organizations. These gifts for people abroad amounted in 1940 to $129 million and rose in 1950 to $238 million and in 1960 to $333 million. This, too, is certainly a pace of growth outstripping the per capita growth of real income, which rose in 1940–1960 by about 50 per cent.

With such a record, the voluntary agencies can well sustain their claim that it was their initiative and example, and later their experience and even their forms of organization, which guided the U.S. government in the foreign aid programs which developed after World War II. Acknowledgment of the importance of the voluntary agencies for government efforts in foreign aid came as early as May 14, 1946, when, by directive of the President, the Advisory Committee on Voluntary Foreign Aid was established. The President's directive gave as the purpose of this committee "to tie together the governmental and private programs in the field of foreign relief and to work with interested agencies and groups." The policy of cooperating with the voluntary agencies was upheld during the ensuing years, reaching its height of intensity and seriousness at the beginning of the sixties. The foreign Assistance Act of

1961 directs that the President "in furthering the purposes of this Act, shall use to the maximum extent practicable the services and facilities of voluntary, non-profit organizations registered with, and approved by the Agency for International Development (AID) Advisory Committee on Voluntary Foreign Aid."

The Act indeed confirmed what was already well under way and was steadily gaining momentum. The AID had already been increasing its reliance on voluntary agencies in its overseas programs. The relationship went beyond mere cooperation. In certain areas of AID activities, voluntary agencies were and are directly entrusted with functions which they perform on behalf of AID. The agencies carry out duties, based on formal contracts, with efficiency and success. Be it a lunch program for school children in some Latin American country taken over by CARE, the improvement of animal stock in Asia or Africa, which "Heifer Project" is undertaking, or care for escapees from Communist countries, the voluntary agencies are fulfilling a growing role. With the establishment of the Peace Corps, this partnership between government and voluntary agencies has assumed a new dimension. CARE, CARE/MEDICO, Heifer Project, Near East Foundation, YMCA, YWCA, the American ORT Federation, and the Unitarian Service Committee all have contracts with the Peace Corps for the administration of projects in rural and urban community development, agricultural extension, education, and health services.

The Advisory Committee on Voluntary Foreign Aid, therefore, does

Bolivian children, participants in a voluntary agency's school lunch program, an activity coordinated with the Alliance for Progress.

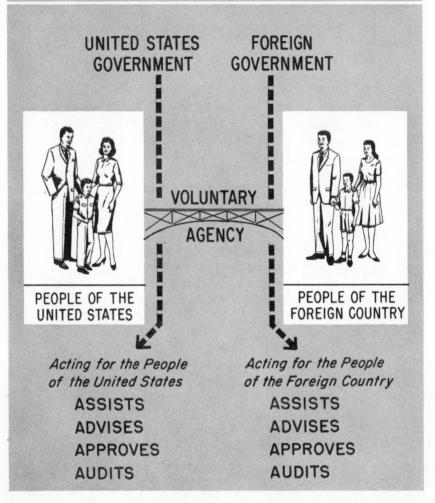

A PEOPLE TO PEOPLE PROGRAM
P.L. 480, TITLES II & III

UNITED STATES
GOVERNMENT

FOREIGN
GOVERNMENT

VOLUNTARY

AGENCY

PEOPLE OF THE
UNITED STATES

PEOPLE OF THE
FOREIGN COUNTRY

*Acting for the People
of the United States*

*Acting for the People
of the Foreign Country*

ASSISTS

ASSISTS

ADVISES

ADVISES

APPROVES

APPROVES

AUDITS

AUDITS

Governments and voluntary agencies form a bridge between peoples for the distribution of P.L. 480 (Food for Peace) commodities.

not lack functions. The Committee's executive organ, the Voluntary Foreign Aid Service, is a part of the over-all AID organization and is attached to the Office of the Assistant Administrator for Material Resources of AID. The functions of the committee are presented, by an official AID publication, as follows:

The Committee correlates the programs of private voluntary agencies in the field of foreign relief and rehabilitation with the programs of the U.S. govern-

A judge shows members the correct method of cultivating peanuts at a 4-H camp.

ment; advises and consults with the Director of A.I.D. concerning the relationships between governmental and voluntary agencies in foreign relief and rehabilitation; and facilitates the organization of voluntary assistance resources and their administration abroad. It has close liaison with the American Council of Voluntary Agencies for Foreign Service, New York, which represents its members and encourages the development of Councils of its members overseas.

Cooperation with the Advisory Committee is by no means compulsory. Voluntary agencies can be active in the field of foreign assistance without any contact with the committee. Those agencies which want to cooperate with this committee have to file for a formal registration which is granted only to agencies which have an active board of directors, a continuing program overseas, purposes other than political or propagandistic, records indicating financial stability and efficiency, and proof that contributions to it are tax deductible.

The benefits of registration are, however, such as to induce agencies to register. The most important benefit, though intangible, is the very fact of registration with a government agency, which gives standing, enhances influence, and increases the support of the American public. There are, as well, more tangible advantages of such a registration. A registered agency is eligible to participate in the Food for Peace program and use food donated under Public Law 480 for distribution overseas; it has the privileges of the overseas freight subsidy program, which means payment of transportation costs of these foods as well as the agency's own supplies. No wonder that over fifty voluntary agencies did seek such registration:

Aid Refugee Chinese Intellectuals, American Bureau for Medical Aid to China, American Foundation for Overseas Blind, American Friends of Russian Freedom, American Friends Service Committee, American Fund for Czechoslovak Refugees, American Jewish Joint Distribution Committee, American-Korean Foundation, American Medical Center in Burma, American Middle East Relief, American Mission to Greeks, American National Committee to Aid Homeless Armenians, American Ort Federation, American-Polish-National Relief for Poland, American Relief for Poland, Assemblies of God—Foreign Service Committee, Boy's Town of Italy, Brethren Service Commission, Catholic Relief Services—National Catholic Welfare Conference, Christian Children's Fund, Church World Service, Congregational Christian Service Committee, Cooperative for American Relief Everywhere (CARE), Foster Parents Plan, Hadassah, Heifer Project, International Rescue Committee, International Social Service (American Branch), Loan Foundation, Lutheran Immigration Service, Lutheran World Relief, Meals for Millions Foundation, Mennonite Central Committee, Near East Foundation, People to People Health Foundation (Project HOPE), Polish American Immigration and Relief Committee, Refuge de Pehts, Romanian Welfare, Salvation Army National Headquarters, Save the Children Federation, Seventh Day Adventist Welfare Service, Tolstoy Foundation, Unitarian Service Committee, United Hias Service, United Lithuanian Relief Fund of America, United Ukrainian American Relief Committee, Universalist Service Committee, Volunteer Border Relief, World Relief Commission —National Association of Evangelicals, World University Service, World Vision Relief Organization, Y.M.C.A. International Committee, Y.W.C.A. World Emergency Fund.

Thus many segments of the population are represented through one or more voluntary agencies. The maximum effective use of contributions through voluntary agencies, especially through coordination of their efforts, is assured by the activities of the American Council of Voluntary Agencies for Foreign Service. The Council coordinates the efforts of the agencies themselves as well as relations between the agencies and governmental, inter-governmental, and international agencies.

In the search for the maximum possible cooperation with non-governmental agencies in the field of foreign aid, the government agencies, most recently AID, have made and are making use of another organization which coordinates some one hundred voluntary agencies in the field of technical assistance. The American Council for the Technical Assistance Information Clearing House (TAICH) supplies valuable information and accumulates remarkable data about innumerable groups in the United States which are busy sponsoring small, but not less effective, projects of assistance, especially technical assistance, all over the world. It is sometimes a small community which has joined an assistance effort, sometimes a group of professionals, and sometimes even a few individuals who, with their limited means, write and advise, and send assistance, tools, and materials.

The story of these agencies' achievements would make a most remarkable record. People who have fled from the countries of the Communist bloc and are entitled to assistance under the regulations of the United States Escapee Program (U.S.E.P.) have found in these agencies friends who provided their shelter, clothing, food, and, later, resettlement for the beginning of a new life in freedom. Thus, 236,898 refugees were assisted in 1952–1962 in Europe and the Middle East alone, while some 345,106 refugees from Communist China were assisted by the Far East Refugee Program of U.S.E.P. and cooperating agencies. Refugees are only one category of people in need. People in areas stricken by natural disasters, children in need of help, people waiting to be cured of their ailments will always find comfort at the hands of representatives of one or more voluntary agencies. Close to six hundred American citizens act overseas as representatives of the various voluntary agencies which also employ about 5,000 local people in the areas they serve.

These voluntary agencies have a peculiar facility for proliferating,

The teacher is a member of "Auxiliares Féminines Internationales" (AFI). At this primary school, the girls benefit from free distribution of "Meals for Millions" Multipurpose Food, a product from California.

Members of the China Youth Symphony Orchestra try out musical instruments presented to them by the China International Foundation of New York.

for, as it often happens, the newcomers succeed in capturing more public attention than institutions which have been in the field for decades. A striking example of the rapid and most successful rise of a new voluntary agency was Medical International Cooperation: MEDICO. Conceived in the mind of a young lieutenant in the U.S. Navy, Dr. Thomas Dooley, after the collapse of the French positions in Indo-China, it started in a modest way. Human compassion and idealism in an individual of the highest caliber, showing something of the qualities of the founder of the Red Cross almost a century ago, have given rise to a concentrated effort in the field of preventive medicine in remote, underdeveloped countries that for centuries were almost completely inaccesible. By 1961, only four years after its establishment, MEDICO founded fifteen projects in preventive medicine in twelve countries.

This was not the only new project which drew considerable attention in the United States and all over the world. The founder of MEDICO became a kind of a legend, a living symbol of compassion for one's fellow man, through the personal story of the young doctor who single-handedly created an institution of world-wide dimensions, who himself fought heroically against a deadly illness that put an end to him in his thirties. But there was another project as well that elicited a great deal of attention in the United States and overseas: "HOPE." It was a modest project in scope but in its motivation it was a monumental manifestation

Aged immigrants assisted by the Joint Distribution Committee.

of the humanitarian spirit. Health Opportunity for People Everywhere
HOPE—grew out of a plan called the People to People Program advanced by President Eisenhower in the spring of 1956. The government reactivated a Navy hospital ship from its "mothball" fleet and renamed it HOPE. It was to become a kind of traveling ambassador of American goodwill, a symbol for all that U.S. foreign aid programs stand for. With the most modern medical equipment and a staff of medical specialists, it carried medical knowledge and expertise in public health problems to countries which needed such assistance badly. Vietnam and Indonesia were first to be blessed by this effort. HOPE became a floating medical school. Local people were taught new techniques for combating malnutrition, tuberculosis, malaria, and yaws. The floating ship of mercy with the American flag very soon became a ray of "HOPE" for sick people and afforded a permanent demonstration of what American presence could mean in faraway lands.

The growing importance of organized labor in the new countries has presented organized labor in the United States with a foreign aid task they have taken up with courage and a deep feeling of social responsibility. George Meany, the president of the A.F.L.–C.I.O., revealed in his testimony before a Congressional committee in 1963 that more than a quarter of the budget of his organization is being spent for programs overseas.

Dean Rusk with Dr. Hu Shih, chairman of an organization to aid refugees from Red China, and U.S. Congressman Walter Judd of Minnesota. Rusk, as president of the Rockefeller Foundation, directed its efforts to help people of many countries.

In the wide array of responses to overseas needs, American foundations also have their share. In fact, they were created to assist others. Their purpose was the support of valuable causes—charitable, cultural, social. The records of their activities show the most characteristic development both of American abundance and of American commitment to social welfare. A nation which gave $1,719,000,000 in 1921 voluntarily for domestic welfare in all its forms, a nation which kept on increasing this voluntary giving—$1,787,000,000 in 1922; $1,859,310,000 in 1923; $2,000,-320,000 in 1924; $2,068,570,000 in 1925; $2,192,680,000 in 1926; $2,219,-700,000 in 1928; and, in 1962, $8.7 billion—has received the most appropriate indoctrination for giving what became later an immensely growing volume of aid to people overseas. The fact that these donations were and are tax exempt is a most convincing proof of official government approval.

It was, therefore, natural for the great upsurge of popular response to the needs of people overseas, which had attained national dimensions during and after World War I, to achieve one of its culminations in the foundations. The Carnegie Corporation of New York, the Carnegie

Endowment for International Peace, the Laura Spelman Rockefeller Memorial, the Commonwealth Fund, and the Rockefeller Foundation have contributed from their resources to the great deeds of relief and rehabilitation in which U.S. aid agencies were engaged.

The change in the scope of U.S. assistance to foreign nations and the growing role of development in the foreign assistance programs have elicited from the U.S. foundations a most understanding cooperation. Among the many foundations engaged in foreign assistance programs, the Ford Foundation in particular concentrated much of its early attention on foreign aid. The older Rockefeller Foundation did not neglect this field and has and is doing much in following the pronouncement in the Foundation's 1938 report that "Friendly relations between nations must be based on an intelligent understanding of the contribution [it spent in 1913–1960 $229,691,683 in overseas operations from its total expenditure of $633,335,056] which each is in a position to make to the other." The Ford Foundation, however, has developed the more conspicuous overseas program. Fifteen years after its establishment, the Ford Foundation started its Overseas Development Program. Proceeding from the conclusion that poverty, sickness, and ignorance are the underlying causes of war and know no boundaries, the trustees of the Ford Foundation decided in 1951 to start a program of supporting overseas development, to be supplemented by an International Training and Research Program. Within ten years of the establishment of this Overseas Program, the Ford Foundation had spent $125 million on it. Starting in 1961, the Foundation increased its regular annual budget for assistance to less developed countries to $20 million. Describing the functions of this program, the Ford Foundation's official report for 1961 states: "The Overseas Development Program helps establish and strengthen institutions important to the long-term growth of developing nations in South and South-East Asia, the Near-East, Africa, and Latin America, and the Caribbean area. Increasingly, the program is supporting projects whose lessons and benefits transcend national boundaries to cover a whole region. Grants have been made in thirty-two countries and territories, including—for the first time this year—Colombia, Guinea, and Tunisia."

And so we see private organizations of all kinds are joining hands in the great mission of helping people in need of various forms of assistance. Their efforts for the sake of foreign nations join the mainstream of U.S. government aid to create the mighty river of aid which flows to the people of almost one hundred states and territories all over the world. "Through these humanitarian activities the historical concern of Americans for their fellow men is demonstrated by effective action overseas," says David E. Bell, the Administrator of the Agency for International Development, in *The Growing Partnership*, a pamphlet on AID and U.S. voluntary agencies. He acknowledges the pioneering role the volun-

An earth block machine, a few hours of instruction provided by a voluntary agency, a man's labor, and $87.63 replaces a house in Korea like this (*above*) with one like this (*below*).

tary agencies have played in foreign aid. Just as those who follow pioneers often overtake them in pursuit of the emulated endeavors, so U.S. aid through government channels has outstripped the voluntary agencies. But the latter remained the grassroots, the affirmation that the United States would have started and continued foreign aid even if there had been no Communist states and no competition for the loyalty of nations around the globe.

The chronicle of Americans' giving, including the billions of dollars they spent on overseas assistance before the establishment of Communist states, provides the proof that Americans' compassion for their fellow men is the mainspring of the U.S. foreign aid program in all its many forms.

ighlights
of
SIDENT KENNEDY'S

New

ACT for

INTERNATIONA

DEVELOPMENT

ON FREE WORLD
AND ASSISTANCE
OGRAMS

by

F. Kennedy
the United States
il 2, 1963

UCATIONAL and
LTURAL
LOMACY
1

Food For Peace

... building a better world

TRAINING
FOR
DEVELOPMENT

FOREIGN
AID
IN
PERSPECTIV

Togethe

we ar

strong

FACT
SHEET

*Mutual
Security
in
Action*

THE
SUDA

INTERNAT

THE ONLY WAR
WE SEEK

t of State

A TASK
TO SHARE

A.I.D.
Participant
Training
Program
for
Foreign
Nationals

Appendices

Appendix A

$$

Recipient Nations Appraise United States Aid

How do the nations on the receiving end of the United States aid appraise the results of the aid programs? Do they appreciate what the United States taxpayer has contributed for the sake of international cooperation and progress—for people he never knew, sometimes even in countries he never heard of? Are they inclined to acknowledge publicly that they were assisted?

These are questions which we think every American would like to have answered and is entitled to have answered. If we accept the tendencies away from the notion of charity and toward the idea of "cooperation," the answer to these questions becomes even more important, for one can give without being asked out of humanitarian feelings or in fulfillment of a moral obligation. But with "cooperation" the inspiration, it is only natural that one of the partners wants to know in what light the other partners look at his investment in this unique revolution for progress.

To get the answer for the American public, and for the American taxpayer, the author asked representatives of almost all the recipient nations to express their opinions on U.S. aid to their countries. No specific questions were asked. No restrictions were set on such appraisals, and only a limitation of space restricted their entire reproduction here.

The response has been generous. Although not all responding diplomatic representatives rushed to turn in their appraisals, many answered most politely, promising full, elaborate evaluations at some later date. Only a few did not respond at all. They should be not only excused but, even more, understood. This inquiry was made on the initiative of a private person, and reluctance to speak is quite the usual trait of diplomats. The Embassy of Soviet Russia answered plainly that the request had been referred to the government in Moscow. This should be accepted without reservations. In view of U.S. aid to Russia in the days of militant Communism, of Lenin, in view of the more than $10 billion of Lend-Lease materials during World War II, and in view of the adopted policy of refusal to acknowledge even the existence of these instances of American magnanimity, no Russian ambassador, no embassy official would or could dare to take upon himself the delivery for publication in the United States of an appraisal of this aid. But even this letter about transmitting the request to Moscow is an answer of significance.

Some answers will not be quoted in full, for to do this would add immeasurably to this book. Perhaps at some future time these answers will find their way to the U.S. public. But the essential portions of these replies are quoted as they were written and submitted; brief ones are, of course, quoted in full.

So "the floor" belongs now to the political or economic leaders who responded in time to be included in this book:

CEYLON: * "Point Four Technical Assistance Program—turning point in the history of international aid"

Ceylon's Minister-Counsellor at the Ceylon Embassy in Washington, Mr. J. H. O. Paulusz, was kind enough to respond to the author's request expressing hope in his accompanying letter that the "material will be of use in the book . . . on U.S. aid."

Indeed it is of use. It tells the story—and is not reluctant to set the U.S. aid as the example and pioneer of foreign aid programs. Wrote former Ceylonese Minister of Finance, the Hon. Felix Dias Bandaranaike, Member of Parliament:

The year 1950 was chosen as it marks the turning point in the history of international aid for two reasons—it was the year in which President Truman first inaugurated the Point Four Technical Assistance Program; it was also the

* U.S. AID TO CEYLON, 1956 TO 1962. The aggregate amount of U.S. aid to Ceylon for the period 1956–62 inclusive was 79.2 million dollars made up as follows:

	(In Millions of Dollars)
Development Grants	10.1
Loans	6.3
Food for Peace	53.9
Other various commodities	8.9 (Approx.)
Total	79.2

(The above figures were obtained from the State Department.)

In the first three years, beginning in 1956, seventeen different types of aid have been listed, mainly of a technical and development character.

As of April 22, 1961, the major activities were: Malaria Eradication, Minerals exploration, Water resources-planning, Hydro-Electric power and Irrigation projects, Nutrition of School Children, Aerial photography and surveys, Airport expansion and the use of American technicians and experts in launching works designed to increase productivity in goods and foodstuffs. There is also the Development Loan Fund, i.e., directed to the development of Highways, Irrigation and Land and Railroad Services in the Colombo area. Contributions have also been made in Rice and Flour ($6,300,000 in 1958 and $8,600,000 in 1959) supplemented by further Flood relief following the disaster of December, 1957. From CARE came Milk and Flour to the amount of $2,000,000 in 1958 and again in 1959.

year in which the Colombo Plan for Economic Cooperation was conceived at a meeting of Commonwealth Prime Ministers in Colombo.

The earlier history of aid was connected with the Lend-Lease, U.N.R.R.A., and Marshall Programs for Rehabilitation and Reconstruction work in European countries which had suffered damage during the war. By 1950, it was generally accepted that technical assistance was needed not only in these countries but to an even greater extent in the underdeveloped countries in which standards of living and economic conditions were still very low. It was in appreciation of this need that President Truman formulated in 1950 his famous Point Four program for international aid. . . .

. . . U.S. assistance to Ceylon commenced on November 7th, 1950, with the signing of a Point Four Agreement between the Governments of Ceylon and America for the acceptance of technical aid from the Technical Cooperation Administration of the U.S. Under the terms of this agreement the two Governments undertook "to cooperate with each other on the interchange of technical knowledge and skills and in related activities designed to contribute to the balanced and integrated development of the economic resources and productive capacities of Ceylon."

. . . This was followed by a Bilateral Agreement signed on 28th April 1956 by the late Hon. S. W. R. D. Bandaranaike on behalf of the Government of Ceylon and His Excellency Mr. Philip Crowe, U.S. Ambassador in Ceylon. The agreement made provision for "such development assistance or authorized related assistance to the Government of Ceylon as may be requested by the Government of Ceylon and approved by the Government of the U.S." It also stipulated that the aid would be given under the General Agreement signed in 1950. The Agreement also provided for the supply and sale of commodities in Ceylon, the proceeds of which would go into a "special account" with the Central Bank of Ceylon to be used partly for expenditure incidental to the furnishing of assistance and partly to finance projects beneficial to Ceylon upon agreement between the two parties. . . .

On behalf of the Government of Ceylon, I take the opportunity of expressing our gratitude to those countries, international organizations, and other foreign agencies which have so generously helped us during this period.

The foreign aid that we have received has assumed several forms, such as capital grants, capital loans, donations of equipment, provision of facilities for technical training of our personnel, and technical assistance in different spheres of activity.

Aid in these forms is, however, only one means by which the economic development of undeveloped countries can be promoted. It is now universally acknowledged that the planned utilisation of a country's resources is an indispensable condition of sound economic development. Planning is of special importance for countries whose resources are limited.

Countries which rely heavily on foreign aid exchange earnings from agricultural exports that are subject to frequent fluctuations in prices need, in addition to the forms of capital aid and technical assistance that they now receive, a reasonable assurance of a stable level of prices for their export commodities over the period covered by their respective plans. Unless measures of this nature are adopted on an international scale by agreement, foreign aid by itself cannot make a real contribution to the economic progress of such countries.

During the early years of the period under review, offers of aid were accepted somewhat indiscriminately without any relation to any program of development. An offer of aid had only to be made for it to be accepted. Almost all proposals for which aid was accepted were outside the annual budget. This policy was unexceptionable as long as the country's own resources were sufficient to finance the approved budgetary program of development, but as the program expanded and these resources proved inadequate, foreign aid had to be utilised primarily to supplement domestic resources in financing the annual program of development. . . .

CHINA (TAIWAN): *"U.S. Aid Played Vital Role"*

In his lengthy evaluation of the U.S. assistance to the Republic of China, Taiwan, Mr. K. T. Li, Secretary General of the Council for U.S. aid states:

United States economic aid to China in post-war years, particularly those after 1950, was instituted in recognition of three basic factors: (1) The traditional friendship between the two nations and the highly disproportionate defense burden borne by Taiwan as an anti-Communist stronghold of the free world; (2) The need to rehabilitate the war-torn Chinese economy and to cope with its short-term difficulties; (3) The need to develop Chinese economy on a long-term basis, aiming at self-support and self-sustained growth.

These three factors worked only to a negligible extent on the Chinese mainland because of the latter's fall into Communists' hands in 1949, which virtually stopped the aid program officially started in July, 1948, with the signing of the Economic Aid Agreement in Nanking. After the Chinese Government re-established itself on the island province of Taiwan in 1950, and with the outbreak of Korean War, the aid program was resumed in the latter part of that year. It was in Taiwan that the aid program began its full-fledged operation and took good care of the three basic factors mentioned above.

In concrete terms, the aid program has contributed, in successive phases, to the rehabilitation of the war-torn economy, to the supression of inflation, to the balancing of government budget and international payments, and to the social, economic, and technical development of the island province of Taiwan. The types and procedures of aid since FY1951 * have undergone several changes as U.S. foreign aid policy as well as local conditions changed, but the amount of dollar or primary aid obligated during FY1951–FY1963 has been kept at U.S. $100 million per year on the average. More recently the emphasis has been shifted from short-term considerations and loans on concessional terms to long-term objectives and a hardening up of loan terms.

The basic role of U.S. aid program, however, has been to help develop Taiwan's economy, as it was recognized that only by vigorously and effectively developing the economy could Taiwan's short-term difficulties and long-term problems be solved. This active attitude was first translated into action in 1953 when the Chinese Government launched the first 4-year economic development plan after the island's economy was more or less stabilized. Since then, a series of 4-year plans have been instituted and implemented and the economy has shown satisfactory progress. With 1952 as base (= 100), industrial production has increased by 205% and agricultural production by 58% by 1962, showing an average annual growth rate of 11.8% and 4.7% respectively. Real national income during the same period has increased by 100%, at an average annual growth rate of 7.2%.

The U.S. aid program has played a vital and active role in the achievement of all this.

* FY: Fiscal Year.

As the situation now stands, Taiwan is more or less in a position to (1) attract foreign investment capital through normal business channels and (2) formulate on the basis of total available resources long-term plans for self-sustained growth. The basic factor for the attainment of this position is of course the efforts of the Chinese people and Government, but there is no question that U.S. aid has played a vital role all the time. It is the attainment of this position that speaks most eloquently for the success of the operation of U.S. aid program in China during the past decade.

GERMANY: *"An enemy country rebuilt."*

In the history of the U.S. aid effort in the postwar reconstruction of countries ravaged by war, the rebuilding of the defeated country of Germany represents a special, unprecedented development in international relations. Instead of demanding war reparations, the United States sent flowing to Germany billions of dollars worth of aid and contributed greatly to what became a real miracle of postwar economic development in Europe: the German prosperity, the German economic growth, which turned West Germany into one of the economically strongest nations in the world.

The appraisal of the role the United States has played in the reconstruction of West Germany is especially significant. The fact that the Ambassador of the Federal Republic of Germany in Washington, K. Heinrich Knappstein, has himself written this appraisal accords the following remarks special importance:

You asked me to give you a short appraisal of the Marshall Plan Aid given to the Federal Republic of Germany, to be published as part of your historical review on American Foreign Assistance; it is a pleasure for me to contribute to your publication the following remarks:

On October 27, 1963, in the presence of the German Federal Chancellor Professor Dr. Erhard and the Secretary of State Dean Rusk, Mrs. George C. Marshall inaugurated in the Opera Square of the City of Frankfurt on Main, Germany, a memorial which carries the following inscription: "In gratitude to, and in lasting remembrance of George C. Marshall, who, as Secretary of State of the United States of America, announced the European Recovery Program of the United States Government. The Marshall Plan for the years 1948 to 1952 which resulted from that has led our destroyed country back to life." This memorial is a visible token of the deeply felt gratitude of the German people towards the General and statesman George C. Marshall and towards the American people for the assistance known as the Marshall Plan which was so vital for the recovery of Germany from the disaster of the Second World War.

This program was of historic significance born out of great humanity and political wisdom, and it was carried out with diligence and generosity. This unique venture led to the reconstruction of Germany and the other participating war-torn European nations, and was meant to bring about the economic and political unity of Europe. It helped to establish free world trade vital to all, and to initiate economic cooperation within the family of free nations.

Under the Laws and Agreements pertaining to the Marshall Plan the United States of America provided for Europe about $13 billion of assistance of which

Germany received about $1.56 billion, Great Britain about $3.3 billion and France about 2.7 billion. In addition to Marshall Plan Aid the Federal Republic received between 1946 and 1952 about $1.26 billion of Garioa Funds. Finally (after the London Debt Agreement of 1953), the Federal Republic of Germany had to repay about $1 billion of those funds; this debt has been repaid almost completely before maturity. The Marshall Plan Aid of 3.18 billion dollars given to Germany was primarily employed to increase the production of coal, steel and food-stuffs and to improve transportation and communications. Later, however, capital was also invested in other sections of the German economy. Further, the program resulted in the stabilization of the German currency and the liberalization of her imports and exports.

The results of this common American-European effort have been recognized and admired all over the world. Thus, the Atlantic Alliance has become a mutual reality to further and to protect the sacred human rights and ideas of the West.

INDIA: *"Assistance so far committed under different programs is $4,349,150,000."*

Among the many special answers which were sent in by representatives of various countries some have preferred to draw on existing materials published in their countries. Though these publications are not kept secret, there is no doubt that few have read them, and certainly even fewer people have seen them in the United States. The fact that the Minister for financial affairs in the Indian Embassy in Washington representing India in the International Monetary Fund, J. J. Anjar, made this material available accords this communication a direct official character, specially provided for this book.

The material presents no appraisals. But the dry facts speak for themselves:

The total value of assistance so far committed under different programs is $4,349,150,000. Out of this, assistance in the form of loans and grants comes to $3,873,960,000 and the rest represents sale of commodities against payment in rupees. . . .

The U.S. assistance has all along been closely coordinated with India's Five Year Plans and has extended to almost all fields of India's development activity. Assistance provided during the First Five Year Plan amounted to $427,310,000. During the Second Five Year Plan, U.S. allocations of aid amounted to $780,770,000. For the first two years of the Third Five Year Plan, the U.S. commitments so far announced come to 980 million against which formal agreements have been signed for the total value of $582,300,000. . . .

A brief account of the nature and quantum of aid received under each program is given below:

INDO–U.S. TECHNICAL COOPERATION PROGRAM

Beginning with a technical cooperation agreement in January, 1952, this program has assisted in financing development activities in such diverse fields as Agriculture and Natural Resources, Industry and Mining, Health and Sanitation, Community Development and Social Welfare, Transportation, Labor,

Education and Public Administration. Projects are selected in support of India's Five Year Plans. From the inception of the program up to the end of November 1962, the fund obligated by the U.S. government under this program totaled $509,560,000, and disbursements amounted to $471,900,000. . . .

P.L. 480—So far the government of India has entered into agreements with the U.S. government for the import of surplus agricultural commodities under Title I of U.S. Public Law 480. The total value of these commodities covered by these agreements is $2,428,300,000. The cost of these commodities plus fifty per cent ocean freight is initially paid by India in rupees. The agreement, however, provides that the bulk of these rupee proceeds would be again made available to the government of India.

From the portion of the rupee proceeds reserved for the U.S. government's own use, the rupee equivalent of $23,401,000 is to be used by that government for assistance to the governments of Burma and Nepal.

Loans from DLF and AID

The Development Loan Fund (DLF), which started its operations in 1958, and its successor organization, the Agency for International Development (AID), have so far extended loans to India for a total amount of $934,900,000. This included $148,600,000 in respect of which direct agreements have been signed with autonomous bodies and private firms. . . .

A welcome feature of these loans is the large scale assistance for the import of non-project commodities for the maintenance of India's economy in the face of the difficult balance of payment position. . . .

U.S. Export–Import Bank Loans

The Export–Import Bank of Washington has so far extended three general lines of credits for a total amount of $225 million to the government of India for assisting in financing the import from U.S.A. of capital equipment and related spares and services in connection with the program of economic development in India, both in the Public and Private sectors.

ISRAEL: *"Americans Showed Understanding to Help Us Develop the State"*

Mr. Teddy Kolek, director general of Israel's Prime Minister's office, who is in charge of the cooperation with the U.S. aid representatives, took care to provide the following statements by Israel's Prime Minister, Mr. Levi Eshkol, and the Deputy Prime Minister, Mr. Abba Eban.

Mr. Eshkol:

There is no need for me to repeat, that, on its establishment and during its first years, Israel was an unique State from the economic point of view and many functions had to be initiated from nothing. There was, therefore, every indication that under pressure of these circumstances and out of lack of experience we would build our economy in such a way that it would be dependent on the various sources of foreign aid.

Fortunately, I can say, that from the very beginning we found that the Americans showed great understanding of our specific conditions and demonstrated outstanding good will in an attempt to help us develop the State in such a way as to lead towards economic independence.

Deputy Prime Minister Eban:

In 1962 the American aid program to Israel passed the figure of $800 million in grants and loans since their inception. They have probably been the greatest single item in our imported revenue over the past decade. An important attribute has been their constancy. The change of Administration in 1952 found us discussing our economic fortunes with Dulles and Dillon, and the response was just as sympathetic. The Secretary of State even had a way of talking without irony about "American–Israel economic cooperation." Since the "cooperation" consisted of the United States giving and of Israel receiving, this seemed to me an imaginative use of the English language. In the larger sense, however, Israel's honest, serious and fruitful use of economic assistance funds came as a positive service to American international policy. The economic aid idea was under constant attack, and Israel's use of it was a pilot plant demonstration of its efficacy. The American people can justly look at the Israel landscape with a sense of having participated in its transformation.

In other areas of American–Israel political relations there were many ups and downs during this decade. I use the words "political relations" because the economic aid programs have always been negotiated and decided on the diplomatic level. It is naïve to assume that such matters are transacted between treasuries. The decisive encounters are between Foreign Offices and Embassies, and the determination to maintain or increase or modify the aid program is a function and consequence of the general atmosphere of relations between the two countries. It is thus particularly memorable to record that the economic program has been almost uninterrupted; and any gaps resulting from political crisis or dissent were swiftly filled.

There were nations in Europe which were plunged in cosmic despair fifteen years ago and are now overflowing with economic vigor and robust independence. Historians can find no precedent for the use of surplus economic power in defense of political ideals and institutions far abroad. The American aid programs overthrew the conservative doctrine of the national frontier as the proper framework for confirming economic energies. The new vision is of growing equalization in opportunity, as advanced economies tax themselves in order to avoid excessive disparities of income and productive capacity.

Asia and Africa are now the main arenas in which this principle stands to be redeemed. Other nations and international agencies have entered the field in which the U.S. once stood alone. America will have no cause to regret her foresight. The ultimate prize may be no less than a family of nations united in a growing equality of dignity and creative growth.

KOREA: *"Honest Efforts by U.S. in Restoring the War Torn Peninsula of Korea"*

The South Korean government responded to the request for an appraisal of U.S. aid by supplying ready-made sources. But, the accompanying letter signed by Mr. Po Lung Kim, Director of the Information Office at the Korean Embassy in Washington, presents in fact a clear and outspoken appraisal of U.S. aid. He writes:

As one of the principal recipients of the United States' foreign aid we are happy to be able to present to you some documentary material which show the honest efforts made by both the UNITED STATES and the Republic of Korea in restoring this war torn peninsula.

The U.S. aid was appraised in the same spirit by the Korean President Chung Hee Park when, evaluating U.S.–Korean relations, he said:

The United States has always lavishly extended immeasurable assistance and cooperation, both materially and spiritually, to our country. Therefore, we Koreans, shall never forget but always cherish in our hearts with gratitude the friendship and prompt and timely assistance rendered by the United States. . . .

But after such unreserved praise come some sober remarks voiced by other official organs of the (South) Korean Republic and included in a publication of the Korean Information Office:

Development grants and supporting assistance for the Republic of Korea have been drastically scaled down in recent years—from $230 million in 1959 to $90 million in 1963. The way of scaling down has been too drastic for the Republic of Korea to attune herself to it. This will not be so for the coming fiscal year, we hope. . . .

Important to the aid recipient is how to obtain the aid at the most opportune time. We repeat, this is no less important than the aid level itself. . . .

Delayed granting can have a harsh impact on recipient nations such as the Republic of Korea, especially at a time when they are in urgent need of foreign exchanges. In a way such delayed action may mitigate the significance of the U.S. aid program itself. Experience shows that by the time aid arrived economic impasses had already developed beyond amelioration. . . . Blame cannot be placed exclusively on the giving side. Neither can it be placed on the receiving side. It's a joint responsibility. . . .

LEBANON: *"I fully appreciate the amount of aid provided by the U.S. Government"*

The Lebanese Ambassador in Washington, Mr. Ibrahim El-Ahdab, did not go into details. His brief statement makes clear nevertheless the unreserved appreciation Lebanon has for the U.S. aid:

I fully appreciate the amount of aid which the United States Government provided in the post-war period for needy people in war-stricken areas, the billions of dollars which greatly strengthened the European economy in grants and loans, followed by technical aid programs. Also, all that has been done by U.S. aid to improve the standard of living in the underdeveloped countries.

I am sure that your book will enlighten its readers on the recoveries made possible in various parts of the world through American foreign aid.

MALAGASY: *"Occidental people must bridge the gap. . . ."*

The aid extended by the U.S. to Malagasy is rather negligible. It totaled only $1 million until June 30, 1962. The remarks of the Malagasy Ambassador in Washington, Louis Rakotolamala, are, therefore, of a general character. But these remarks are perhaps even more interesting than a detailed appraisal of the practical results of the U.S. aid. They shed light on the broad political aspects of Western aid to undeveloped countries. It could be said without exaggeration that in this respect the Malagasy statement expresses the views of a majority, if not all, of the undeveloped countries:

It is certainly indispensable for Occidental peoples to bridge the gap which separates them from nations which are on their way to self-development. But their effort will be vain unless they recognize clearly that there can be no question of the new nations' adopting their values, their manners, and their ways of thinking. The emerging countries can borrow their scientific and technical knowledge; that is all. . . . So, if the American people really want to collaborate and to achieve, progressively, world unity and freedom, it is indispensable for them to learn to know the inner minds of their partners to assimilate their ways of thinking and of feeling.

Appendix B

$$$

Report on a "Special Relationship"

The great American contribution to the recovery of Western Europe was best symbolized by the aid the United States has extended to the United Kingdom. It is a special privilege to have an outstanding spokesman of this leading U.S. ally himself evaluate the great saga of U.S. help to Great Britain.

The author is Sir Eric Roll, K.C.M.G., M.C., the Economic Minister at the British Embassy in Washington, scholar, writer, and the United Kingdom executive director of the International Monetary Fund and the International Bank of Reconstruction and Development. His past services have kept him close to problems of economic cooperation with the United States. Sir Eric was kind enough to write for this book the following, which we include in full because this report is, in many ways, representative of the way the United States assisted Western Europe first in war and later on the way to economic recovery:

Whatever divergent views there may be about the "special relationship" between the United States and Britain, there is one context at least in which the links between the two countries in the past two decades have been particularly close, if somewhat one-sided. It is in the matter of financial and economic aid, which during World War II and immediate post-war years was flowing abundantly and eastward across the Atlantic.

The aid given by way of loans is being repaid. The service on these debts is being punctiliously honoured. And as a counterpart of the whole of that aid, whether given as loans, Lend-Lease or under the Marshall Plan, there can be set an economically healthy Britain which today stands side by side with the United States as a strong and dependable ally in the greater community of the free world.

The story of this particular special relationship begins with the outbreak of World War II. It was soon apparent that if Britain was to emerge victorious in the contest a great deal of essential material, whether food, raw materials or ammunition, would have to be obtained from the United States. In the days of "cash-and-carry" the wherewithal to pay for these purchases had to come in large measure from Britain's slender gold reserve and by mobilising the dollar and other foreign securities of British citizens. Over the whole period of the war Britain, on balance, lost gold to the amount of $615 million and sold overseas assets, including dollar securities, to the amount of $4,500 million.

ACT OF FAITH

This, however, was but a drop in the bucket of Britain's requirements. By the end of 1940 Britain had committed nearly all her available dollars on work actually in hand in the United States, including the building of American factories. By the same date British orders and commitments stretching far into the future amounted to more than $10 billion, which was far in excess of any resources that Britain might conceivably mobilise. This was an act of faith, both in ourselves and in the United States. It was well expressed by the Prime Minister, then Mr. Winston Churchill, in one of that famous series of personal messages, "From a Naval Personage," to the President of the United States: "We shall go on paying dollars for as long as we can, but I should like to feel reasonably sure that when we can pay no more, you will give us the stuff just the same."

The loss of all our gold was a prospect which raised certain major issues of principle and awakened some doubts about the future of the international financial system. This was well put by the late Lord Keynes, who was in the British Treasury at the time and who argued that it was in nobody's interest, and certainly not that of the United States, that Britain should completely denude herself of gold.

If the convention by which gold was used as a means of settling international payments came to an end, the United States' own stocks might become valueless. This is how he put it: "The convention depends on not all the gold being in one hand. When in the game of beggar my neighbour, all the cards belong to one player, that is the signal for the game to come to an end. The pack becomes worthless pasteboard; the fun is over."

Mr. Churchill followed this up with a message couched in his own incomparable and vivid eloquence. After reminding President Roosevelt that the moment was approaching when we would no longer be able to pay cash and assuring him that we would shrink from no proper sacrifice to make payments, he added: "I believe you will agree that it would be wrong in principle and mutually disadvantageous in effect if, at the height of the struggle, Britain were to be divested of all saleable assets so that after the victory was won with our blood, civilisation saved and the time gained for the United States to be fully armed, we should stand stripped to the bone. Such a course would not be in the moral or the economic interests of either of our countries."

"Most Unsordid Act"

The help that was to be forthcoming in such profusion and that was to earn the Churchillian phrase "the most unsordid act in history," began with the Johnson Act and the Lend-Lease Act of 1941. The Johnson Act made it possible for Britain to raise a loan of $400 million from the Reconstruction Finance Corporation, a U.S. Government agency. This loan was secured by a mixed bag of dollar assets, which had remained unsold. That loan, together with interest of $64 million, was repaid by September 1951, almost five years ahead of schedule.

But it was through Lend-Lease, introduced by the United States as a policy "for the defence of the United States," when the United States was not yet at war, that the really massive help began to flow. "Give us the tools and we'll finish the job," said the British Prime Minister. The idea was introduced to the American public by President Roosevelt with the famous parable of the man lending his fire hose to the neighbour whose house was on fire.

After the Japanese attack on Pearl Harbour in December 1941 and the entry of the United States into the war, both the scope and character of Lend-Lease were immensely broadened. Fighting side by side, both the United States and Britain determined that financial problems should not be allowed to obstruct the use of their joint resources in the way which would most rapidly secure victory. Lend-Lease became not so much a method by which the United States aided the Allies as the weapon by which the total strategic and economic resources available to the Allies were most effectively deployed.

It was evident that a larger proportion of Britain's population could serve in the armed forces and engage in the manufacture of war equipment if Britain received some of her food and other bare necessities of life under Lend-Lease. Had this aid not been forthcoming Britain would have had to divert some of these resources of manpower and industrial equipment to manufacture the exports required to pay for these essential imports; for it must be remembered that by then the British reserves of gold had been exhausted (in 1942 they fell to a bare $12 million at a time when the outstanding cash obligations of Britain to the United States amounted to about $1,000 million). It would in the circumstances have been senseless in a joint war effort to compel British workers and machines to earn the wherewithal with which to pay for imports instead of engaging directly on the battlefront or in the industries that provided the necessary munitions of war.

TORRENT OF HELP

This equation of sacrifices should be recalled before we move to the next phase of American help to Britain, that which opened immediately after the war was over and which involved the credits totalling $4,400 million which were negotiated in 1945. The Lend-Lease operation should be recalled in this context, because it was thanks to Lend-Lease that Britain was able to throw to the winds virtually the whole of her export trade and as a result found herself at the end of hostilities deprived not only of the most saleable of her foreign assets, including the dollar securities, but of the export trade and overseas markets that were and are the very basis of her economic existence.

To say all this in explanation and justification of the torrent of help which the United States gave to Britain during the war, is not, however, to diminish in any way the sense of admiration with which the magnitude of that assistance must be viewed. Between March 1941 and the end of August 1945 the British Commonwealth received Lend-Lease aid from the United States valued at $30 billion, of which the share that went to Britain was $27 billion.

Lend-Lease was not wholly a one-way traffic. Britain provided the United States with reverse Lend-Lease supplies and services, including some essential raw materials produced in the Commonwealth. This reverse Lend-Lease totalled about $5 billion, which left the account weighed heavily toward the United States to the tune of $22 billion as between the United States and Britain and $25 billion if the whole Commonwealth were included.

When the end of the war came and the settlement of this vast account was considered, the United States generously decided to wipe the slate almost clean. Of this vast debt all that remained was $620 million mainly in respect of goods that were in the pipeline when hostilities came to an end and that were not eligible for further Lend-Lease treatment. This amount of $620 million was added to a line of credit of $3,750 million which the United States Government made available to Britain in 1946. It is now being repaid in annual instalments.

Apart from this $620 million the whole of the balance arising from this reciprocal aid was wiped out. An appropriate acknowledgement was made by Mr. Churchill in his address to the United States Congress on January 17, 1952. "During the war we bore our share of the burden and fought from first to last unconquered, and for a while alone, to the utmost limit of our resources. Your majestic obliteration of all you gave us under Lend-Lease will never be forgotten by this generation of Britains or by history."

WEAK AND VULNERABLE

The end of Lend-Lease, in spite of the generosity of the settlement, left Britain in a weak and vulnerable position. The weakness was not merely in the virtual disappearance of export trade. There had been immense physical losses. The destruction on land was valued at more than $6 billion. This included 210,000 houses totally destroyed, 250,000 houses rendered uninhabitable and more than 3,500,000 damaged. Losses of ships and their cargoes amounted to $3 billion. In addition to this the sale of overseas assets amounted to $4½ billion. Britain had also accumulated vast liabilities to other countries, some of them in the Commonwealth, in the course of waging war and buying supplies in their territories. These liabilities amounted to more than $11½ billion.

All told, Britain's wartime losses were estimated at nearly $30 billion. Time was bound to elapse in the process of demobilising the wartime economy of Britain and putting it once again on a normal peacetime basis, able to earn its keep in the world markets, to sustain its population and pay for its imports by an adequate flow of exports. A vast process of transition had to take place and the necessary external finance had to be found.

In this emergency Britain turned to the United States and negotiated a line of credit of $3,750 million. To this was added the loan of $620 million in respect of the Lend-Lease settlement. The total of $4,370 million is being repaid in annual instalments, the last of which is due in the year 2005. The terms were generous. Interest was fixed at 2 per cent., which was decidedly below the commercial rate. In addition the United States agreed that if in any year Britain's balance of payments position, as measured by certain defined standards, made repayment of the loan especially burdensome, Britain could apply for a waiver of the amount of interest due in the instalment for that particular year. This waiver has been invoked on only two occasions and the amount in question is due to be paid at the end of the instalment period.

The line of credit of $3,750 million was intended by both the United States and the British Governments to provide against Britain's balance of payments difficulties for several years. At home Britain was achieving a substantial Budget surplus and her domestic financial position seemed sound. The whole purpose of the credits was to meet the difficulties that confronted Britain in her external balances, and in particular to give time for Britain to build up again the volume of merchandise and invisible exports that would enable her to achieve once again a satisfactory equilibrium in her balance of payments.

PENT-UP DEMAND

This intention was unfortunately not realised. This was in part due to one of the clauses of the loan agreement which required Britain to make sterling freely convertible for current payments transactions into any currency within one year after the credit became available, that is, by July 1947. This condition was duly implemented and sterling became convertible. But, as has already been pointed out, heavy sterling liabilities had been incurred towards other countries during the course of the war. Much of this was represented by sterling balances in British banks.

There was at that time an enormous pent-up demand throughout the world for goods and materials that were then obtainable only against payment in dollars. This worldwide demand for dollars was further intensified by the widely prevailing belief that the dollar was a stronger and safer currency to hold than any other. As a result of this Britain found that as soon as sterling became convertible, in accordance with the terms of the Anglo-American Financial Agreement, there was a violent run on the currency. From many countries of the world came orders to sell sterling and buy dollars. The line of credit which had been put at Britain's disposal and was intended to serve for a transition period of several years began to melt like snow in summer. By August 20, 1947, a bare five weeks after sterling was made convertible, the British Government had to ask for a waiver of the convertibility clause. The convertibility of sterling was then suspended, but an unduly large proportion of the dollars had already disappeared, though it should be added that the converse of this was a reduction in the sterling liabilities of Britain to other countries.

In spite of this mishap, the line of credit was of immense value in allowing Britain to make the transition from war to peace in less harsh conditions than would otherwise have obtained. The conditions that had to be endured by Britain in the immediate post-war days were, nonetheless, severe. Rationing of such basic commodities as meat, butter, gasoline, clothing, candies, had to be maintained for many years; but had it not been for American aid, the prevailing austerity would have been even grimmer.

We now come to what is undoubtedly the most generous and remarkable chapter of U.S. aid to Britain and to Europe. It is the period of Marshall Aid, which lasted from 1948 to 1951. The United States had given help to European countries through large but isolated transactions such as the line of credit to Britain, but soon came to realise that this was not the best way to help Europe in its immense task of reconstruction. To begin with it became apparent by 1947 that the dislocation of world trade was more severe and deep-seated than had originally been recognised, and that the world outside the United States suffered from what then looked like being a chronic dollar shortage. This shortage meant that persistent obstacles were being placed in the way of freer trade with the United States, not because countries like Britain did not want American goods, but because they could not afford to pay for them. The United States, moreover, realised that by giving their help in piecemeal fashion they were not contributing to that collaboration between the recipient countries which was absolutely necessary to their satisfactory recovery from war ravages.

THE MARSHALL PLAN

It was against this background that on June 5, 1947, General George C. Marshall put forward the entirely new, imaginative and generous proposal that led to the plan that will for ever be linked with his name. The then Secretary of State said that if Europe would formulate a comprehensive programme for co-operative action to ensure the wiping out of its dollar deficit over a period of years, the United States would do what it could to cover the dollar needs of the countries concerned while the programme was being carried through. It was, in fact, an offer of help to Europe, but to be given on the condition that Europe would help itself.

Mr. Ernest Bevin was then the British Foreign Secretary, and he appreciated both the generosity and the constructive potential of this offer. He seized it, as he said, "with both hands." It was on his instructions that British experts met other European colleagues in Paris, and there hammered out a European recovery programme which would make Europe eligible for and deserving of the help that had been promised by the United States. No less than 17 European countries joined this programme and formed the Organisation for European Economic Co-operation, whose initials O.E.E.C. were to become familiar in the economic history of Europe during the ensuing years.

The European recovery programme was launched in April 1948, and it proved of momentous political and economic value to Western Europe. One of its first successes was the establishment of a European Payments Agreement which soon made way for the European Payments Union, under which payments between the countries of Europe were settled partly in credit, partly in gold or dollars. In this way a real measure of convertibility was secured as between European currencies, and with American help they were taken a long step towards full convertibility with the dollar, which most of these currencies have since achieved.

285

Under the Marshall Plan Britain had by December 1950 received help to the tune of $2.7 billion. Of this, $1.7 billion was in outright gifts, about $620 million was "conditional aid," that is dollar aid given on condition that Britain provided corresponding sterling aid to other European countries. The balance of about $337 million was a loan, which is still being repaid in six-monthly instalments and with interest of 2½ per cent.

By far the greatest part of the Marshall Aid allocated to Britain was used to purchase essential foods and raw materials. Food and animal feeding stuffs accounted for $853 million, petroleum products for $331 million, raw materials and semi-finished products for $1,018 million, tobacco to $232 million (an essential ingredient for British morale in those days of austerity), and machinery and vehicles $182 million. The rate of aid to Britain was cut after mid-1950 and was completely suspended from the end of 1950, which was 18 months before the target date for the conclusion of the European Recovery Programme.

To Avoid Economic Collapse

This programme had been launched after exhaustive Administration and Congress studies which had led to the following conclusion: "To avoid economic collapse Western Europe must have long-range assistance on a comprehensive scale; the material and spiritual resources of the countries of Western Europe give promise that with such aid they will be able to achieve recovery. With skilful management the resources and productive capacity of the United States are equal to the extraordinary task; if aid is not extended, free institutions everywhere, including those in the United States, will be put in jeopardy." (First Report to Congress of the Economic Co-operation Administration.)

This Marshall Aid was put to highly constructive use in Britain. Insofar as it was canalised to the easing of payments between European nations through the European Payments Agreement and later the European Payments Union, it helped to clear the channels of international trade that had previously been choked by exchange regulations of all kinds. This was to prove of special benefit to Britain, dependent as she is on international trade for her economic existence. It also brought special benefit to Britain's international banking business, which was then beginning to pick up again from the effects of war and post-war restrictions on payments. Seen in its widest European context, the Marshall programme was the first real step towards that closer integration and economic unity of Europe which was to make such giant strides in later years and in which Britain has played her part—albeit not as full a part as the British Government might have wished.

In its more domestic context the aid received by Britain under the European Recovery Programme was an essential ingredient in the impressive economic recovery and expansion that occurred during these years. Between 1947 and 1950 industrial output in Britain increased by about 30 per cent. while the numbers employed in industry rose by less than 7 per cent. These two figures provide a measure of the improvement in productivity. To this improvement equipment received from the United States, as well as technical aid provided under the Economic Co-operation Administration, made a notable contribution. The dollar costs of the Anglo-American Council on Productivity were met under the European Recovery Programme. A number of productivity teams were sent out from Britain to the United States under its auspices.

Boost for Agriculture

It was not only industry that benefited from Marshall Aid. Agriculture also prospered. Productivity on the land was rising fast. The number of tractors increased by 50 per cent. during the Marshall Aid period. Feeding-stuff shortages were countered by better methods of growing and treating grass. Little by little the grip of austerity on the British people could be eased, one by one the controls could be lifted and rationing abandoned. In 1951 the President of the Board of Trade was able to claim that he and his colleagues had "made a bonfire of controls."

There can be no doubt that Marshall Aid laid the basis for the recovery which Britain has made in the subsequent years—and what a recovery it has been. Industrial production is now 66 per cent. higher than it was when Marshall Aid began. British exports have risen by 70 per cent. in volume.

Although over the intervening years there have been periods of stress and difficulty, the balance of payments is now in good fettle and in a position to meet the service on the loans which the United States has made to Britain. Sterling has been riding high in the exchange markets and has shared with the U.S. dollar the considerable responsibility—burdensome at times—of providing the rest of the world with one of its two key or reserve currencies. With the restoration of convertibility of sterling for all current transactions and a large measure of freedom for capital operations, the banking structure of the City of London has regained its importance and London can again claim to be one of the great, if not the greatest, international financial centres.

The next chapter in the long history of U.S. assistance to Britain falls under the heading of Mutual Security. Some of the weakness in Britain's economic position in the early 1950s arose directly from the new defence burdens assumed during and after the war. Britain's concentration since the war on increasing exports and her determination to curb imports to achieve a balance in overseas payments, emphasised the burden of defence expenditure incurred outside Britain on the balance of payments.

The United States in these circumstances agreed to give aid to Britain to ease the special burdens imposed by the defence programme which Britain had assumed as a member of the North Atlantic Treaty Organisation. Under the policy launched in 1949 the United States provided help to her allies under the Mutual Defence Assistance Programme. Through this programme, which covered the two years 1949–1951, sums totalling $2,357 million were allotted by Congress, and of this Britain was provided with some military aircraft and $112 million to cover the purchase of machine tools to help defence production.

MUTUAL SECURITY ACT

This programme was succeeded in 1951 by funds made available under the Mutual Security Act which became law in October of that year. The total amount of aid provided by Congress under this Act for the year 1951–52 was $7.3 billion, of which $5.8 billion was for military aid and $1.5 billion for technical assistance and economic aid. For Europe alone military aid was $4.9 billion and economic aid about $1 billion.

At first Britain was not deemed to be deserving of any aid, since in 1950 and the first part of 1951 the gold and dollar reserves of the sterling area had been rising. Later in 1951, however, it became clear that the gold and dollar surplus earned earlier had been due to temporary factors and that Britain, by plunging into a full defence programme, had become involved in higher dollar expenditure than could be covered out of current income. These arguments were substantiated during the defence sharing discussions in Paris in the Fall of 1951, and Britain therefore applied for aid both on the economic and military sectors of the available funds. The net receipts of defence aid over the period 1951–58 amounted to $1,004 million, which included a loan of $48 million which is being repaid with interest at 2½ per cent.

A final item of U.S. assistance to Britain was the Export-Import Bank loan of $500 million at the time of the Suez crisis. Of this, $250 million was drawn. Sterling was then under serious pressure and assistance was obtained from the International Monetary Fund. The closing of the Suez Canal gave rise to the need to increase British purchases of materials, including oil, from dollar sources of supply. It was, therefore, a justifiable operation for the Export-Import Bank to extend a loan to Britain to finance such purchases. The loan was amply secured by the dollar securities in the ownership of the British Government. These in large part were the securities that had been pledged during the war for the already-mentioned loan from the Reconstruction Finance Corporation and freed from their lien when the Export-Import Bank loan was repaid in October 1959. The market value of these securities had over the intervening period risen to between $800 and $1,000 million, and they therefore provided an ample margin over and above the $250 million that was borrowed from the Export-Import Bank. It would, however, have been a difficult and also improvident operation to have sold some of these securities to mobilise the dollar cash that was then needed. The intervention of the Export-Import Bank was, therefore, welcome and extremely useful.

SECURITIES FREED

The collateral securities have again been freed. They remain in the ownership of the British Government. They represent a substantial second line of reserve for the defence of sterling and at the same time a portfolio of dollar investments which have been improving in value in a very satisfactory manner.

Looking back on the financial relations between the United States and Britain over the past quarter of a century, we find, therefore, that on balance a flow of assistance has poured eastward across the Atlantic reckoned in billions of dollars. If we endeavour to exclude from this the normal, two-way movement of capital and investments dictated by normal commercial considerations and to identify the outright aid or loans made on exceptional terms, we arrive at a net total which reaches towards the $30 billion mark. The question that must be raised by the magnitude of this figure is whether the investment and the pouring-out of real resources which this represents, has been worthwhile for the United States.

The greater part of this figure is represented by net Lend-Lease aid, and in this context the question hardly arises. World War II was a total war in which the balance of forces swung violently and for a time was precariously poised on the edge of defeat for the Anglo-American alliance by the forces which then opposed it. Victory was gained by the fullest utilisation of the resources—human and material—available.

It can, in fact, be shown that in the waging of total war,—that is, in the fullest diversion of man and woman power to the war effort, on the battlefield, in the ships, in the factories—Britain did more than any other belligerent country. In this Britain and the Allied cause were helped by the vast flow of aid, military and civilian, which poured from the United States under Lend-Lease. That aid was not investment. It was an outright contribution to the overall objective of victory—victory not only in battle, but for the kind of world in which we wanted to live and in which, thanks to the effort and sacrifices made in those years, we are fortunate to be living today.

The other kind of aid which was given to help the reconstruction of Britain may be somewhat more difficult to justify, especially when the attempted justification comes from the side of the recipient. But it can be said in the first place that every dollar which went out of the United States in this way must have gone back by way of purchases of goods and services. Britain has not hoarded dollars or gold. The dollars she received or borrowed, she has spent. The dollars sent out of the United States were like homing pigeons: they returned to the country whence they came; in their voyage they have benefited Britain; but they have also benefited the U.S. producers of wheat and cotton, machine tools and manufactures on which the dollars were spent.

Money Well Spent

Let it further be said that the dollars have been well spent. The prosperity and vigour of Britain today is proof of that. The United States and Britain are allies not only in political and military terms, but in the world of economic and monetary relations. The pound sterling and the U.S. dollar are inter-dependent currencies. The strength of Britain's economy is but one facet of the value of Britain as a member of the Atlantic Alliance. None of the dollar aid granted to Britain has been diverted into corrupt hands or cyphered bank accounts. Every cent has been accounted for through the sternest and most meticulous accountancy mechanism of which any national fiscal system can boast.

It must also be stressed that every dollar borrowed from the United States is being paid back in strict accordance with the respective loan agreement. There will be no default on these obligations.

But when all this has been said in reassurance and in justification of the aid given to Britain by the United States, the final sentiment must be one of appreciation and gratitude from Britain. Warm recognition of this has been given practical shape in the Marshall Scholarships awarded under Britain's Marshall Aid Commemoration Act of 1953 which have enabled young people from all over the United States to go to British universities to study for degrees or pursue postgraduate studies. From 1954 to 1962 there were 144 Marshall Scholars.

Rarely in the history of international relations can one country have given so much help to another as the United States has, over the past 23 years, given to Britain. There may have been very good reasons why it should have been given. The gifts may have redounded to the interests of all concerned. But the gifts came not from some vague, impersonal overflowing horn of plenty, from "a government"; they came from the people of the United States, from those who paid taxes and used their savings to subscribe to government bonds and thus provided the dollars out of which the necessary appropriations were made.

It is this personal facet of the aid which should be stressed and which will be remembered as long as gratitude has a place in human emotions.

Appendix C

$$$

U.S. Foreign Assistance
Obligations and Loan Authorizations

July 1, 1945–June 30, 1962

Total Economic and Military Assistance $97,133,000,000
Foreign Assistance Act Program $62,627,000,000
Other Assistance $34,506,000,000

U.S. AID TO FOREIGN ASSISTANCE ACT COUNTRIES BY REGION AND COUNTRY
OBLIGATIONS AND LOAN AUTHORIZATIONS, CUMULATIVE
FISCAL YEAR 1946 THROUGH FISCAL YEAR 1962

	Millions of Dollars		Millions of Dollars
Near East and South Asia	$17,847	Africa	$ 1,845
Latin America	6,824	Europe	44,706
Far East	21,837	Non-Regional Funds	4,079

COUNTRY BY COUNTRY, ACCORDING TO REGIONS

Near East and South Asia

Afghanistan	$ 219	Nepal	$ 48
Ceylon	79	Pakistan	1,854
Cyprus	17	Saudi Arabia	46
Greece	3,359	Syria	96
India	3,867	Turkey	3,815
Iran	1,294	U.A.R. (Egypt)	608
Iraq	68	Yemen	23
Israel	882	Cento	27
Jordan	350	Regional Funds	1,106
Lebanon	88		

Latin America

Argentina	$ 618	Mexico	$ 767
Bolivia	262	Nicaragua	70
Brazil	1,955	Panama	101
Chile	743	Paraguay	59
Colombia	410	Peru	476
Costa Rica	90	Trinidad and Tobago	20
Cuba	52	Uruguay	87
Dominican Republic	46	Venezuela	276
Ecuador	143	Other West Indies	2
El Salvador	41	British Guiana	4
Guatemala	163	British Honduras	2
Haiti	100	Surinam	3
Honduras	46	Regional Funds	281
Jamaica	9		

Far East

Burma	$ 93	Laos	$ 442
Cambodia	336	Malaya	23
China, Republic of	4,350	Philippines	1,737
Hong Kong	30	Thailand	767
Indochina, Undistr.	1,535	Viet Nam	2,447
Indonesia	682	Western Samoa	*
Japan	3,682	Regional Funds	444
Korea	5,269		

Africa

Algeria	$ 15	Niger	$ 3
Burundi	5	Nigeria	44
Cameroon	16	Rhodesia and Nyasaland	36
Central African Republic	*	Ruanda	1
Chad	*	Senegal	10
Congo (Brazzaville)	1	Sierra Leone	4
Congo (Leopoldville)	160	Somali Republic	28
Dahomey	6	Sudan	65
Ethiopia	186	Tanganyika	18
Gabon	*	Togo	6
Ghana	156	Tunisia	293
Guinea	13	Uganda	5
Ivory Coast	5	Upper Volta	3
Kenya	18	Zanzibar	*
Liberia	128	Other French Communities	
Libya	192	and Possessions	6
Malagasy Republic	1	Other Portuguese Possessions.	13
Mali, Republic of	6	British Territories	1
Mauritania	2	Regional Funds	47
Morocco	352		

Europe

Austria	$ 1,176	Norway	$ 1,133
Belgium–Luxemburg	1,983	Poland	523
Denmark	908	Portugal	478
France	9,414	Spain	1,698
Germany (Federal Rep.)	5,001	Sweden	109
Berlin	132	United Kingdom	8,705
Iceland	71	Yugoslavia	2,397
Ireland	146	Regional Funds	2,581
Italy (including Trieste)	5,790	Non-Regional Funds	4,074
Netherlands	2,464		

* Less than $500,000.

The shift in the emphasis on particular areas of U.S. aid distribution is best illustrated in the figures of aid in fiscal year 1962 (in millions of dollars): Near East and South Asia—$2,292,8; Latin America—$1,365,7; Far East—$1,323,6; Africa—$523,9; Europe—$698,7.

Index

$$

Index

297

Loans, 78–81, 151
Lodge, Henry Cabot, 5
Logan Act, 5
Lutheran World Relief, 76
Luttwitz, Von, 3
Luxembourg, 36

"M's," two (money and materials), 5
"MacArthur rice-thresher," 234
Maintenance-of-Value clause, 82
Malagasy, 279
Malaria, 223, 226
Malaya, 128
Mali, 151
Malone, Senator George W., 41
Management Inspection Staff, 92
Mansfield, Senator Mike, 65, 175
Marshall, George C., 34–36, 41
Marshall Plan, 35, 37, 40, 43, 49, 52, 55, 65, 78, 79, 81, 83, 121, 131, 150, 175, 177, 181, 214, 241, 242, 275
McCormick, Vance, 9
McElroy, Neil H., 139
McNamara, Robert L., 103
Meany, George, 128, 263
MEDICO, 262
Merchant Marine, American, 43
Military aid, assistance, 131–33, 138, 147
Missionaries, 244
Molotov, V., 36, 37
Morocco, 151
Moscoso, Teodoro, 181
Moscow, 248
Moscow Conference, 34
Moscow Economic Conference, 149
Mossadegh, Dr. Mohammed, 227
Mutual Aid, 23
Mutual Defense and Assistance Program, 49
Mutual Defense Assistance Act, 134
Mutual Security Act, 57, 58, 65, 135
Mutual Security, Mutual Security Program, 121, 131, 140, 142

Nanking Economic Aid Agreement, 274
Nasser, President Abdel G., 61
National Conference on International Economic and Social Development, 130
National Rural Electric Cooperative Association, 89
NATO, 50, 131
Naval bases, 18
Nelson, Governor Gaylord, 130
Nepal, 125, 151, 223, 226, 227
Netherlands, the, 36, 127
Neutrality Act, 16, 253
Newfoundland, 18
New Times, Moscow, 53, 159, 178, 241
New Zealand, 127

Nigeria, 231
Nixon, Vice President Richard, 112, 139
Non-governmental, 88
North Korea, 151
Norway, 36, 47, 127
Nourse, Edwin G., 37

Office of Foreign Relief and Rehabilitation Operation (OFFROI), 24
Office of Lend-Lease Administration, 20
Officer-training program, 143
"Operation Pan-America," 168
Orenburg, 12
Organization for Economic Cooperation and Development (OECD), 127, 201
Organization of American States, 168, 169
ORT Federation, 257

Pakistan, 114, 125, 151
Participant Training Program, 89
Passman, Congressman Otto E., 92, 94, 104–06, 109, 124
Patterson, Robert P., 40
Peace Corps, 178, 204–22, 257
Dutch, 217
Peace Corps Secretariat, International, 217
Peaceful competition, 149
Peace Treaty, 10
Peru, 208
Petrograd (Leningrad), 12
Philippines, 133
"Pipeline," 124
Point Four, 67, 85, 149, 192, 227, 228
Poland, 16, 30, 31
Population explosion, 125, 126, 184
Portugal, 36, 127
Pravda, 36, 159
Private assistance, 242–45, 248
Program Review and Coordination Staff, 92
Protestants, 249, 256
Public Law 480, 71, 76, 77, 122, 260
Puerto Rico, 125
Punta del Este, 171, 172, 174, 185

Rakotolamala, Ambassador Louis, 279
Recipient Nations, 271
Reciprocal Aid, Reciprocal Aid Agreement, 23
Red Cross, American, 75, 250
Reed, Philip, 40
Relief Administration, 12, 13
Republican, Republicans, 35, 39, 44, 85
Reverse Lend-Lease, 23
Rhodes, Representative John J., 103
Riddleberger, James W., 100
Rift, Russian-Chinese, 155
Robinson, Henry, 9
Rockefeller Foundation, 265

JACOB A. RUBIN

is a journalist and author of long standing. After earning his degrees in law and diplomatic studies, he started a career in journalism. He has served as editor and political commentator with many newspapers. Mr. Rubin has visited numerous countries and thus had an opportunity to observe, on the spot, the conditions in which people in Asia, Africa, and Latin America are living.

During World War II, Mr. Rubin saw action in North Africa and in the European theatre of war. In 1953 he joined the corps of United Nations correspondents. Lecturer and radio commentator, Mr. Rubin is the author of many books, among them *Nationality Problems in Postwar Europe, At the Gates of Hades, Poland Revisited, Country Without a Curtain.* His latest book, *Pictorial History of the United Nations* (with forewords by U.N. Secretary General U Thant and Presidents of the 15th and 17th U.N. General Assemblies, Ambassadors Frederick H. Boland and Sir Mohammed Zafrullah Khan), earned praise from critics and the international diplomatic community.